Chantel A. Ferraro

THE ONLY GIRL ON THE FLOOR

a memoir

The Only Girl on the Floor

Paperback : 979-8-9969924-0-9
Hardcover: 979-8-9969924-1-6
EBook: 979-8-9969924-2-3

For Michael, Lily, and Noah.

Thank you for being my babies
and my reasons why. I love you most.

Author's Note

This book is a memoir.

It reflects the author's present recollections of experiences over a period of time. Some names and characteristics of individuals, places, and events may have been changed, modified, or disguised to protect the privacy of those involved.

This book contains subject matter relating to self-harm, eating disorders, childhood sexual abuse, and rape. While I have taken great lengths to ensure this subject matter is dealt with in a responsible manner, it may be troubling for some readers.

Discretion is advised.

Table of Contents

What's Wrong with Me?

I absently traced the square floor tiles with my finger. The dingy grout and the chill of the hard tile was what I deserved. From my vantage point on the kitchen floor, I had an up-close look at all the forgotten crumbs that had fallen from the toaster. *I don't even clean right anymore.*

Lying on the floor in the fetal position isn't how I planned to conclude my 28th birthday, but the damage was done; I did the one thing I promised myself I would never do. *What have I become?* I was unable to grasp the reality that I was a mother, a wife, a sister, a daughter, a preschool teacher, and had real career potential as a makeup artist. Instead, I just felt hollow.

Mike was talking to one of the police officers who showed up after I made a scene. He looked completely distraught and depleted.

"We're going to have to take her to be evaluated," the officer said.

Mike nodded. He was holding our daughter, a not-quite-two-year-old who was more interested in the buttons on the police radio than what was happening around her.

When I arrived at the hospital, I was evaluated and put on a 72-hour hold for further evaluation. I never meant for things to get this out of hand. I had threatened suicide in the chaos, so they did what they had to do. I now had zero control over my circumstances and to make things worse, I couldn't see anything. I had cried so hard my contacts popped out, and it wasn't like the cops were going to wait patiently for me to pack my overnight bag. I tried to convince the intake nurse that I was fine now, but she wasn't having it. Fortunately, Mike would be allowed to drop off my glasses, but not until later.

It took several hours before I was finally able to meet with a psychiatrist for my evaluation. When she asked me how I ended up there, I gave her the Cliff's Notes version. I wasn't really on board with the whole therapy thing at the time, and we only had 45-minutes. How detailed could I really get? So I took a deep breath and listed the recent chronology of events as an explanation.

I had a miscarriage, and then shortly after that, I had become pregnant again, and I never quite felt comfortable with the pregnancy because I was worried I would lose it again. When I finally gave birth to my daughter, she almost died of sepsis and I couldn't bring her home for a while. The entire year after her birth, I struggled with fears of losing her and my new life as a mom and wife of two children.

What I told her was all true, it just wasn't the whole story. What would she say if I told her that the moment that I found out I was having a little girl my entire childhood flashed before my eyes? I didn't believe I deserved to have a daughter. Because of my own chaos, I had no idea how I was going to mother her. Having my son was hard, but he was a boy. I figured I had Mike to fill in if and when I was lost. But a little girl? I was terrified. I had a complicated relationship with my mom. I had no real, long-lasting girlfriends growing up, and I didn't have a single female in my life that I trusted to share all the fears I had of raising a little girl. How could I avoid repeating history? Being who I thought she needed felt impossible. Everything felt impossible, but I wasn't about to dive into all that.

She diagnosed me with postpartum depression, gave me a prescription for Wellbutrin, and suggested I use the journal they gave me at intake to write down my thoughts and feelings. I found out that I could be released a day earlier if I showed that I was not a threat to myself or others, so for the rest of the day, I was on my best behavior. I followed the rules and went to group therapy. I took out the journal and began to write:

October 29, 2003. What's wrong with me?

ONE

Cigarettes & Strawberry Shortcake

★

If These Stairs Could Talk

I always thought the house I grew up in was unique. Turns out, bungalows like mine, made of those brown and rusty-red bricks were actually an architectural staple in the city of Chicago. But I wouldn't have known that yet, I was just three. It was 1978, and my parents were over the moon to have been able to scrape together their hard-earned savings and check off one of those boxes in their quest to live the "American Dream": buying a house.

They were young, but they had goals. My mom was particularly determined to move us out of our reputedly haunted apartment, and I'm grateful for it. Even though I have no memories of any encounters with the spiritual world, Mom was uncomfortable with the male ghost that liked to hang around my crib. Maybe that's why I've always been drawn to ghost stories and haunted houses. Or maybe because my birthday is close to Halloween, it's just part of who I am.

The houses on Kilbourne Street all sat on narrow lots where every house was different from the next. Some were made of wood, and some were brick. Some were single-family homes and others were three-flat apartment buildings. Some had stairs that led directly into the house and some had porches. My house had stairs leading to a small, covered porch that held so many conversations and discoveries. So many Halloweens. So many firsts.

Those stairs hold many of the best childhood memories I have, like the day I scraped my knee after falling off my Strawberry Shortcake bike. I was five, and Dad said it was time for me to take off those training wheels and learn how to ride on two. After falling what felt like a hundred times, I eventually did; but those steps were there for me to find comfort in between those falls. And when I was twelve, I kissed Elvis on those steps. His name was actually Elvis, I promise. It was my first real kiss. His smelly baseball jersey and his big fat gross tongue is something I can never forget. I'm sure I pissed off the neighbors by playing George Michael's song "I Want Your Sex" at max volume on my pink boombox every single day. Dancing to Madonna's "La Isla Bonita" with a friend in lace tights and a skirt way too short for my age to get the attention of anyone who'd look.

I learned a lot about life out there. Who needed school when I could watch the world from that porch? People running to the bus stop at the corner, vagrants having passionate conversations with invisible friends, kids playing in the street (I always wished they would ask me to play but they never did), I learned about the world from a distance.

Oh, if those stairs could talk.

The entire house was a labyrinth of beautiful moments and dysfunction and life lessons that have taken me years to dissect.

When I was four, bored and exploring, I wandered up to the attic. Behind my mom's old prom dresses and a couple of old coats, I found a small door that was just my size. I opened it and saw something glimmer in the dark. Hiding among the spiders in that dusty cubby hole was a metal dollhouse that I still have today. It was a treasure trove up there!

When I grew out of the dollhouse stage, I found my peace and quiet on the roof outside of the attic windows. I hid up there with my thoughts and watched the world go by. I became comfortable being alone. I taught myself to smoke on that roof—just me and my pack of Newport Lites. I watched the maple tree in front of our house, the one that used to barely cover our main floor front windows, begin to cover the sky in front of me.

The main floor of the house was where everything happened. The front room was where Santa Claus left me my first Barbie doll under our fake, snow-sprayed Christmas tree. The orange shag carpeting was where my bare little toes twirled and danced on Saturdays when Mom would play her Kenny Rogers and Diana Ross records on the stereo. And the tiny little bathroom next to my bedroom had the best acoustics. I sounded awesome singing Debbie Gibson's "Only in my Dreams" in the shower. At least I think I did, anyway.

But I think the reason I remember it the most was because it was the only home I ever knew my parents to be good to each other in. My siblings never got a chance to know the mom and dad I knew those first six years of life. And with tightly clenched fists, I had fought to hold on to those days for as long as I could.

The Only Girl on the Floor

As a little girl, I was obsessed with my mom. She was every bit of a Libra. Beautiful, glamorous, popular, and confident. The life of the party. The fun friend. She was the oldest daughter of eight and the only one out of them who chose to graduate high school. My dad fell in love with her long, strawberry blonde hair one afternoon after watching her do cartwheels in the yard across the street from his house. She smoked Kool cigarettes. She lived on Tab and RC cola and loved Scooby Doo and The Pink Panther. At work, she had a mirror on her desk with one of those red labels that she stamped herself. It read "Lorenda's moment of pleasure." Some might have thought her to be conceited, but her carefree attitude would've just laughed it off as jealousy.

Every morning before school, I would eat my cereal and watch her get ready for work. She would set her hair in hot rollers and apply her makeup at our kitchen table. Good Morning America would be on our TV in the background those mornings and it always amazed me how she could multitask. She'd sip her cup of coffee, take a drag of her cigarette and brush that Mary Kay grey on her eyelids almost at the same time. She was so cool to me. Like Sandy was at the end of the movie Grease. Mom's long golden curls would have made her perfect for a Clairol commercial and I wasn't the only one who believed that. Even a group of my second-grade classmates once told me she looked like a movie star. I was proud that she was my mom and when I was little, I really enjoyed being her daughter.

Saturdays were my favorite days with her. It was the one day of the week when she traded in her hot rollers for a bandana. Instead of eating at the kitchen table, we took our cereal bowls into the front room and watched cartoons together. Saturday was also when cleaning day was fun for me. Mom would open up all of our windows to let the breeze in. I loved it especially when it rained. The sheer curtains in our dining room swayed gently in the breeze as I danced around them while listening to "Burning Love" by Elvis on moms record console. Home was best to me when it smelled of Pine Sol and rain. As she swept, I dusted. When she vacuumed, I danced some more. Saturdays were the best. The only day better was my birthday.

I was due on October 24th, 1975. Unsurprisingly, I showed up on the 28th instead. I think it was the Scorpio in me that wasn't about to let anyone be right. Mom would say, "I told everyone at work that I would dress you up in a clown costume if you were born on Halloween!" Every year on my birthday she'd tell me this story.

I was the only baby girl born on the hospital floor that day. She had endured thirteen painful hours of labor and refused the pain meds that she was offered, for my sake.

She'd mention how the nurses began to think I was some sort of celebrity with all the visitors that came to the hospital to see me that day. And in typical fashion, her father, my grandpa, arrived at the hospital, drunk as a skunk, and smelling like it too. Apparently, he was proudly toting a huge plastic doll that he had picked out of a dumpster for me on the way to the hospital. I have always wondered what it looked like, but the elusive "dumpster doll" never made it into any of the pictures of my baby album because my mother didn't allow it in the hospital room.

As crazy as that story is, I loved when she would tell it to me. It felt like a movie, and for a moment, I was her favorite character. She always said she wanted a little girl and knew God would give her one. She never even got an ultrasound confirming that I was in fact, a girl. Yet that never stopped her from telling the world that she was having a baby girl.

"But what if you were wrong?" I'd asked her.

"I knew I wouldn't be," she asserted.

Growing up and hearing her say that didn't mean much to me when I was little, but looking back today, there is something beautiful about her confidence in that statement that I never realized until now. It's almost as if she was trying to make sure that I knew that she knew who I was before I was born. She was confident in it. More importantly, it showed that I was wanted. She wanted me.

From time to time, I have looked through my baby album in hopes to connect some of the images in my mind about the day I was born. But none of those yellowed 4x4 prints told the story anything like Mom did. Maybe it was just how I interpreted it. She always seemed so happy when she told it, and I longed to see that somewhere in the pages of my album. There was only one photo of my mother smiling that I could find. We were in a pool, and it was several months after I was born. The rest of them reflected a very young, not smiley mom. Maybe it was a generation thing, because my father's pictures weren't much better even if he did smile in a few. Dad's shaggy hairstyle and wire rimmed glasses, his "deer in the head lights" expression, reflected more like a serial killer trying to look normal, than a new dad holding his daughter. Grandpa's goofy look was the only picture that tracked with the original story Mom told, but he was a drunk. Since he was always drinking, he always looked the same. But there were no pictures of any of the crowd that came to visit me that day and none of my mother's mother.

Not one.

The Miscarriage That Lived

Within the four walls of oak paneling, my bedroom was like an amphitheater of an eighties childhood. I had a Strawberry Shortcake canopy bed with the matching ruffled curtains that hung in the window. There were rows and rows of dolls and stuffed animals on shelves, a Holly Hobby kitchen sink, and a porcelain tea set that sat on a little table next to a wooden rocking chair that was just my size. It was everything a little girl could dream of. My parents were doing it. They worked hard and much of the evidence could be found all over my room.

Because my father worked so much, the time I saw him the most was before I went to bed. I'd be already in my pajamas with my teeth brushed, anxiously waiting for him to come home. Apparently I was always excited to see my dad. Even when I was a baby, my mom used to put me in a dress and prop me up on the couch before he would get home so that I would be the first thing he would see when he walked in. Hearing her tell me this story was like listening to a little girl tell me how she used to play "house." To me, we were a picture-perfect family. As soon as I heard his keys turn the lock in the front door, I would run as fast as I could to greet him. Most nights he would scoop me up and carry me into the kitchen where my mom would be pulling his dinner out of the oven that she was keeping warm. As he briefly told her about his day, I would lay my head on his shoulder. I loved to hear his voice reverberate in his chest. It was strong and direct.

This self-proclaimed bookworm had collected books his whole life. Reading was my dad's gift to me, and I cherished it. Of all the books he read to me, my absolute favorite was *The Witch of Hissing Hill.* It came to me as part of the Weekly Reader book club. (My dad signed me up as soon as I began preschool.) I had tons of books, and he would read one book to me every night. But once I received this one in the mail, it wasn't long before this would become *the* book. He read the characters with voices, and energy, and offered color commentary as he read. Even as he grew tired of reading the same story over and over, that became part of our game. I would run to my bookshelf and grab it. He would dramatically throw his head back and act almost wounded, "*again*?" he would demand in an exaggerated way, and I would giggle all the way to my bed. I especially loved it when my mom would sometimes come in and sit on my bed to listen to the show too. Growing up the second oldest in a family of eight kids with a father that never learned to read, there wasn't any story time happening in her house growing up. It's not like she *couldn't* read. She read *The National Enquirer* cover to cover; we had a ton of them stacked up on the floor in our bathroom. She just didn't enjoy it like Dad did.

Whenever Dad finished up reading our story, he would tuck me in and give me a hug. I can still remember the smell of his t-shirts. The concoction of Old Spice cologne, metal, and cigarette smoke. Even though he hated smoking and never smoked a day in his life, he seemed to always be surrounded by people who did. His mom, who I knew as Busia (bush-ah), was a chain-smoker. He once told me how when he was young, he broke all of her cigarettes in half to get her to quit. He must've known that she loved him, because that was a brave move. Busia was a tough Polish broad who loved her Raleigh's Plain. When she took care of me, there'd be days when she'd have me run down to the gas station with a note to give to the cashier because they couldn't sell an eight-year-old two cartons of cigarettes without it. She was a straight shooter and a hardworking Chicagoan who didn't have time for people's foolishness. To many, she could be abrupt and rough around the edges, but I understood her. I saw her heart. The woman spoiled me even when I didn't deserve it. The first time she ever told me no; I threw myself down on the sidewalk screaming and crying in front of a Sears department store. Boy, was she embarrassed. If it were my parents, my three-year-old butt would have been spanked. They would have dragged me kicking and screaming to the car and taken me home, but Busia's patience with a spirited, bratty kid like me often came at her own expense. Yet, she never hit me. She just lit herself a cigarette, sat on the bus stop bench or whatever seat was around and let me scream it out. That's how she taught me things. If anything, that day I learned what it felt like to lay on an unforgiving cold cement sidewalk. I'm grateful because today I now know I could never live outside.

But all joking aside, my father said she put up with more than she should've with me because she said I was the little girl she never had. All of her family had died before I was born, and she lamented about it often when I was growing up. Busia would say a lot of things, and Lord knows, she never did sugar coat it. The truth was what it was, and it was hard to hear at times. Especially if you're not mature enough to understand it all. By the time she was married to my grandfather she was considered an "old maid." Being in her early thirties they had tried many times to have a baby. After failed attempts and several miscarriages they finally conceived my father. She opted to never try again after. He was her one and done. He became her world from that moment on, and I know she loved him deeply. She often bragged about how smart he was and how close they used to be when he was little while also complaining about how he's always too busy to come see her now that he's grown.

What I loved about her openness was that I never questioned where I stood with her; she told me. She told me with hugs, food, and of course, her words. I know she loved my dad, too. I'm not sure if my father felt the same love from her that I did, though. He was rarely around when Mom picked me up from Dza Dza and Busia's house. He jokingly referred to himself as "the miscarriage that lived." Talk about sad. All those Gen Z 's on Tiktok who say they have cornered the market on dark humor haven't met my father. But I'm not sure he had a choice in feeling the way he did. He was an only child whose mother suffered a set of traumas that she dealt with in the only way she knew. She ruminated on it.

Interestingly enough she married my grandfather, Dza Dza (ja-ja), who was the total opposite. He was a man of very few words. He did save the good ones for cussing at the dogs though. Dza Dza was also Polish, and a World War II veteran. I learned much later that he was one of the soldiers responsible for cleaning up the dead bodies. That could explain a lot of why he never had much to say to anyone. PTSD wasn't even recognized as a mental disorder until after I was born and by that time, he was already set in his ways surviving the only way he knew. By himself, on his own. Even if he was married and a father, he lived a lot of his life isolated from us all. He was a mystery to me. Sometimes, my curiosity would try to spark some sort of reaction out of him in hopes to get to know him more. Unfortunately, there were no pranks I ever played on him that brought me any closer to learning anything other than a new cuss word. But swearing was something, and it did make me laugh. He might've tried to, but he didn't scare me. He might've been a grumbly guy that just wanted to be left alone, but on weekdays after work, he would make me his favorite bologna and cheese sandwich, and we would watch the People's Court together.

I once asked my father if he ever knew what Dza Dza's favorite show was when I was growing up. He didn't know, and nothing more was said about it. I suppose there wasn't much he could say, because Dza Dza just wasn't that way. I always knew my father's favorite song was "Cat's in the Cradle" by Harry Chapin. Whenever it came on the radio in the car, he would turn it up. I never really listened to the words until I was in my teens, but I grew to understand more about the "miscarriage that lived" through the words to that song.

What My Mother Knew

I was always being dropped off somewhere to be watched by someone. This aunt or that cousin or a grandparent or a sitter. Eventually it was preschool, but all I ever wanted was to be home with my mom like we were on Saturdays. My mom said that women like her were meant to work. I know my mom cared about me, but she also cared about working. She was not going to be stuck at home like her mother, so she became the woman she saw on TV and in magazines. When she found out that Mean Miss Monika didn't allow me to use the bathroom when I needed to, she yelled at her and threatened her, but she still went to work. After that, I didn't need fresh clothes after naptime as often, but it's not like daycare felt any safer to me. Now, Miss Monika didn't look at me. Ever.

As if being pawned off on other people all the time wasn't bad enough, I also had to listen to them complain about how my parents never came back to pick me up at the time they said they would. I learned quickly that I was an inconvenience or a burden to everyone around me. I hated it. I would pretend to be sleeping as the sitters verbally bashed my parents. I just wanted to be somewhere I belonged. I threw a penny in every fountain I came across and made a wish. I prayed the Our Father every night, like the priest at school taught me to. I hoped and prayed and wished for the day I could be at home.

That day came when my Aunt Beatrice moved in with us. My mother described her as my grandmother's favorite daughter and the sister that was the closest to her. Apparently, there was some sibling rivalry and jealousy between the two of them growing up, but what large family doesn't have that? Aunt Beatrice had pulled some crap to get my mom in trouble, and my mom was the one who got beat for it. Mom must have gotten past it since she was trusting her to watch me now.

Having my aunt live with us meant I could be home more now, but it also meant that my parents came and went as they pleased. Outside of work, they now had time for multiple bowling leagues, painting classes, and girls' night out after work. There was little, if any, consideration for my aunt who might possibly want to have her own life outside of raising me. That roof over her head came at a cost, and that cost was me. So now, instead of feeling unwanted in other people's houses, I felt that way at home, too. I would listen to my aunt complain about my parents not coming home when they said they would, and I felt very clearly that I was still a problem. I didn't ask to be born, but here I was, the one keeping *everyone* from having a life.

When Aunt Bea got mad and cried and yelled and scared me, I prayed. I asked God to do something to get my mom to quit her job so that she could be home with me and no one else would have to stay with me anymore. Then one day it finally happened: My mom became pregnant. After six years of being alone, I was finally going to have someone to play with! The happiness this brought me didn't last, though. Shortly after my mom found out she was having my brother, the vibe in our house got weird between my parents. There was a lot more fighting, more door slams and tears. Aunt Bea moved out suddenly, and I didn't know why.

I spent many nights hiding under my Strawberry Shortcake blanket covering my ears, trying to drown out the screaming and crying that echoed from our kitchen all the way through the wallpapered hallway and into my bedroom. My parents were too angry to notice me anymore. After my brother was born, things between my parents got even worse. The sound of the mushroom coffee cups lifting off the kitchen table, as my father pounded it in sync with his words. The huge hole in the plaster wall that later had to be fixed because my dad punched it. And now that Aunt Bea wasn't around, I was the one Mom left my baby brother with when she needed to run out for a few minutes. It was hard getting up for school on those days because I wasn't getting much sleep. Every day was chaos, but surprisingly, it was the silence in the car as my mother drove me to school that made me the most uncomfortable. I couldn't believe it, but I was actually missing my aunt being around. At least she talked to me. At least she saw me.

One morning they were fighting again, but this was the worst I had ever heard them. I opened my eyes and tried to figure out what was happening. I watched my mother hurry from their bedroom to the kitchen and pour coffee into a cup. I could smell the coffee as she breezed through the hallway quickly into their bedroom with a cup in each of her hands. She set both cups down on their bedside table, and turned to flip on the light.

What transpired in the moments that followed have never left me. I watched her jump on top of my father, who was still lying in the bed. She straddled him, and punched him in the face as hard as she could, over and over, screaming and crying.

"WHY?! Why, Bob?" She wailed.

My father did what he could to block her fists as she went to town pounding him everywhere she could reach, a hammer of fists. As he figured his way around her wallops, he found his "in" and all it took was one hard punch to the side of her thigh to stop everything for a moment. She got up from the bed, sobbing, and ran into the kitchen.

I was frightened about what I had seen and what I still might see. I got up the courage to get up from my bed and walk toward the kitchen. Standing in the doorway, the cold floor beneath my little bare feet, the lace trim of my white nightgown with the pink flowers brushing the middle of my calves, I watched in horror as my mother grabbed a steak knife from the kitchen drawer and pressed it into her throat. I froze.

"Momma, please no!" I cried, as my dad tried to wrestle it away from her.

She looked at me blankly and said, "Chantel, please just go back to bed."

I inched backwards, but I refused to take my eyes off of her until I saw her put the knife down. The house became eerily quiet then, but my mind was anything but. I got myself back into bed, and the thoughts came flooding in. *Why would Mom want to die? Did she not know how much I love her? Doesn't she love my baby brother? What about my Christmas play? I am going to be the angel that said, "Fear Not!" I had the most lines in the entire play. She was making my costume. Didn't she want to see me in it? Doesn't she love me?* My world spun in a blur around me, as I tried to make sense of what I had just seen.

No one ever said anything to me about what I saw that morning. For a very long time after, I struggled to turn off the mental picture of my mom holding a knife. I regretted ever praying to God for my mom to be home. I regretted ever telling my parents I wanted a sibling. Maybe life really was better when Aunt Beatrice watched me. Sure, she yelled at me and was mean when my parents didn't come home on time, and her weird boyfriend made me uncomfortable, but anything would be better than this.

In an attempt to create some semblance of normal family life, my parents took me to see the movie *Gremlins* in the theater one afternoon. It was almost Christmas time. All around us were lights and decorations, but I could only feel the tension between my parents as we got our tickets and popcorn, and found our seats. On our way out, my parents argued about something, and I remember trying to climb into the back seat of our car quickly, without spilling any of the popcorn I still had left. I focused on the red and white stripes of the bag while they yelled at each other. In a blink, the yelling stopped and my mother started the car, peeled out of the parking space, and drove as fast as she could directly towards a brick wall at the end of the alley. My father and I screamed for her to stop. I wasn't belted in, so when she slammed on the brakes, I ended up on the floor of the backseat, surrounded by spilled popcorn. Thankfully I wasn't hurt–not physically, anyway–but for a long time I couldn't remember what that movie was even about.

One morning, shortly after the car incident, I found my mother in front of her bedroom window with every one of our photo albums wide open. She was surrounded by pieces of torn paper. I picked up a piece to look at what it was, and staring back at me was Bea's face. Mom was tearing her face out of every photo she was in.

When I asked my mom why she was doing this, she didn't answer. Later that same day, Beatrice showed up at the door. I hadn't seen her for a while, and I thought she looked different. I let her in, and noticed her round stomach. My mom was in her room making the bed when my aunt went in to speak with her.

I watched how my mother looked at her; the pain she felt was immediate: "How could you?" she cried.

"I'm sorry, Lorenda, I'm sorry. I'm so sorry."

I wouldn't see my aunt for a long time after that. She had a baby. I guess the weird boyfriend I didn't like was his father.

A while after Bea had her baby, Mom started to become happy again, and things were better for a while. I didn't understand why that was until years later. I found out that my father had an affair with my aunt while my mother was pregnant with my brother. When Bea also became pregnant, it wasn't clear who the father was: her boyfriend at the time or *my* father. This would make a stellar episode of the Maury show. They could call it "Cousin or Brother?"

The results are in!

[dramatic pause]

DAD…

[more dramatic pause]

You are *not* the father!

[cheering and bleeped expletives]

TWO

Surviving Seven

★

No Talking in Class

First grade was a total set up. I should have gone to my neighborhood school (my neighborhood Catholic school, that is), but my parents screwed up my entire grammar school life by being late to my neighborhood school enrollment. It would have been nice to get to know other kids in my neighborhood after spending twelve hours a day at daycare, but that didn't happen. Instead I became an outsider at my school. Nevermind that I was already an awkward, chubby girl with orange hair and a name I hated, I was going to be the new kid. Great. They all went to kindergarten together like they were supposed to, while I was at the daycare version of kindergarten across town. But when school started, I put on my uniform, pulled my white socks up to my knees, buckled my brown leather shoes, and hoped I might make a few friends along the way.

I remember learning quickly that there would be no outside play time, no time for coloring, and no talking in class. My teacher, Mrs. R, was a thin woman with stringy blonde hair and severe dark circles under her eyes. She didn't seem to like me very much, but I'm not sure she liked anyone. Not long after school started was picture day, the only day we could wear something other than our uniforms. I couldn't believe how different everybody looked in their dressy clothes. The boys wore ties and their hair was slicked back; the girls all wore a dress and some even had curls in their hair like me. My mom bought me a pink, ruffled apron dress from Sears that had a little bell sewn into the slip. The bell jingled as I walked, and twirled around. That little bell made me feel special and all the girls around me in line were fascinated. Well, all the girls except one.

The girl in front of me was a very tan, blonde girl, wearing a dress with white ruffles and a blue tulip embroidered on it. I would have told her it was pretty but she slugged me in the stomach out of nowhere. I guess that was her way of saying she didn't like me or my dress with the bell. I remember feeling her fist go straight into my gut and immediately hunching down to catch my breath. Doubled over in pain, my face in line with that embroidered tulip, I noticed that her patent leather shoes were dirty. In hindsight, maybe there's more to her story, but at that moment all I knew was that she was mean and that I didn't want people to see me cry. When she walked away, I turned and leaned my forehead on the cold brick wall and couldn't fight back the tears anymore. The other girl who saw this happen didn't know what to say, so she did as we were taught to do in class: she stopped talking and faced forward.

I tried to tell the teacher about the girl in the blue tulip dress, but she ignored me and scolded me for getting out of line. *No talking. Face forward. Don't cause problems.* It would become the foundation for my people-pleasing tendencies. I didn't know why that girl didn't like me. I hadn't ever talked to her before. I just wanted friends, and even though I have no memory of actually having friends that year, my teacher wrote on the back of my first report card that I was talking in class too much, and that I needed to work on it. I told you she didn't like me. The only time I remember ever seeing her smile was when she met my dad at parent-teacher conferences. Anyway, I was getting in trouble "for talking in class," but if I even looked in a direction other than forward, or opened my mouth to breathe, it resulted in a disciplinary homework assignment. I'd have to write, *I must not talk* 25 times in a row, along with my other homework. *I must not talk. I must not talk. I must not talk.* Over and over again.

The morning after parent-teacher conferences I got a warning for talking, and by the afternoon I had earned myself a punishment because I got caught breathing again. This time, Mrs.R wrote a note for my parents and stapled it shut. I hated being in trouble at school, and I definitely didn't want to be in trouble at home. Things at home were a mess, and I was so afraid of making things worse. After school that day, I opened her note and tried to read what it said. It was written in fancy cursive, and I hadn't learned that yet, but I made out what I could: *blah blah blah…* talking…*blah blah blah…*problem…*blah blah blah…*

Oh, no. My parents had to sign it.

Friday nights for my parents meant bowling league, so I asked my mom while she was in a hurry to get ready if she could just handwrite her name a few times on a piece of paper for me. I remember her asking me why and I told her that I wanted to learn how to write in cursive. When she asked me why I wanted her to write her name and not mine, I claimed it was because I liked her name better. I liked the cursive *L*. My scheme worked.

I put my teacher's note on top of the paper that my mom wrote her name on, and I traced her cursive as best as I could. On Monday morning, I confidently put that note on my teacher's desk and spent the rest of my day being good (being quiet and sitting still). Because the teacher didn't say anything to me that morning, I thought for sure I was in the clear. When my dad answered the phone during dinner, I didn't know why he turned to look at me. I had no idea that my teacher had our phone number. I suppose I was supposed to learn a valuable lesson that day about honesty or something. I already wanted to be good. I already wanted to stay out of trouble. I only plotted the coverup to save myself more punishment. I learned the word "forgery" that day, and I was sent to my room with a spanking. No matter how hard I tried to be good, and how desperately I wanted to do things right, I found myself in trouble. Somehow I was always a problem.

The Purple Pencil

So, let's talk about my genetics for a sec. I was born big-legged, with red hair, and had bad eyes resulting in wearing huge Daisy glasses. Even though strawberry blonde is a desirable hair color now, back in the early 80s, it was another thing that made me different from everyone else in school. I hated it. I was just that fat girl with yucky orange hair that didn't look like anybody else.

Then my mother gave me the name Chantel. Who does that? I tell you what, not someone who has their daughter's school social life in mind. Every time I cried about kids making fun of me for my name, she would tell me the same story about why she chose the name Chantel. There was a girl in her seventh-grade class who was smart and beautiful and I guess my mom hoped that by giving me the same name, I might be like her. But it was 1981; Gen X kids were ruthless. They didn't care about the story behind my name, they only cared about being cool, and having a name Chantel was not it. They called me *chan-delier, show-and-tell, she can't tell*, and later, *chan-ty liner*. I mean, sure, those are clever insults, but when you're little, it just sucks. I wanted a name like Lisa, Heather, or Angela. To anyone with those names, congratulations! You're in the top ten and most likely not bullied for your name. Unfortunately for me, the name Chantel didn't even make the top 100. I hated my name just as much as I hated my hair color. Couldn't I have just one thing that everybody else had so I didn't have to feel so different?

As decades go, the 80s were big—big hair, big shoulderpads, bigger-better-everything. Consumers were moving on from the earthy, mushroom brown and orange palette of the 70s with its bell bottoms, and macrame-everything. The world was becoming big and bright—think Cyndi Lauper—and we kids were the perfect target market for gimmicky, neon-iridescent, school supplies. Because we all wore uniforms at school, our accessories were the only way to signal our coolness, and I had an uphill battle. If you weren't very good looking, but you had great snacks to share with others at lunchtime, you still had some friends. If you didn't have cool shoes on, but you had a cool pencil case, you had friends. I just had to figure out what I could bring to the table so that somebody would like me.

With my home life being so chaotic, I was becoming more and more desperate to fit in at school. I learned that teachers like quiet, attentive students, so I was quiet and attentive. I also made sure my hair looked nice every day because it seemed like that mattered as well. Other kids might still make fun of the color of my hair, but at least it was clean and brushed. I created a formula in my head of how I needed to be in order to belong. I was about to take my people-pleasing to a new level.

One day I brought a brand-new package of colored pencils with me to school. I loved art, but at Catholic school, artistic expression was limited to an occasional Friday afternoon, twenty minutes before we were sent home with a coloring page of Jesus and the disciples. Out of the entire package I brought to school that day, the iridescent purple pencil, the best one, by far, would be my ticket to coolness. I just knew it. No one else had this color, and everyone wanted to try it. I finally had something to offer; I finally felt special.

Jennifer sat at the desk right across from me. She was a bigger girl, tall and broad. Jennifer also wanted my purple pencil, and I ended up giving it to her out of desperation for loyalty. I wanted a friend at all costs. To the right of me sat a boy named Jack. He made fun of me with the other boys, and said that I was chubby. I didn't like him, but what choice did I have? The teacher sat me next to him. Our desks were placed side-by-side in two rows, facing each other, so it looked like we were all sitting at a big Thanksgiving dinner.

One day Jack dropped his pencil on the ground, and when he picked it up, he brushed his hand along my leg. I flinched a little and looked at him, but went back to being a model student and thought nothing of it. Then it happened again another day, but this time he left it there. I froze because the teacher was teaching, and I knew that boys should not be touching anywhere near my skirt. I knew that this was not OK, but when I looked at Jack, he smiled at me. He moved his hand further up my skirt. I was desperate for anybody to like me, and even though Jack was mean to me in front of our peers, I was willing to accept that maybe he secretly liked me. So, I let him do it.

This went on for a couple of weeks until the day Jennifer dropped her pencil under the desks and saw what was happening when she bent down to get it. In hindsight I'm kind of glad she saw it and not the teacher because I was so afraid of getting in trouble. I will never forget the look on Jennifer's round face when she popped up from under the desk and looked at me. Her mouth fell open as she placed one hand over it and raised the other one in slow-motion.

"I'm going to tell the teacher on you," she whispered.

I silently begged her not to. The panic welled up inside of me and I fought back tears. In my head, everything was going to fall apart. I had been doing well in school and I did *not* want to upset my parents—things were already bad enough at home. Jennifer lowered her hand, but still made me suffer by acting like she might tell somebody. It's only now that I realize that she never cared to tell on Jack. Just me. By the end of that day, she gave me only one option: give her my new purple pencil and she would keep her mouth shut. Jennifer kept her word; she never told anyone that she saw Jack rubbing his hand under my skirt. Shortly after this incident, our desks were rearranged like they were every quarter, so Jack didn't touch me anymore. He probably thought he was special, but he wasn't the first boy to do that to me.

The First Time

When I turned six, I got a nightgown for my birthday. It had a Zebra with pink cheeks on it along with a silly joke:

"What's black-and-white and red all over?"

"An embarrassed zebra."

I had plenty of pretty, frilly nightgowns with bows and satin trim, but this one was my favorite. A simple, t-shirt style nightgown with pink baseball sleeves, and a funny joke.What's not to love? I wore this nightgown every night. It was quickly becoming pilled and faded, but I didn't care.

One night when Mom and Dad were out bowling, Aunt Beatrice was watching me as usual, and she was upset that my parents were late again, as usual. This time she had her weird boyfriend over and we were all in the front room watching TV. The room was dark except for

the glow from the TV screen. I should have been in bed, but I was lying on the floor in front of the TV, half asleep.

At some point, Aunt Bea left the room, probably to go to the bathroom, and her boyfriend moved from the couch to sit beside me on the floor. He didn't say a word to me, but he looked around to see if she was there. I went back to vacantly staring at the TV. I don't remember what I was watching, I just remember feeling his hand. It started at my foot and ended up in a place inside of me that I had never felt someone touch before. I completely froze. Those few moments felt like years. When he heard my aunt's footsteps, he jumped up and moved back to the couch as if nothing happened.

I wish I had just gone to bed when I was supposed to. That was the last time I wore my zebra nightgown.

You Get What You Pay For

I didn't like going to my grandma's house, but like most things when you're a kid, I had no choice. Mom was back at work now, and school was out for the summer, so my baby brother and I had to go somewhere. Daycare for both of us was out of the question – Dad was building a business, which meant money was tight. I was hoping we'd go with Busia, but her arthritis was getting bad and chasing after my baby brother was a lot of work even without the pain of arthritis. So we ended up with Grandma, because she was the only cheap option we had, and you know what they say: you get what you pay for.

Remember the movie *What's Eating Gilbert Grape* starring Johnny Depp? Grandma was the spitting image of the mom. You know, the one whose body was too heavy for the emergency service people to remove when she died, so her kids saved her and themselves the embarrassment of her having to be removed by a crane, so they set the house on fire and left her in it? Grandma was that big, too. She also never smiled, but maybe that's because she didn't have any teeth. Mom said she was pretty when she was young, but I had a hard time imagining a different version of her. The grandma I knew was a scowling woman, one who scratched and picked at her psoriasis sores until they bled, and wore a house dress that was too small and revealed her expansive belly which hung to the floor between her legs when she sat down. I remember thinking how uncomfortable that had to be, and because I was often face-to-face with her enormous belly button, I always wondered what kinds of things lived in the depths of that terrifying cavern.

She was talented with yarn though. She crocheted blankets and dolls of all sorts. Busia once told her she should take her handmade items to the market to sell. She said she didn't crochet for that reason, and then Busia called her stupid and that made her cry. They didn't talk much. I wish she would have taught me how to crochet. It could have given me something to do that summer instead of staring into the void of her belly button hole and watching *The Price is Right!* But that would have required something of her that I don't think she was capable of giving.

Mom once said she didn't think her mother loved her. Looking back, I actually think I believe her. Grandma never looked happy to see us when we came around for the holidays, yet Mom always made a point to visit her anyway. After Aunt Beatrice had an affair with my dad, Grandma took her in and seemed to take her side. It gave her another reason to dislike my father; something she had made up her mind about a long time ago. The feeling was mutual,though. Dad never had a kind word to say about the woman who raised my mom, and for good reason. He knew about how Grandma broke my mom's hip when she was only three. He knew about how Grandma beat her regularly throughout her childhood. When my mom was seventeen, one of those beatings left a scar on her left eyelid. For my dad, who lived across the street, that was the last straw. He knew my mom needed to get out of there and the only way my grandfather would allow that was if my dad married her. So that's what they did.

Mom would say my grandma was just jealous of her because she was my grandpa's favorite, and because she never had the opportunities my mom had. She wasn't wrong. Grandma and Grandpa met when he was fourteen and she was sixteen. At that time, she already had a son who was rumored to be born from a rape when she was only fourteen. When she and my grandpa got married, Grandpa took him in as his own. I never got to meet him because he was murdered before I was born, and everyone in the family says Grandma was never the same after. I have to assume that she was once different from the grandmother I know, otherwise the grace my mother extended to her doesn't make sense. Even then, I struggled to reconcile my mother's decision to leave my brother and me in the care of someone who was clearly not right in the head.

That summer we spent with Grandma, my brother was kept in a playpen all day long. Sure, he was a bit of a holy terror, but Grandma had no patience with him. The only time she would interact with either of us was when we needed to be fed. She only held my brother if he wouldn't stop crying, and it was far from a loving embrace. She'd snatch him out of his playpen and roughly pat his back while mechanically rocking him to sleep. She never allowed him to roam around the rooms and play. She didn't ever play with either of us, or take us outside. She barely spoke to us. There was a park just across the street, and *sometimes* I could go swing on the swings. But only if she was in the mood to sit in the room where the window faced the park and she could see me without having to get up. Most days I would alternate between staring out the window at the lucky kids playing outside, and learning the latest about Vicki's multiple personality disorder on the soap opera *One Life to Live*. I clocked a lot of time on that couch, pretending I was somewhere else. I hated it there.

The loneliness and boredom from sitting on the couch at Grandma's eventually became desperation for anything else. JD was someone who lived with my grandmother at the time, and while I only ever remembered seeing him leave his room to get a bowl of Chef Boyardee ravioli, or to refill his pop, I hoped that he might be better company than Grandma. I hoped he would at least talk to me. I hoped he might go to the park with me or play Monopoly with me, but he never wanted to. It was still just watching TV and being bored, but at least now I wasn't bored and alone.

One day, after weeks of pestering him to play a game with me, and then giving up when he wouldn't, *he* asked *me* to play a game with him. He didn't have to ask me twice; I was dying to play anything! Anything to make the dog days of summer go by faster. He told me that I probably never played this game before but that it was fun, and he would teach me. It was a pretend game. He was the mechanic, and I was the customer who needed her car fixed. The game required me to pull down my pants and let him touch me wherever he wanted.

His bed was stained and smelled musty and sour, like dirty socks. I don't know if there were curtains, but the window was cracked and taped over. An Iron Maiden poster hung on the dirty walls along with a carnival mirror, featuring John Travolta from *Staying Alive*. The huge TV sat on the floor, on a dirty brown shag rug. Everything in that room was dirty, but the smell is something that still triggers me: dirty laundry that has been sitting in a basket too long.

I hated that game. I didn't want to play it, but I didn't want to be alone either. He would tell me what to do and I would do it. It was uncomfortable, but I pretended to be someone else. I told myself it was a game. It was just a game.

Until it wasn't.

I was sitting in my grandmother's front bedroom eating cereal and watching Oprah with her. Oprah was on every single day at 9 AM on Channel 7. If she wasn't on at my house, she was on at Busia's house, or my aunt's house, or your aunt's house–it was Oprah. She was on everywhere. And on this day, she was on at my grandmother's house. She was talking about her childhood sexual abuse and the more she shared, the slower I chewed. Everything she said she felt, I felt, too. I knew something was wrong but I struggled to put the pieces together about things that just didn't make sense to me. I needed to talk to someone. I wished I had Busia, but I was stuck with Grandma. I told her about how Aunt Bea's weird boyfriend touched me when she wasn't around. I told her about the "mechanic" game that JD always asked me to play in his room.

"You're a liar," she interrupted. "Don't you ever say these things again." She nearly hissed at me: "If you ever share this with anyone, you could ruin everything. Now get out of this room!"

So much for Oprah's approach.

I already felt weird and gross and dirty, and now my grandmother confirmed for me just how bad I really was. I now felt the shame of those dirty spots on my soul on top of every other bad feeling I had. There were so many dirty spots after all those times, how would I ever feel pure again? And summer was far from over. I would have to come back to Grandma's the next day and the next day and the next day. JD would ask me to play the game and I didn't know how to say no.

The Crown

Ms. Geri's School of Dance was a staple in my neighborhood. Any kid who wanted to dance, danced there. I was obsessed with memorizing every routine and every song from *Annie* and *Mary Poppins.* I dreamed of being an actress and a dancer one day. I wanted to go to this dance school so bad. I knew that my parents would have to sacrifice to make it happen, and I wasn't going to hold my breath. After all, I had just endured a horrible summer at Grandma's because money was tight. The only reason that ended was because Mom saw a mark on my baby brother from where Grandma had hit him. Anyway, now that I was back in school and taking the city bus, I got off by Busia's house. She would meet me at the stop every day and the first thing she would ask me is if I was hungry. The answer was always yes. I was tasked with making my own lunches this year, and while my mom never told me *not to* eat lunch, she also didn't make sure that I did. It wasn't that she was being negligent about it, it's just that skipping meals was such a normal thing for her, that she extended that practice to me, even though I was just a kid. All of this is to say that by the time I got to Busia's stop after school, I was always starving and couldn't wait to stuff my face with whatever we were going to get that day.

Mom must have figured out the money because she agreed to sign me up for dance. On our way there, I remember her telling me that Ms. Geri was the real deal. I peered through the studio's front window, both eager and intimidated. The studio walls were lined, floor-to-ceiling, with photos of every class Ms. Geri taught, photos from every recital Ms. Geri produced, and professional headshots and poses and awards from everything Ms. Geri had accomplished as a professional dancer. I loved looking at all of the costumes and hairstyles and I imagined what it would be like to see myself costumed and in full makeup on those walls, too. Ms. Geri was so cool. She had an alternative pixie cut that looked like Pat Benetar in the video for "Love is a Battlefield." She always wore an off-the-shoulder hand cut sweatshirt over her black leotard and nude tights and jazz shoes, like the girl in Flashdance. The real deal. And I was in. I was going to be one of Ms. Geri's dancers.

I picked out a purple leotard–the kind with suspenders that go over a cropped t-shirt–and I had my hair pulled back into a messy ponytail, and I was ready to go. Little did I know that the standard dance uniform was a simple black ballet leotard with pink tights. Look, I get that my mom wanted me to have some choice, but she didn't do me any favors by not suggesting that I go with a classic look here. My mom didn't get to participate in dance when she was my age. It just wasn't an option for her, so this was all new territory and she had no idea what she was getting us into. She also didn't spend much energy trying to learn about it. She had done her job as a mother: she found the money, signed me up, and dropped me off, and I had better be grateful.

So week after week, I lined up at the bar, looking in the stupid mirror at myself, wearing my stupid purple leotard, with my hair in a stupid messy ponytail. Every other girl had her hair pulled up into a perfectly polished bun and wore the perfect black leotard and pink tights. Ms. Geri instructed us to be mindful of our form and our foot positions, but all I could see in the mirror was that I was different. I was the only red head with big legs. I was the only one wearing a lavender leotard and a messy ponytail. I didn't fit in here. I didn't fit in anywhere. I wanted to quit. I wanted to disappear. I wanted to be invisible. My head spun with all the ways I didn't belong, but then I would catch a glimpse of sparkle. Up on a high shelf, there was a crown. It was the most beautiful crown I had seen in my entire life–more beautiful than the first communion dresses and sparkly rosaries–and I just *had to* have my turn at wearing it.

This crown was handmade. It was a silvery material with hundreds of sequins hand-sewn onto it. When the studio light hit the crown just so, the sequins would cast a glittery reflection all around the room. It was magnificent. The only time we could wear the special crown was on our birthday. At the end of the class, if it was your birthday, Ms. Geri would seat you in a chair in the middle of the dance floor, and delicately place the crown on your head as if you were a princess. Then she would play the special birthday record and everyone would join hands and dance and sing around you while the crown sparkled like a magical halo around the special birthday girl. I couldn't wait until it would be my turn.

I spent the weeks leading up to my birthday hating the huge mirror at the ballet bar, and hating my hair, and hating my glasses, and hating my legs–I hated my legs the most. People in my family always had something to say about my legs. I was a chubby baby, and even though I eventually outgrew most of my baby fat, it stuck around in my cheeks and legs. When I started school and became an easy target for teasing, the other kids made fun of me for my hair, my name, my glasses, my round face, *and* my legs. God, we 80s kids were mean! But as I stood there in dance class, analyzing the other girls and picking myself apart, I became convinced that something was wrong with me. There must be some reason why I'm so different–why I can't just fit in. Maybe everything the kids at school say about me is true. Maybe my grandma was right when she said I would just make trouble. Maybe I deserved to feel so disgusting and bad because maybe I really *was* bad. The fear of ruining everything, and the shame my grandma so graciously lavished on me when I told her what was going on became heavier each day. I hated myself. I hated how I looked, and I hated how I felt, and I thought that somehow, maybe, wearing that crown, even just for a moment, would let me feel special and beautiful and maybe that magical sparkly glow that it reflects onto the floor could surround me and change me. I just had to wait for my birthday.

I always loved my October 28th birthday as a kid. A Halloween-themed party with costumes and cake was amazing. My mom ordered the best cakes from the bakery–Miss Piggy, or Cabbage Patch Dolls, or Strawberry Shortcake, of course–my mom liked going the extra mile to make my birthday special with a really cool cake. This year was different, though. I told my mom that I didn't want a cake and that I didn't want to have a party either. I hadn't gotten the nerve to tell her that I didn't want to dance anymore because I didn't want to disappoint her. I practically begged to be in dance class. But I also held off telling her because I wanted to wear that crown at least once before I quit.

When it was Halloween week at dance, we were encouraged to wear a costume and bring a bag of candy to share. I chose to be Strawberry Shortcake for the fourth year in a row. It was one of those cheap plastic costumes that you could buy in the Halloween aisle at Woolworths or Walgreens that tore after one day of trick or treating. But because I loved it so much, Mom bought it for me every year anyway. The costume came with a weird plastic mask that I never wanted to wear, so Mom found me a cute pink bonnet and drew freckles on my cheeks with her eyebrow pencil instead. I was in my costume, and I brought my bag of candy, and I watched the clock tick slowly as I pushed through our dance routines, anticipating the Halloween party and my turn wearing the special birthday crown. I tried not to look in the mirror, so I looked up at the crown on the shelf to make sure it was still there, and I looked around the room at the other dancers. I've got to admit it was pretty funny watching a girl dressed as Cookie Monster do the splits, and another girl dressed as a Care Bear, the grumpy one, do a perfect pirouette.

As the class went on, my mind spun with the words *just ask her, Chantel!* I worried that we were going to run out of time, or that maybe she'll forget–or worse, maybe she didn't even know that today was my birthday at all. She never really looked at me. I kept hoping she would ask me. I kept hoping I could wear the crown for just a few minutes and feel something different. I kept hoping that I could feel special. But she never reached for the crown that day. We went from practicing our routines, to sharing the candy we brought, to going home. I never got my turn in the beautiful, sparkling halo, and I never told her.

I finished the season and participated in the recital, because I didn't want to disappoint my parents, but something inside of me broke that day. I took off my dance shoes, and put them in my bag with my candy along with any hope that I might really be a dancer one day.

My First Lesson in Love

Baz was a boy in my class who sat in the desk right in front of me. He was new to our school, and for some reason, our teacher did not like him. Honestly, I don't think she liked any of us. But when Baz came into the picture, she found her target and never missed. Every day she'd find a reason to yell at him or make some mean, condescending remarks about how he said things, and I felt bad for him. I never understood why she disliked him so much, I just understood what it felt like to be an outsider.

Baz wasn't a "looker." He was a chubby, pale-skinned boy with red cheeks and black hair. He had just moved to America from Poland. He smiled at me one time when he turned around to pass back a lesson handout. His eyes were clear and blue and that was all it took–I was in love. No stupid teacher was going to yell at my Polish prince and make him feel bad without me doing something about it. So, one day after religion class, I got the nerve to write him a letter. In the best cursive I could, I wrote about how I thought our teacher was evil and how unfairly she treated him.

I wanted to show him that he wasn't alone, which really meant that I saw an opportunity to feel less alone. I thought we could be some sort of alliance.

In this note, I told him about how our teacher wanted to be an actress and had bragged for months about being an extra in some new movie being released next year called *Sixteen Candles*. I remember thinking that it was cool that she could be a movie star one day, but because she wasn't a warm and fuzzy person, I was like, who cares? I wrote about how she told us whenever she could that people told her she looked like Olivia Newton John. I guess her blue eyes and short blonde bob with bangs did remind me a little of Sandy from Grease, but this was an obsession and it was annoying. On Fridays, when we could listen to music in class, guess what she played? The only records we had to choose from were by Olivia Newton John. What about Michael Jackson? Culture Club? We all loved the songs "Beat it" and "Karma Chameleon" why couldn't we listen to those! I put all of this in the note to Baz, and then some. When I had finished writing it to perfection, I carefully signed it *love, Chantel*, and drew a heart next to it. I folded it up into a square and handed it to him just before lunch was over. He looked confused, but then again, he always kind of did.

As class started, I remember watching Baz open the letter and I freaked out. Didn't he know he was going to get in trouble for reading it in class? It wasn't long before our wannabe Olivia Newton John caught him and made him bring it up to her desk.

Of course the class was filled with whispers and giggles as we all watched her eyes dart left to right reading everything I had said about her. I wanted to run but instead I just looked down at the lesson we were supposed to be studying and prayed to disappear. *I'm going to get in so much trouble!* I thought.

She shifted her seat and leaned over to look around the rows in front of me to make eye contact. But I refused to look up. She never said anything to me about the letter, but she rearranged our seats right away. Baz never said anything about the letter either. Actually, he never said anything to me at all. That dummy probably didn't even read it, and here I was stuck with the humiliation that my teacher knew more about the first love of my life than the actual person I loved. He had no idea. To make matters even worse, I was now sitting in the front row facing her desk.

Maybe it all happened for a reason. Maybe it was God trying to straighten out my priorities. Our grade was preparing to receive the Holy sacrament of Communion and Brother Bob said that the only one we should be in love with was Jesus anyway, and I really tried hard to do what I was told.

My First Confession

"Bless me father for I have sinned. This is my first confession." I knelt, head bowed, hands folded, just like I was taught. The confessional was dark and wooden, heavy with incense and shame. I was in third grade.

As a Catholic girl who attended Catholic school, I spent a lot of time sitting in the pews, looking up at the carved Jesus wearing a crown of thorns. I always felt so bad for him–he didn't do anything wrong, so why did he have to suffer? It wasn't fair.

My Catholic upbringing also meant experiencing my First Holy Communion and all that went with it. This was a time when little Catholic girls got an entire pageant, *I mean mass*, dedicated to dressing up like miniature brides to eat a wafer. Now, I understand the significance of the religious sacrament, but to my eight-year-old mind, it was about the presents and the party.

Leading up to First Communion, we learned and memorized all of the prayers–the Apostle's Creed, the Our Father, the Rosary…blah blah blah. But the most important thing about the whole process for me was picking out my dress. One Saturday morning, my mom and I drove to church to walk through aisles and aisles of tables laid out in the church basement – beautiful dresses in satin, silk, and taffeta, hand-beaded, adorned with sequins and lace. I wanted it all. I wanted to feel fancy and special and important. Veils and gloves and patent leather shoes, rows and rows of white leather-bound Bibles all beckoned to me, but the crystal rosary beads glimmering in the sunlight like magic–those were the real prize! I wanted to be a princess–I wanted to be God's princess. Even though I clearly didn't fully grasp the magnitude of religious sacrament, I wanted to be a good girl. I wanted to do everything right.

It would not be until my 30s when I would really understand that communion was not about a party where I would eat cake and receive religious gifts and money. Actually, now that I think about it, all of this production is pretty ironic considering what it is really meant to symbolize. Back then, this was what everybody did. Well, this was what everybody who was Catholic and living in my neighborhood of Chicago did.

Before the party, though, there was one thing to do first. It was called reconciliation. In other words, I needed to properly repent for my sins. We were taught that we could not receive our first holy communion until we knelt in front of a priest in a box, behind a curtain. The priest, I learned, had been chosen by God to absolve me of all the things I had ever done wrong in my life. He would be behind a curtain so I couldn't see his face, and after listing every bad thing I did, he would tell me my penance (this many Hail Marys, this many Our Fathers, etc.) And then it was time for the party.

We rehearsed the process and for weeks, we chanted the words *bless me father for I have sinned* over and over again to practice. In between *bless me* rehearsals, Brother Bob tried his best to teach us about sin. I wasn't a perfect kid, but the sins we learned about were really big ones. I never killed anybody. I never stole anything from a store or another person. I never used the Lord's name in vain even though everybody around me did–especially Dza Dza. I never swore once! Brother Bob explained that sin was like black spots on our hearts and on our souls, something that needed to be washed away. He drew a heart and then scribbled over it to illustrate his point. I didn't understand this with any nuance, but I could feel the black spots on my heart, and I understood that to be good was to be pure.

So, the week of our first confession I was a little stressed. There were a few things that I felt that I could share with the priest that I have done wrong, but the perfectionist in me thought crap, what if I miss something? We are being taught that we have all these black marks on our souls that could not receive communion if they weren't washed away. And the only way they could get washed away is if a priest absolves us of them.

When the day came for my first confession, I knew my lines perfectly. I kept repeating in my head, *bless me father for I have sinned, this is my first confession.* I was nervous and didn't want to make a mistake. *What if I forget one of my sins?* I worried that if I forgot then I wouldn't be able to wear my dress or have a party. My mom would have spent all that money for nothing. My tendency towards perfectionism might have been honed by this experience.

As I waited quietly in line, I watched each child go into the confessional booth. The second they knelt; a little light above the door turned red. After they were done, the light turned green. I don't know if the priest handled that or if it was triggered by the kneeling, but it was a good system. When it came time for me to enter the booth, I remember being nervous and shaky, but I rattled off my first line perfectly.

"Bless me father, for I have sinned; this is my first confession." I did it. I told the priest that I thought my brother was a terror, and sometimes I pinched him. To be fair, though, I prayed for someone to play with and instead, my brother arrived as *a baby.* What was I supposed to do with *a baby*? I told him that sometimes I talked back to my parents. From there, I wasn't sure what else to say, but I could still feel the black spots. Brother Bob said if we could not come up with a sin to confess to just feel free to pick one of the Ten Commandments. Whew, the dress could be worn, and the party would go on!

"I have committed adultery," I said to the priest.

There was a long pause on the other side of that carved wood screen and privacy curtain before he responded with the typical absolution and my plan for redemption: Six *Hail Marys* and Two *Our Fathers* and I would be pure as the driven snow, ready to receive my first communion the following week. That was it; I was now absolved. My heart no longer had those gross, dirty spots on it. But I didn't feel any different. I thought the priest would ask me why I said that. Even if I was just picking one of the commandments like Brother Bob told us to do. It's possible that my life could have been different if he asked any follow-up questions. But he didn't.

It's true that I didn't understand the meaning of that commandment, *thou shalt not commit adultery,* but I knew it had to do with grown ups being naked and breathing heavy. Or at least that's what I thought. Maybe I picked it up through my environment, considering everything that was going on with my parents. Whatever the reason, it felt familiar when I read it, so it stuck. I remember seeing warnings of "adult content" on cable movies and being sent out of the room. If there was anything over a PG rating, my dad wouldn't allow me to see it. He was strict like that, which is funny, given his behavior throughout my life. My mom sent me out of the room, too, but she let me watch some of the movie. I loved listening to the record from *Flashdance* when my mom would play it on Saturday mornings, so I wanted to watch the movie with her, even though it was rated R. She only let me watch some parts and made me promise not to tell Dad. This is how I began to associate people being naked and kissing and breathing heavy with the word adult and that's pretty close to the word adultery, so there you have it.

We all know that when parents make something off limits, it becomes more interesting to children; so, if I ever got a chance to sneak back into the living room to watch the scenes *with adultery,* I obviously would. I know I said I wanted to be good, but I was also a typical kid.

Rated-R meant off-limits, bad, adult content, adultery, naked, kissing, touching – it all got jumbled up in my head and that confusion with sex only got worse. I didn't understand sex when I was eight, but knew it was off limits. And while I didn't fully grasp what was happening to me and around me, I knew it was bad, and therefore I was bad. I had hoped my first confession would make that feeling go away, but it didn't.

THREE

Bullies & Body Issues

★

I Hate Everything … Except Busia

After my grandmother told me that I would ruin everything if I spoke up about what happened to me, I decided that it must have been my fault. I didn't stop my aunt's boyfriend, I just froze. I went to JD's room all those times. I agreed to play the game. I didn't say no. This secret had a power over me that held on and didn't let go.

I didn't dance anymore so I didn't have to look at myself in the mirror all the time, which was fortunate I guess because I still hated my legs and my hair. I learned to hate more parts of myself, too. I learned to read every signal in my environment, studying every look and expression, so I could navigate certain dangers. A subtle shift in tone from either of my parents' could dictate how I felt about myself that day. I was in a state of constant anxiety, walking on eggshells around everyone. I couldn't put a name on what it was, but I was feeling it in every part of my body. Any feeling of fullness in my stomach after I ate a meal, left me feeling disgusting and upset about my lack of self-control. I wanted to eat less so that I could be skinny like the girls that everyone seemed to like in school. Like the other girls I envied in the mirror at dance class. I hated wearing my uniform skirt to school because my thighs touched as I walked now and when they rubbed together, I sometimes got a rash. Most days, I just felt awkward and gross and that everything about me was *wrong*.

Even though I did a lot of praying, God never stopped the kids from making fun of me. He didn't lift the feelings of shame that I had, and he wasn't helping my parents get along any better at home. The only prayer he answered was that I got to spend time with Busia. Even though her arthritis was painful, she knew my parents needed someone to care for my brother and me. I don't know if my mom told her about the mark my grandmother left on my brother, she just stepped in without complaint, knowing that it wouldn't be for long. My mom was pregnant again, and would soon take time off from work to be home with us kids for a while anyway.

I loved being with Busia. Before my brother was born, she took me on many adventures around the city of Chicago. The cabs she would call to take us to our daily destination had blue leather seats and always smelled like a combination of stale cigarettes and whatever air freshener was hanging from the rear view mirror. If we were going to Sears, I was definitely getting a new dress or a toy of some sort. If we were going to the Brickyard Mall, we would definitely be stopping by the Lisa Frank store. Busia would give me ten dollars to spend on the coolest stickers. The walls were a technicolor explosion of pastel and neon leopards, dolphins, and kittens peeking out of high top sneakers. The hardest part was always choosing which stickers to get. On the days our trip was a straight shot to the destination, we would take the bus. My favorite adventure was when she took me to Lincoln Park Zoo–in the winter! I'm sure I complained about my toes freezing in my boots, but it was the only time I ever saw the polar bears playing outside. These are fond memories now, but back then, these were the moments that kept me going.

When I told her the kids at school were making fun of me for being fat, she said that I would need to get thicker skin, and then she took me out for hotdogs to make me feel better. She didn't exactly help me in the weight department, but at least she offered me comfort. Whether it was a hotdog and crispy fries from Jimmy's, a Mr. Submarine Turkey Sub, or the infamous Burger King Whaler, which Busia simply called a fish sandwich, we spent a lot of our time together eating and talking. For as gruff as she could be, she and I would talk for hours. I could tell her anything–well, *almost* anything. I didn't tell her what I told my other grandma; I chose to carry that shame in secret. But being with Busia made it easy for me to forget–for a little while, anyway. Because loneliness was something we seemed to have in common, she had a way of making me feel less alone in the world. She understood me. She saw me.

It's not that she talked about being lonely, but Busia never had any friends that I knew of. She only had us and Dza Dza, and boy did they fight. My dad said there wasn't a birthday or Christmas that he remembers that didn't include a soundtrack of yelling and swearing, and I believe him. When I was with them, I either saw constant bickering, or no interaction at all; they simply coexisted. Dza Dza steered clear of Busia, and Busia steered clear of Dza Dza. I once asked Busia why they fought so much, and she simply replied that he disgusted her. My mom told me that she thinks it was because Busia caught him talking badly about her to his sisters one day and she never forgave him. My aunt once said it was because he was getting too friendly with some neighbor down the street. All my dad ever said was that they had a hard life.

I don't know what kind of dreams Busia might have had for her life, she didn't talk about that. What I do know is that when Busia would tell me stories about her life, they were stories that just *felt* lonely. When Busia was a young girl, her much older sister had a child that died of whooping cough at only three years old, and the embalming process was done at home, in the family kitchen. As if that isn't unsettling enough, little Busia happened to see what was removed during this process because it was plopped in a bucket behind the couch. That's not something you can unsee, and whenever Busia told me this story, she went into grizzly detail. A few years after that incident, her sister died, and before long, before she ever met Dza Dza, Busia was the only one left of her family.

I heard that story many times growing up. I knew that I was the little girl she never had, my father reminded me of this any time I was being a brat, but even if my dumb kid behavior seemed like I didn't appreciate her, she was the most important, stable, and safe relationship I had growing up. I never questioned if she wanted me around or loved me. She was my light in the darkness.

Busia was tough because she had to be. And maybe by the time I came into her life, she was able to soften just a little–just enough to show me what love is supposed to be. Maybe by caring for my brother and me, we helped her hold onto some thread of some other life. A happier life, without so much loss and conflict.

Nobody Hits My Kid But Me

I was ten when my sister was born. At first, I was hopeful she'd be more normal than my rambunctious brother who seemed hellbent on destroying everything I owned, but my excitement didn't last long. I was glad my mom was home now, but I was growing more jealous of my siblings by the day. My sister was glued to my mom's hip during her first few years of life, and actively disliked everyone that wasn't my mom. I don't know if babies are capable of manipulation, but every morning when I poured myself a bowl of cereal, the charade began. My sister would stare me down from her highchair at the kitchen table until I looked at her. Then, as soon as I met her gaze, she would start screaming. I learned to roll my eyes and laugh it off because it was ridiculous how much she couldn't stand the sight of me. But it was my mom's response that made me begin to hate her.

"Chantel, just don't look at her!" She would snap.

Did I not have a right to exist in my own house anymore?

My sister's screaming would be so obnoxious that my mom would plead with me to put the cereal box in front of my face so she would just stop. I ate countless bowls of cereal hiding behind the box. *Don't upset the baby. Don't show your face. Don't be a problem.* It was ridiculous, but it was also infuriating to me that my mom never bothered to correct my sister, or even entertain the possibility of finding another solution–you know, something other than: *Chantel, just hide your face.* So there were some times when I took things into my own hands.

When Mom wasn't looking, I'd stick out my tongue or pinch her as I passed by. I was pissed. I was pissed that my brother was allowed to break all my stuff without consequence. I was pissed that my baby sister bullied me into hiding my face in my own home. I was pissed that my siblings got a lot more of my mom than I ever did at their age. I was pissed that my dad regularly introduced me as their built-in babysitter. I was pissed about pretty much everything. And to top it all off, I was pissed with what I had to deal with at school every day. There wasn't a single place where I could just *be.*

Richard was a whiz kid in my class that was good at everything. He also was a huge brown-nosing tattletale and unfortunately, he sat right next to me. Every day we had math homework to do in a workbook. Sometimes our teacher would come around to check if it was done and sometimes, she didn't. The only thing I hated more than my hair, my name, my legs, and my siblings was math. I was never any good at it even though I was in the accelerated kids group. Weeks had gone by and I hadn't done my homework. I didn't understand it and Mom was busy with my siblings and my dad wasn't home much at all anymore to help.

I don't know why Richard decided on this particular day to tell Ms. Dabrowsky that I hadn't done my homework, but one day he did. He raised his hand and told her that she needed to see something. She turned to come over, and I knew I was in trouble. As she leafed through my workbook and saw how many pages were blank, she huffed with disappointment and then boiled over. She was an older lady, scrawny, leathery, hard and loud with a raspy voice. It was well known that she was a yeller and she could be heard all the way down the hallway and in the bathroom. Whenever she would go off, all the other teachers would shut their doors in unison and continue their lessons. I don't think she had it out for me in general, but on that day I was going to be made an example of.

She grabbed my arm and pulled me out of my desk and up to her podium, screaming the whole time. I focused on her leathery mouth, frosted light pink lipstick and spittle collected in the corners as she spat her disappointment at me. What I got from her tirade was that lying was something she would not tolerate. She was disappointed and was going to make sure that nobody else in the class would repeat this behavior. She slapped my workbook down on her podium and whacked me several times on the butt in front of the class. It did hurt a little, but not as much as it humiliated me.

When the school called home that day to report an incident, the focus was on how I messed up. My mother was informed that I hadn't done my math homework for several weeks. Nothing was said about the spanking. When I got home and told my mother what had actually happened, she was dumbfounded. Not that I hadn't done my homework, but that a teacher would ever spank a kid at school. The next day she marched into that office with my baby sister on her hip, and demanded an immediate meeting with Ms. Dabrowsky and our principal. Because the school allowed corporal punishment, there was no further action to be taken, but my mom let them have it. *No one hits my kid, but me* was the message she had for them. I realized that, in her own way, my mom had my back. My mom made it clear that if Ms. Dabrowsky ever spanked me again, there'd be hell to pay. Her threat must have worked, because she never did, and for that, I'm grateful.

Starving with Sister Carmella

My fifth grade teacher, Sister Carmella, was a frail, spindly woman with crusty yellow nails and bad teeth. I always thought she looked like the Wicked Witch of the West. I was intrigued by the nuns at school, their limited clothing options, the bad shoes (was that a mandate or something?), the fact they never wore makeup—it was all so strange to me. But the thought that they would never be married? I couldn't fathom a life where I was forbidden from kissing my one true love, actor Corey Haim. After I saw the movie *Silver Bullet*, I tore his picture out of my *Teen Beat* magazine and pinned it to my wall. *One day, Corey. One day.* Anyway, being a nun and missing out on love sounded like pure hell to me. Maybe that's why she was so miserable. I swear, there was not an ounce of human warmth in that woman.

Other than being the most boring teacher in the school, she also was the strictest. It's one thing to sit still and barely breathe during lessons, but even during lunch? Come on! Kids should be able to talk to their friends at lunch, and if I had any, I would definitely want that, but my school didn't have recess, or even a cafeteria like a normal school. We had nothing to give us a break from the prison of the classroom, so we just sat at our desks quietly.

Every day I watched Sister Carmella peel back the Saran wrap from her sandwich, and eat just three bites before wrapping it back up and returning it to her desk drawer. Everything about this woman was dry. Dry sandwich, dry lips, dry personality. She ate as slowly as she talked, and her sandwich, which appeared to be two slices of bread with nothing on it, always left crumbs on her thin, wrinkled lips. When she'd pop open her daily can of Diet Coke, she would take a sip with such satisfaction you'd think it was a sin. I never brought lunch, so I would just sit there, starving, watching Sister Carmella with equal parts fascination and disgust.

The real reason this classroom lunchtime was so terrible though was because I had to sit next to two boys whose calling in life seemed to be making fun of me. You'd think I would be used to it by now, but they were the kind of boys who deliberately poked at people to get a rise out of them, and if you delivered, they would become relentless. These two boys made my days at school a living hell. I ignored them for as long as I could, but the day they called me *fatso*, that was it. There was no way to hide my reaction. That five-letter work was my breaking point, and they knew it.

Of all the things the kids made fun of me about, being called fat was what I hated the most. The absolute worst thing I could be was fat. As adolescence set in, I was beginning to see curves in all different areas of my body. While I would've preferred to have filled out more in my boobs, unfortunately for me, my weight was evenly distributed everywhere, and I hated it. I couldn't care less about being smart, fun, kind, or unique. You know, traits that actually matter. Instead, I fixated on what I thought being a girl—being a woman—was really about. I was determined to be beautiful, popular, and thin. The mirror became my obsession.

Where my bedroom walls once had framed pictures of Strawberry Shortcake, and dried palm fronds behind a statue of the sacred heart of Jesus, now were covered floor-to-ceiling with fashion magazine clippings, and pictures of music artists I listened to on the radio. My Barbie Townhouse was a convenient shelf for my new double cassette boom box radio, and I shoved my Cabbage Patch dolls to the side to make room for the new white wicker vanity I got for Christmas. I used to love watching my mom do her hair and makeup, and now it was my turn to join the world of chasing feminine beauty standards. I studied myself in that mirror. I scrutinized every problem I could find and tried to figure out ways to fix me.

Even though I wasn't a teen quite yet, I convinced my Mom to get me a subscription to *Teen Works*. This was like an encyclopedia, an ultimate how-to guide for being a teen. With my subscription I received two huge binders in the mail, and then every month they would send a new insert on topics like skincare, how to apply makeup, how to act around boys, how to exercise, how to be thin–I mean *healthy*– and more. Everything an 80s teen girl needed to know, they covered. My mother had stacks of magazines and tabloids with instructions for targeting her body's "problem areas," and warnings about not "letting yourself go," —

she subscribed to it all. Literally. I suppose this was just me following in her footsteps.

She loved to read about the lifestyles of celebrities, and sometimes I wonder if she had the dreams of being one herself. She once told me that her dad would call her and her sisters his queens. Whenever a beauty pageant was on TV, he'd call them into the living room to watch it. It was clear that this was the standard they should aim for. My mom's obsession with looks started young, but let's be honest, it was all around us. I don't think any of us girls ever had a chance to escape it back in the 80s. The Women's Liberation Movement meant women were becoming more and more successful in the workplace, but the message blaring at us was a twisted version of women "doing it all." Yes, you can work! Yes, you can be a mother! Yes, you can be whatever you want! Oh, but you also have to do it while maintaining a perfect figure. She referred to applying makeup as "putting her face on" and it did serve as a mask of sorts. With her makeup on, Mom smiled and carried herself differently. I saw firsthand how to internalize those beauty standards, and my dad encouraged it. I took that all in very seriously.

My dad was building his own tool and die business then, and he was gone all the time. "The Miscarriage That Lived" was now calling himself a "Work-a-holic" He loved those labels. As a young child I saw my dad as the most intelligent and hard-working guy around, but as I grew older, I realized how incredibly vain he was too. He seemed to care more about what people thought of us than anything. Especially when we went out to eat at restaurants. His eyes were never on us but instead would be entirely focused on the waitress that served us. He always made a point to get her name and call her by it every time she returned to the table. If any of us ever accidentally spilled our glass of milk, or spoke a little too loudly, he'd spend the rest of the time criticizing us for embarrassing him—especially my mom. Yet when "Waitress Amber" stepped up to help, he would put on such an act, showering her with gratitude for having to deal with a family like ours. His words towards my mother taught me very clearly that a woman's worth was conditional. How much she weighed more than anything else, even beauty. My mother's weight fluctuation after having my sister was a running argument my dad brought up at almost every meal. It never mattered how much Mom did for Dad or how beautiful she was, the thing he made abundantly clear to us all was that he wasn't going to stay married to a fat wife.

I used to enjoy family pizza night on Fridays, but I grew to hate how I felt after eating it. Eventually, my sister would grow to hate pancakes on Sunday mornings because, according to Dad, thin people don't eat those. Food became the enemy in our home, so I decided that the only way to avoid the drama of food was to just not eat it, to convince myself to hate it.

In this new season of instability and criticism, I tried to block out as much of their fighting as I could, but some things you just can't stop hearing because they repeat in your head even when people aren't speaking. Being the built-in babysitter didn't make it any easier either. It meant I would come home from a terrible day at school and then I was expected to watch my siblings. There were times my mom was so busy helping my dad with his business that she wouldn't come home at all, she would just call to make sure we didn't burn the house down. Generally, we had to fend for ourselves in those days. Even when my mom did cook, she only cooked for my dad and left us with whatever was in the pantry. Usually Spaghetti-Os and cereal. It's not that I missed family dinners. I didn't; they only involved fighting and I was beginning to realize I didn't want to eat, even if I was hungry. My self-loathing was growing at an alarming rate, so between the whispers and pig snorts from the mean kids at school, I was in tears by lunchtime every day.

Sister Carmella sat directly right in front of our desks, but she would never intervene. She'd eat her three bites and read whatever book was in front of her. It was only the day I got the nerve to yell back at them to shut up that she finally looked up. I was sent to the principal's office. Not them. Eventually the bullying expanded beyond lunchtime and I would run out of class crying while she was teaching. I'd sit on the hallway stairs or in a bathroom stall until I got myself together. She never once checked on me—nobody did. I was alone, convincing myself that I was the problem, that I was ugly and fat and unlovable and that no matter how hard I tried, no matter how much I starved myself, it would always be that way. I was too young to know what suicide was, but I was beginning to feel like I either had to be thin and pretty and perfect, or not be alive at all.

FOUR

Just Not a Happy Girl

★

The Christmas Mullet

As if middle school isn't hard enough, I made it harder by convincing myself a mullet would solve all my coolness problems. The infamous "business in the front and party in the back look," though considered super cringy today, was actually pretty rockstar in the 80s. My parents had just gotten cable TV and the channels, MTV and VH1, became my whole life. The music video for "Kids in America" was my inspiration for the haircut; I wanted to look like Kim Wilde. I was completely obsessed with her blonde, choppy fringe, and I was fully determined to become someone different from who I was. Kim Wilde's iconic pop star style embodied my vision, and that was that. The only problem was that I was a chubby redhead with gaps in my teeth. I felt pretty mature for my age because of everything I had experienced, but I was only ten. What did I know?

Sure that my pop-star-fashion-icon dreams would come true with a new haircut, I decided that I would use my Christmas money to make it happen. I just needed to get there. I hated asking Mom for things, but I couldn't drive myself, and it was super cold out so I couldn't take the bus like I usually did. Mom agreed and drove me to the local Fantastic Sam's because they took walk-ins. I had no idea that the trendy and skilled stylists at the salon my mom went to would be any different from the blue-eye-shadow-and-moo-moo-sporting woman that was about to cut my hair for $10. Kids make bad decisions all the time, but there was no conversation between my mom and me about whether or not this haircut was a good idea. My mom knew I was having a hard time at school; I exhausted her daily with my crying over what the kids said to me. But I guess she was having a hard time with my father, and must have figured hey, if it would make me happy and shut me up, she might as well just let me do it. Awesome.

I loved my mother, but I was becoming more resentful of her because I felt so alone. I always thought my mom was supposed to be who I would look to for guidance, but she didn't know what to do with me. I shamed myself relentlessly for not being able to keep it together on some days because she made it apparent that she could not deal with both me *and* my father. I was being bullied by kids at school; she was being bullied by my father at home. Instead of feeling seen and supported, like those mother-daughter duos in the movies that are all *it's you and me, kid*, I got the feeling that she didn't really believe me. When I told her how the kids treated me at school, she acted as if she could not fathom that it could be so miserable. Her perspective was that I had so much more than she did growing up, and that I should be grateful. Her family was poor, and it's true that I had toys and clothes, and everything that *looked like* stability, but she always had many friends regardless of her circumstances. I, on the other hand, did not. Her advice to me during the years I was bullied was minimal and simple. I needed to focus on the common denominator in all those situations: Me.

Little did she know that I was well aware that I was the problem, and I was determined to fix it–determined to fix *me.* I wanted to be invited to birthday parties. I wanted to have friends to play with. I wanted to like myself, or at least be able to fend off the bullies so they wouldn't think I was weak. I remember Busia telling me that my dad was bullied as a child. If I had a better relationship with him, maybe he could understand where I was coming from. But he wasn't my approachable dad who read to me anymore, so I never felt like I could tell him what was really going on unless it was related to my academics. It's complicated to both love and hate your parents.

Apart from the bullying, and the chaos at home, though, I always had this lingering feeling that I couldn't quite grasp at the time. What I could understand was that it made me feel alone and gross. It would come up in boring everyday situations like going to the restroom at school. Just pulling down my pants to pee made me think of the game I agreed to play with JD all those times. If I got a whiff of dirty socks, I'd think of my grandmother's house the day she told me that I would ruin everything if I told anyone about JD and the game. I always felt ashamed and embarrassed; I never felt safe or at ease around other people. I was sensitive and emotional–unmanageable at times, and I hated it. I didn't want to cry all the time. I wanted to be happy. I didn't want my parents to feel like their daughter was incapable of feeling grateful for what they provided, so I came up with a list of how to fix myself:

1. **Be stronger. Stop crying all the time.**
2. **Do things myself. Mom has enough on her plate.**
3. **Be happy. Your parents do a lot for you.**
4. **Show that you're grateful. You have so much more than they ever had.**
5. **Be pretty and skinny.**
6. **Lose weight to be skinny, so I can be pretty.**

I read enough of my mom's tabloid magazines in our bathroom with all the ads for diet pills and hair dye to absorb the constant message: "if you look good, you'll feel good," and I believed it.

When I arrived at the salon, I was so excited–delusionally hopeful, even. Back then, we didn't show the stylist a perfectly curated inspo board on Pinterest. Instead, there were huge hairstyle catalogs in the waiting room. They were filled with photos of models sporting different hairstyles at different lengths, all of them posed and angled in dramatic lighting. When the stylist was ready, you'd just point out the haircut that you wanted and assume they had the skills to do it. The Kim Wilde mullet was popular, but there wasn't a picture of anything even close to that anywhere in these books! Panicking a little, I did the best I could to describe what I wanted. The stylist who reminded me of the funny lady from *Three's Company,* "Mrs. Roper," convincingly assured me that she knew what I wanted. So, like an idiot, I trusted her.

She spun me around so my back was to the mirror. As she snipped and snipped, my attention alternated between the old, black-and-white TV playing the show *Love Connection,* the sound of water from the shampoo station, and the constant whine of hair dryers. When she asked me to look down to improve her angle, I became immediately concerned. There was an awful lot of strawberry blonde hair on that tile floor, and it was feeling a little too drafty near my ears.

I was dying inside. Right before she turned me around to see the results, she brushed off the remnants of what was once attached to my head and beamed with pride.

It can't be that bad. I reasoned. *She's smiling! She's proud! It can't be that bad. Please don't be that bad.* She flipped me around, and when my eyes met themselves in the mirror, I confirmed: It's not that bad. It's way worse. Instead of looking like Kim Wilde, I looked like Chunk from *The Goonies.*

She cut it super short in the front and left the back long without blending it at all. Nothing about it was feminine. Nothing about it was rockstar.

"Soooo? What do you think?" she said.

She was an adult, and I was alone, so I said what anyone who was contemplating throwing herself off a bridge would say: "It looks fine."

I had no idea how I was going to style it for school because it looked too short to even fit the curling iron that I had. It took everything in me not to lose it as I paid the cashier.

The second I left the building, I stepped outside where the icy Chicago wind froze my tears to my cheeks. Here's one more thing for the kids to make fun of me about. Here's one more thing for my mom to say I'm unhappy about. I felt like Charlie Brown when he says *nothing ever works out for me* but instead of saying those words, I just repeated, *I hate me, I hate me, I hate me.* I remember thinking that death might be a better option than returning to school. That's an extreme response to a bad haircut, I know, but I was sinking deeper and deeper into self-loathing. I pulled my stupid hood over my stupid head and tried to pull it together for my mom. When she pulled up, she smiled and motioned excitedly for me to pull my hood down. My siblings were sitting in the back trying to see it as well. Seeing my mom so happy for that second made me feel even more guilty for not matching her energy. The second she saw my face, however, her smile faded. First to concern, then quickly to aggravation. I already knew what I was about to hear and the minute I got in and refused to pull my hood down it began.

"Chantel, you know, it wasn't convenient for me to drop you off and pick you up. At the very least I thought this would finally make you happy."

The disappointment tightened in my throat. No matter what I tried, I continued to disappoint her. The whole way home she talked about how my moods were always so up and down, that I was becoming unbearable. The predictable lines were all there: she was giving me all the things she never had as a child, and I was ungrateful. My unhappiness was more likely because I was spoiled than because of any kids at school. No matter what she would try, it was never enough. I was never happy. I knew what she would say before it filled the air between us, but her words were sharp.

I leaned my forehead against the cold passenger side window and closed my eyes; the cool glass helped me remain calm as her words continued to stab and slice at me. One experience after another of how I have disappointed her. She complained, finally, that it was hard to be her and that she was giving up. Her voice faded out, and I began to feel numb. The vibration and cold on my forehead was my comforter. Nothing she said I didn't already know, and nothing I did to make things better ever worked either. Why bother anymore?

When we finally reached home, my mother summed up what she felt about me with a sentence that I'll never forget:

"You're just not a happy girl, and I really don't think you ever will be."

I got out of the car, and took a deep breath, thinking to myself once again that maybe it would be better if I were dead. Fortunately, by the time I got to my room, my exhaustion got the best of me. Contemplating my death would have to wait until after I took a nap. So, I threw my coat on the bedroom floor, crawled under my bed covers, and instantly fell asleep. That's the one thing my parents said I was good at: Sleeping. So, I did. I slept through dinner and didn't wake until the next day.

The Black Eye

I can't say that I looked forward to going back to school after Christmas break, but being at home wasn't great either. I expected that going back to school with a horrible mullet was going to invite a whole new wave of insults, but now I was heading back to school with a horrible mullet *and* a black eye.

I didn't want to lie, but I also didn't want to explain to anyone that it was my mom who gave it to me. At one point I thought maybe it could be a good tale to tell. I could say something like, I was walking through an alley when a bunch of creeps jumped me. They not only gave me this black eye, but those sickos even cut my hair! It sounded good to me, anyway. But no one ever asked me why I had a black eye. Not even the teachers. No one said anything about my awful haircut either.

The first day back, I kept thinking about what happened. It was weird to feel safer at school than at home. Although I had seen my mom lose it before with my father, and I knew that she could let it fly, I had never been on the receiving end like this. It's true that I was a pain in the ass sometimes. I pushed my mom's limits when I didn't think the response "because I said so" was a legitimate reason, but this was different.

It was normal for her to crack me across the mouth without a second thought whenever I would talk back, or to use my father's belt to whip my ass when I was being a brat. I hated when the belt hit my thighs instead of my bottom. The swollen welts were meant to be a reminder of whatever I had done. I was sent immediately to my room, and I would hide myself under the blanket in my bedroom when my spankings were over. The smell of downy fabric softener from my blanket surrounded me and somehow provided some comfort after these punishments.

I never really counted how many times my mom hit me, but it definitely increased after my siblings were born. On this occasion, I pushed my brother out of my room so I could work on styling my new haircut. I also wanted to protect him from burning his hand on my curling iron because he wasn't at an age to understand that it was something that got hot. Not sure if he even knew what hot felt like yet. But his reaction was enough to make my mom absolutely lose her shit that day. The look in her eyes when my brother started crying was one I had never seen before.

I put my hands up above my head to shield her swats at it while screaming, "I'm sorry I'm sorry!" As I twisted and turned, begging for her to stop, I saw my father sitting at the kitchen table. Just sitting there. She then threw me down on the floor, straddled her legs over me and only stopped once she realized her diamond ring had cut into my face.

The next morning when I got ready for school, I was met with the typical silent treatment I always got when I was being punished. Typically, I would feel guilty and try to apologize in hopes to gain her acceptance, but I didn't have it in me this time. I had very little care in me about anything at all that morning actually. I felt numb. I no longer cared what the kids would say to me about my hair. I didn't care if they called me names again. All I thought to myself was I hate my brother, I hate my hair, and I hate me. And I wondered why my father just sat there.

You Got It All

During the first week of sixth grade, I met a girl named Rose. Apparently, she was in the same first grade class with me, but she had transferred schools for a few years, so I never knew her. As the weeks went on, she would even entertain a conversation with me at lunch! She was different from any of the girls I had met or tried to be friends with at school before. She seemed to be quieter and more reserved, but I wouldn't describe her as shy. She had green eyes and perfect hair, but it was her unfiltered facial expressions that set her apart from everyone else. I studied every girl around me to try to crack the code: how do I fit in? So I remember noticing that she often had her hands up by her face, and she tugged on her lips whenever she was concentrating or got anxious.

Rose sat behind me in class, and most days, she brought a thermos of Spaghetti-Os or Chef Boyardee ravioli for lunch. It smelled delicious whenever she unscrewed the cap. She once asked me why I never brought anything, and I simply told her I was on a diet. I wondered what it would be like to be like her, to be thin and eat anything without guilt. Sometimes she would share part of her lunch with me if she couldn't eat it all. That was weird to me–to eat only part of something. Even though my dad was hard on us all about healthy food and being thin, he also didn't tolerate waste of any sort. I was expected to clean my plate, but whenever I ate, there was not a morsel left to be found. Still, no matter how much I ate, there was still something I was trying to fill.

The conversations between Rose and me were surface level at first, but I didn't care. I was just glad someone was talking to me. It was when our teacher Ms. G made us official class helpers and had us do different projects together for her, that I began to feel like *maybe* I actually had a friendship blooming. The first school dance of the year was coming up, and Rose told me that I should go because it would be fun. It was that simple for her. Why wouldn't I go? Even though I was hesitant, she convinced me that it would be okay because she would be there, too. I took the invitation seriously. I wanted to go, but only because Rose would be there.

When I got home that day, I told my mom about the dance and begged her to take me to the mall to buy a new outfit. I wanted to go to the GAP, or Merry Go Round where all the cool clothes were, but instead, we only went to *her* favorite store, Lerner. Ugh! The few things I actually did like were too small for my awkwardly developed body, and the ones that did fit made me look like a 40-year-old divorcee headed to the office. What could have been a beautiful mother-daughter bonding experience was a nightmare. As my mom scoured the racks for items for me to try on, I tore myself apart in the dressing room.

"Okay, let's see!" She was trying to make it fun.

I opened the door to show her each outfit she picked, and even if she thought it looked good, it didn't matter. I felt awkward and uncomfortable and just wished I could find clothes that made me feel okay. Mom's patience didn't last very long.

"Chantel, if you don't dry it up and get yourself together I'm never taking you shopping again." She perceived my mood as me being ungrateful. She reminded me how she never got to do things like this when she was my age.

But it wasn't that I was ungrateful, she just had no idea how much I hated the reflection staring back at me in the mirror. Even though her weight was an issue now, according to my father and her stack of magazines, she wasn't fat when she was a kid. Even though she was poor, she had friends. And even though her mother was awful to her, she was still her father's favorite. There's no denying that my mom experienced difficult things, but those things didn't translate to any empathy for me. She didn't get that every time I looked at myself in the mirror, I not only saw the fat red head with the dumb name that the kids at school pointed out every day, but I also saw the girl whose grandma said I would ruin everything if I told anyone about the things that made me feel gross and dirty inside.

Eventually, I got it together and picked out a white sweatshirt with a cool modern graphic on it. I decided to layer it over a red and white striped button-down man's shirt (a fashion idea my *Teen Works* book gave me) where the collar and shirt tails hung out like a cool accent. I chose a pair of ill-fitting black stirrup pants, and finished it with my black criss-cross ballet flats from Payless Shoes. I was as ready as anyone like me could be. Even though nothing could make my awkwardly grown out mullet look great, I did the best I could to curl and plaster it with a few sprays of mom's Aqua Net hair spray–the purple can, this stuff was like glue. On the way to the dance, it seemed as if Mom was excited, even giddy to drop me off that night. She genuinely seemed to want me to have a good time even if preparing me to get there was a nightmare.

As I entered the school gymnasium, I felt like I was somewhere I had never been. Most of the lights were off with the exception of some colorful ones from on a light tree the DJ brought. The dance floor was pretty empty at first, groups of kids huddled in clusters talking and laughing. Rose wasn't there yet, and I didn't know what to do. I stood by the window of the kitchen where the teachers and parent volunteers served hot dogs, chips, and pop. I fidgeted and shifted, and obsessively scanned the room until I saw her.

"Thank God she's here!" I said aloud. She was with a girl from another class. When our eyes finally met, I smiled and waved at her, and instantly my enthusiasm for this dance morphed into rejection and disappointment. Rose looked away, as if she didn't know me at all. I didn't know the other girl, but I knew she was closer to cool than I was. The tears were almost instant. *Great*, I thought to myself, *now what was I going to do? Cry in the bathroom all night?*

I spent a lot of time crying in bathrooms during these years. Things were getting complicated in school, and fast. There was a group of popular girls beginning to form in our 6th grade class, spearheaded by the new girl in school, Heather Vera. I don't know what school or planet she came from, but we worshipped her. Her bright blonde hair made her green eyes pop and when she laughed, she did this little thing with her tongue that drove the boys in our class crazy. She was pretty, smart, and outgoing, and she wasn't wearing a training bra like the rest of us were. There were rumors all around school that she was caught by the school janitor with her shirt wide open while making out with her 8th grade boyfriend in the cleaning closet. I don't know if it was true or not, but I just wanted to be like her. We all did. She had great nails to accent all the gold rings on each of her fingers, and her uniform shirt was see through just enough for us all to see her lace texture of her bra and the sparkle of her gold rope chain necklace where a crucifix dangled. She was a force from the day she enrolled, and it was clear: either accept her authority or be destroyed by it. Just as I was finally figuring out how to survive everyone that came before her, now I had a new hurdle to face. How was I ever going to be cool enough to be her friend?

It was obvious Rose had the same quest because the girl she walked in with was one of Heather's friends. Even though I was hurt by her rejection, I understood it. We all just wanted to belong and only the strong would survive. After sitting in the bathroom stall waiting for the chatty girls in there to leave so they wouldn't see me, I got myself together and headed back out to the gym. I tried to make eye contact once again with Rose, but it was clear that she was blind to my existence that night. There was no other option, I went out into the hall, put a quarter in the pay phone, and called my mom.

"Mom, you need to come pick me up."

My mom was not happy to hear my voice on the other end of the call. She literally just got home from dropping me off and was putting away some groceries. I told her about Rose ignoring me and not having anyone to talk to, but her response was clear: I was a disappointment.

"Chantel, I'm not coming to get you until I'm done. I cannot believe you cannot find any friends to hang with right now. I don't understand you. Why would you choose to go if you don't have any friends?"

I didn't say anything.

"You're going to have to wait," she said.

"Ok I will, but please come soon!"

As I walked back through the gymnasium, a girl out of nowhere ran up and startled me. I had classes with her here and there throughout elementary school, and she did go to the same dance school as me, Ms. Geri's, but we had never really talked before this moment. Her ash blonde hair was pulled back into a tight ponytail and her smiling, freckled cheeks complimented her sweet demeanor. While all of us girls were dressed to impress, trying to be like everyone else, she was confident in her jeans and t-shirt. A little out of breath from playing tag with a group of boys, she asked me where I was going. It was like she noticed I was upset.

"I'm headed to the stairs outside to wait for my mom to come get me," I said.

She looked at me weird, "Why would you leave? The dance just started."

I wanted to tell her that Rose was a terrible friend, and that I feel like a total nerd and I hate my life right now, but instead I shrugged. She took my hand and pulled me across the dance floor to the edge of where all the kids (and Rose) were dancing.

After scoping out everyone around us, she asked me, "Out of all the boys in the gym, who would you like to dance with if you could?"

Is she nuts? I wondered. "Why?"

"I'm going to set you up with one of them."

She was so matter-of-fact about it. As the lights from the mirror ball bounced around the gym and the house music bumped, a huge smile spread across my face. She waited as I thought about my answer. And then I saw him. The boy I wished saw me in the mornings before we headed to our classes. He was a year older than me, dark brown hair, long eye lashes that framed his gorgeous blue eyes. When he smiled, I melted. But who am I kidding? This girl is crazy if she thinks he would ever dance with me. First of all, he had no idea who I was. Secondly, he didn't even seem to care that we were at a dance at all. He was running around the gym with some other boy, as if they were the only ones there. But those tight black acid-washed jeans, gym shoes, and Metallica T-shirt sure made him look good. Oh, to put my hands through in his spikey hair and look into his eyes.... that would be a dream for sure.

"On it!" Melissa replied. Before I even had a chance to stop her, she ran off on her mission. So there I was, awkwardly standing alone again, next to groups of kids dancing and chatting. I still couldn't process what the heck just happened, but I wanted to see what might.

Oh no, I thought. *I got to call my mom.* I ran back to the pay phone and dialed home. Luckily, she hadn't left yet.

"Mom, don't come to pick me up. I'm fine now," I said.

"I wasn't going to, Chantel. I have to wait for your father to come home before I come get you anyway."

"Ok great! See ya!" *Click.* I never hung up a phone so fast in my life.

I ran up to Melissa to see how it was going. I thought for sure we had our work cut out for us, but with her, nothing seemed impossible. *Who is this girl?*

I was beginning to not care if she got him to dance with me or not. I was just happy to have a reason to stay. She and I ran around the school, following Jeff and his friend everywhere they went in hopes of getting their attention. Laughing was something I hadn't done in a long time. Every now and then, I would look over at Rose standing near the group she was trying so hard to be a part of. With everyone's eyes on the new girl, Heather, they didn't seem to really care if she was there or not. It made me a little sad for her, but I just kept going. I had a boy to chase, and a new friend to chase him with!

I honestly don't know why Jeff agreed to dance with me, but he did. And he did it without us having to beg him. Maybe I wasn't as gross as I thought I was. Maybe one day Jeff will marry me. But if not, I was happy for that moment. It was the very last dance of the night, a slow dance. I wrapped my hands around his shoulders, and he put his around my waist, and we swayed without looking much at one another, as "You Got It All" by the Jets played. I completely forgot about Rose. I looked over at Melissa as we stiffly swayed from left to right. She smiled at me with pride. It was a job well done for her. She got a cute guy to dance with the sad, fat girl.

When my mom picked me up that night, I told her all about it. She was giddy to hear about all that had transpired after our phone call. I wished Melissa was in my class. Boy, she would have been a great friend to have around, but we were on opposite ends of the building, and we never really connected after. But she gave me hope that night. Maybe I could be a part of the popular girls one day. If I work on it. If I really work on it.

No One Loves Fat Girls

My mom was always a sucker for dramatic docuseries, and she really liked the actress Meredith Baxter Birney, from *Family Ties*, so when she saw a preview for the made-for-TV movie, *Kate's Secret,* she made sure to set our VCR to record it, just in case we missed anything while it was playing live. The movie was about a housewife who, from the outside looking in, led a perfect existence. Of course, as the title indicated, she had a secret: she was bulimic. It was the first time I had ever learned of anyone doing something like this. The only knowledge I had of what an eating disorder was came from the story my mom shared with me about the famous singer, Karen Carpenter, and her battle with anorexia. I didn't know that an eating disorder could be any different than starving yourself. I didn't know that there could be a way to get thin and still eat. This was a revelation. A terrible one, but a revelation nonetheless.

After watching that movie, it was all I could think about. I even went to the library and checked out books on eating disorders to get all the information I could. Sixth grade already had me in the practice of writing research papers, so going to the library and checking out books was something that I did regularly, and even liked to do. Now that I had a topic that actually interested me, it was even more fun to check out books. I read all about the things that could happen with an eating disorder and filtered all of this through my own twisted logic that if I tried this I was going to be well informed. My theory was that if I knew the risks, I could avoid the consequences. *I wouldn't let it get that far*, I told myself. It was just a temporary solution until I got to the weight that I wanted to be then I would stop. This research consumed my thoughts by the end of the school year, and suddenly it was the last day of 6th grade and summer vacation was about to begin.

My mom didn't usually pick me up from school, but she needed me to babysit and it was the last day of school so she thought *it might be fun* to pick me up instead.

I waited for her in the chaotic school parking lot, surrounded by classmates talking and laughing about their summer plans: Sleepovers with friends, baseball games, and getting ice cream from the ice cream truck on those warm summer nights in Chicago that we all loved. I had a plan for what my summer was going to look like, too, and I was eager to get started. I noticed a blonde girl staring at me from across the street. Her name was Jessica. I didn't know her very well, and I didn't think anything of it at first. But then I realized that she was looking at me and then turning to another girl next to her and laughing. I swallowed my anger and did my best to ignore it.

My mom was late, of course, but I finally saw our Jeep pull into the lot, and smiled to myself about how nuts my mom is. She was waving out her driver's side window, singing "yoo-hoo" to make sure she got my attention and *everyone else's* too. She loved to embarrass me in public. Most of the kids had been picked up already, but Jessica and her friend were still in their spot across from me, and I had no other option but to walk by them as mom pulled in closer for me to hop in.

"Hey, is that your mom?" I heard someone ask.

"Yeah," I said, holding my backpack straps as I jogged to the car.

"She's even fatter than you!" the voice said with a laugh. It was Jessica.

The jarring comment put me at a full stop and then I exploded. Before anyone knew what was happening, I dropped my backpack on the street and charged her. My mom, having no clue as to what was happening because she didn't hear the insult, yelled my name and some other words I can't remember because I hauled off and punched Jessica straight in the gut, and pushed her to the ground.

"Don't you *ever* call my mom a name again" I screamed in her face,

Jessica's head was down, and her friend was consoling her as I stormed back to the car. My mom was standing half out of the car door, still confused about what just happened.

As I got in, I interrupted the immediate interrogation "Mom, I just want to go home!"

"What did she say to you, Chantel?"

"She called you fat, mom! She called you fat."

I wiped my face and tried to breathe again, and Mom got quiet for a moment.

"Well, looks like you told her!" she said with a smile. "I don't think she'll say anything to *you* again."

I just shook my head and turned the radio up to avoid any more conversation. I know she was trying to encourage me, but deep down I was convinced she really didn't get it; Jessica was one of many. Mom knew there were bullies, but she thought I was a bit of a crybaby and wanted me to toughen up. She also didn't have time to deal with it.

This was the day I decided to change myself.

To have friends, I would need to be thinner. To please my dad, I would need to be thinner. To be happy, I would need to be thinner. I didn't care what the real ramifications were if I became bulimic, I simply considered it to be a solution. I was determined to become someone else before school started again in the fall. Coming up with this plan made me feel, for the first time, in control of my own life and future.

I woke up excited to start my new plan. The first thing I did was get on the scale. I was 4'8 and 115lbs and completely distraught seeing that number for the first time. The last time I was at the doctor was in 4th grade and I was 104lbs! I had no idea to take into consideration that different bone structures, height, and muscle mass also play a part into how much I weighed. I was solely focused on the numbers that I thought would be best for me. Anything under 100 pounds would be better than where I was. Every girl at my school that was well-liked looked like they were under 100 pounds and even if the most popular girl in school Heather was heavier than that, she carried it in all the right places.

That morning, I had decided that for breakfast I would eat an apple. An apple was 100 calories, and my goal was to eat 500 calories a day-no more no less. I got that number from one of the eating disorder memoirs that I had read, and it seemed like a good number to start with. That library also had a book of calories and nutritional information that I had checked out to help me.

When I was in the kitchen eating my morning apple, Busia, who was there a few days a week during the summer, would notice and ask me "don't you want anything else?"

"Nope! I'm OK, I'm not hungry." I replied as I walked back into my room. This was not like me at all, and Busia recognized it immediately. I had always been a good eater and some of our best memories and conversations together were done while sharing meals together. This was going to be harder than I anticipated. I had to be strategic. If Busia was around and I was in the kitchen with her, in order to not draw attention to what I was or wasn't eating, I would have to make our conversations shorter. The best thing to keep this all to myself was for me to stay in my room. No conversations meant no explanations. I had control. I'd put on my radio and look in the mirror and focus on each part of my body I wanted to change. The main focus was the fat on my thighs. I wanted skinny legs. No more bullies making fun of them. No more jokes from my father saying I have good "Polish stock" like him, knowing how much he hated fat people.

My second focus was my face. My chubby cheeks and round face had to go. It might've been cute when I was a baby, but as someone entering the seventh-grade next fall, I needed to lose the puffiness I saw when I smiled. I wanted to look like the models in the magazine pictures I pinned to my bedroom walls.

I had written up an exercise routine for myself. Thanks to my *Teen Works* books I learn how to work out all my different body parts. I counted my jumping jacks, push-ups, and sit ups. Did all the things I learned in gym class at school. Even though I wanted so badly to go with my mom who had recently joined the Richard Simmons health club, I wasn't old enough yet. I would be 12 in a few months, though, and I prayed that maybe she would sign the waiver and let me go with her. But for now, it was 500 jumping jacks, 50 push-ups, and 75 sit ups a day. It was the one time in my life I was grateful that I didn't have a ton of friends. I had a lot of time to work on these goals. As long as I accomplished them without distractions. Well other than my siblings who were constantly banging on my bedroom door asking me what I was doing. I would just turn up my stereo as loud as possible and pretend that I didn't hear them. I focused and did what I needed to do to change and it paid off. I did so well my first week. I lost 5lbs!

Then the day came when Busia almost screwed it all up. It was lunchtime, I was in the kitchen again. Busia asked me if I wanted to walk down to the corner to get a hotdog with her and the kids. Jimmy's hotdogs and fries were my absolute favorite thing to eat. But I had to resist. I needed to change. But it made me angry.

"No, I'm not hungry," I snapped. I grabbed an apple and went back to my room.

I hated treating Busia like this, but the sacrifice would be worth it. I was no longer going to be a loser at school. Shopping with Mom was going to be more fun because I would finally be able to buy clothes I liked and that were age appropriate. I just had to power through even if I was becoming moody and exhausted. One day Busia would understand. She'd see that I was happy, and she'd be happy for me. As for my mother, she never questioned why I slept most of the time now, or chose not to eat. But I was grateful for that. I didn't need her interfering with my plans.

By the end of the second week, I was struggling and by 9pm every night while everyone was getting ready to go to sleep, I was wide awake and starving. If there was some leftover macaroni and cheese in the fridge and my hunger got the best of me, I ate it. Once I was done, I might move on to bread with butter, and then cookies. Instantly after consuming them, the self-hatred would scream, "You a fat pig! What's wrong with you!?" Desperate times called for desperate measures, so I first drank a huge glass of water. I had read that if I drink water immediately after a binge the food would come up faster and easier. It's also important to bring a glass of water along with you into the bathroom just in case I got dry. Another thing I read was, if anyone is home, run the water from the bathroom shower or sink. That way nobody hears you. I always did that. Then it was time to get gross. Stick that finger or two down your throat and jab it hard until it all comes up. If my throat hurt afterwards I looked at it as the punishment I deserved. I was that fat idiot who brought this upon myself. When I was finished, I brushed my teeth, rinsed my mouth and gargled with mouth wash, washed my hands, all while staring at my swollen red face and eyes that looked like I had been punched repeatedly. I thought to myself, tomorrow would be a new day; hopefully the scale would say something good to me. This went on all summer long.

The new day of the week I looked forward to the most was no longer Saturdays but Sundays. Sunday was the day when my mom was home now. Even though most of the time we spent together on Sundays was in the car running errands, I never minded because that was our time to be together. Driving through the city in the summer with the radio on and the windows down blowing the summer breeze through my hair was truly glorious. So glorious that even my noisy siblings didn't bother me much. Getting out was good for us all after being in the house all week. Before we went grocery shopping, we'd always stop by my grandma's house to visit for a few hours. Sundays seemed to be the day most of my mom's siblings would also be there visiting.

When we walked into the house there was a gasp from one of my mom's sisters when she saw me walk into the kitchen. Seeing how visibly thinner I was starting to look now that I was getting older, she had a look on her face I had never seen before from anyone: concern. Mom told me in the car later that one of my aunts wanted to know why I had lost so much weight and that she told them that I was watching my weight now and reassured them that I was fine. I was completely elated! Someone noticed! Mom bragged about it! I was working so hard, and it was paying off.

Built-in Babysitter

As the summer weeks went by, my parents were busy with the tool and die business my father had been building and were rarely home now. Understandably, Busia was becoming more and more frustrated by their absence, as the days went on. Although she wasn't as dramatic as my Aunt Bea, who used to talk to herself as she paced and cried when my parents didn't come home when they said they would, Busia wasn't happy with the inconsistency and lack of respect for her time. Busia always said trust is everything and when people lie to you over and over again, they cannot be trusted. Hearing about Busia's frustration, my mom encouraged her to leave earlier. I was going to be twelve that October, and like most generation X kids, I would be considered more than qualified to be in charge.

So Busia left earlier and earlier and my parents came home later and later. I know they were working hard, but some days it seemed like they forgot they even had kids at all. Now that they could leave me alone with my siblings, they made sure to take full advantage of it.

My obsession with diet and exercising meant that I actually didn't mind stepping into my "built-in babysitter" title. I could be left alone, no one bothering me, wondering if I ate that day or not. I was psyched to think I could have the freedom to be alone and do anything I wanted in exchange to just to make sure my siblings just didn't die.

Check. Done.

I didn't know how to cook, other than macaroni and cheese and hot dogs, but all I really needed to know was how to read since much of the food in our pantry had the recipe on the back of a cardboard box. I wasn't eating much those days, so it never mattered to me whether we were sitting down to a family dinner any longer or not. And usually, we were not.

Sometimes they stayed out until the wee hours of the morning because they needed a date night. Sometimes my mom would call and say that they'd had a terrible argument and wouldn't be home for a while. But most of the time it was simply, "We have to work, Chantel."

I tried to make the best of it with my siblings that summer. We'd watch cartoons, play Monopoly, and sometimes we would take walks down to the park when Mom allowed. She did have *some* consideration for safety, after all.

After my brother was born and Aunt Beatrice left, my mom would leave me home alone with my baby brother if she had to run out for "just a few minutes." Even though that usually meant at least an hour, part of me felt special. Mom said I was a big girl now, and I could take care of my little brother! The other part of me, that was still just seven, was afraid that something bad might happen. What would I do? Well, one of these times, I learned the answer.

I was sitting on the couch watching TV as I was told to do. It was the time of day when the iconic "do you know where your children are" PSA came on to remind parents that they had children. My brother was asleep in his bassinet when I heard heavy footsteps come up onto the front porch of our house. I could hear police sirens in the distance, but I didn't think anything of it because I lived in Chicago. I heard sirens more than I heard birds chirp. It wasn't unusual. It also wasn't unusual for my mom to leave our front door open. We had a glass storm door outside of our front door that not only provided additional insulation in the winter, but allowed for our actual front door to be left open wide during the winter to allow light in. When she had left that evening, I must've forgotten to lock it, and before I knew it, those footsteps would make their way into the front hallway of my house. Just as I heard the door open, I felt my heart fall into my stomach. I saw a man hastily close not only the storm door, but the actual door behind him and tuck himself in the corner of our hallway, hiding behind the coat rack. Just as he was doing that the sirens of the police cars became louder as they zoomed down my street. I got up from the couch to get a good look at him and all I remember is he was wearing a black hat and black clothes, and I screamed. I don't remember much of his face because he was too busy covering his mouth pleading with me to shush and to stop screaming. I was terrified. I didn't know how to protect my baby brother. After we could no longer hear the sirens, thankfully the man ran out of the house.

Mom came home soon after to find me crying on the couch under my Miss Piggy Blanket. My baby brother was still asleep somehow. When

I told her what had happened, she assured me that it wouldn't happen again. I don't remember if she hugged me or not, but what I do remember was not wanting to be left alone again for quite a while.

Maybe this memory was part of mom's reasoning for why she told us to stay inside, but I'm pretty sure the shock of a man barging into our house to escape the police had more of an emotional effect on me than on anyone else involved. More recently though, there had been another strange incident that could have contributed to her caution.

I was taking the trash out when a blue van came creeping slowly down the alleyway of my block. There were two men in the van. I stared at them as they passed by and smiled at me. I often saw people behaving strangely in the city; it was just part of the deal. I dropped the garbage bag into the can and began to put the lid back on, when I noticed the van that was now about three houses down from me and had stopped. I stood there for a second, just watching to see what they were doing. A few seconds later, a middle-aged man jumped out of the passenger side of the van and ran up to me. Startled, I froze as I watched him pull down his pants and grab his private area. Violently jerking it back and forth a few times, I stood there in shock not knowing what to do. The moment I saw the white stuff dripping down his hands and then pants is when I came to and started screaming.

I ran into the house, and told my mom what happened. Her response was not what I expected: she *laughed.* To be fair, it could have been one of those shocked, no way kinds of laughs, but I was terrified and seriously grossed out, and she laughed?

By the time she got to the alley, the van was gone. I was still upset and confused and kept asking, Mom what was that white stuff!? She didn't tell me, but she did call the cops to file a report. I didn't get a license plate number, so there wasn't much they could do. No one was ever caught, and no one ever brought it up again. I'm pretty sure my mom never even told my dad about it.

★

FIVE

Boy Crazy Girl Gangs

★

Seventh Grade BS

After begging and pleading all summer along, my mom finally caved and allowed me to put bleach in my hair. Because she wasn't about to waste any money on the strong possibility that I could still hate my hair after it was blonde, the only option I was given was to allow her to frost my hair herself with one one of those home bleaching kits that included a plastic cap with hundreds of tiny holes, and what looked like a really thin crochet hook. I stared at our horrid kitchen wallpaper, a repeating pattern of brown birdcages and yellow flowers, and winced as my mom poked and pulled my hair through each of those teeny tiny cap holes. Sometimes beauty is pain, and I was committed to going blonde. No one hated blondes.

The new Chantel was going to walk into that school on the first day of 7th grade and show everyone that she was not the girl she used to be. She was thinner, blonder, better. The old Chantel was dead. I even gave Rose a call over the summer. We started spending time together, and had a sleepover where we bonded on all things cool. I never told her how much it hurt me that she acted like she didn't know me at the school dance, I just wanted to move forward and be someone new.

Just before school started, I took my siblings to the park on the corner like I had many times in the past. I was wearing a royal blue crop top and a white denim mini skirt that had a zipper up the back. It was the first time I ever wore anything that exposed my stomach, but I was feeling confident now that I had lost weight and grown two inches. As I tried to keep my siblings from dilly-dallying all over the place, a car drove by and the pile of boys inside all leaned out the windows and whistled. The driver, probably the dad of one of the boys, even honked the car horn. Startled, I looked around me to see who else was there, but it was just my siblings and me. My little brother pulled my hand to keep walking. It took a moment to process what just happened. I had never experienced anything like that before, and after feeling invisible for so long, the attention felt good. I wore that top and skirt as much as possible after that day. If I could have worn it to school. I would have. This was the new me! Even my dad said I was looking good and should keep it up. That was high praise coming from him.

My mom said that because I was becoming a woman, I was now allowed to wear *mascara*. That was a game changer being so fair all my life. Rose recommended Maybelline Great Wear so that's what I got. I was obsessed with it. It's funny that my mom made a fuss about mascara being allowed because I was "becoming a woman," but didn't bother to teach me anything about what that might actually mean. I knew enough about periods to know that I was in no rush. The idea of bleeding once a month grossed me out, and when I saw her blood-soaked pads in the bathroom garbage? No, thank you. She insisted it would happen soon since I had been so moody the past few months, and while she didn't elaborate, she did make a point to tell me that once I did, I could get pregnant. She noticed that I was suddenly getting attention from some of the boys in my neighborhood, so I think she was trying to warn me.

7th and 8th grade was in a different building from the younger grades. Now, we had lockers where we could hang pictures, and a mirror to check our hair in between classes. Because we had different teachers for different subjects, we weren't in just one classroom all day. The best part of it all was that now, I would get to meet a new group of students because I was in specific classes based on my test scores. The boys who used to torment me by calling me fat were now in different classes. Even so, I wasn't fat anymore, so what could they even say now? Besides, I was getting attention from older boys everywhere I went. I couldn't roll my eyes hard enough at the thought of these pathetic little boys thinking their opinions mattered. Not anymore. It was going to be different now. It was going to be better.

That morning, I took inspiration from Heather, the popular girl in 6th grade, and rolled up my red plaid uniform skirt so that it would lay a few inches above my knee. It was against the rules, but I didn't care. I pushed my grey slouch socks down my calves and left my white blouse unbuttoned low enough to see my bra if I moved the right way.

I had my mom drop me off way down the street and took my time walking up to the building of my new school life. As I opened the doors and began to walk through the halls of that school building for the first time as a junior high student, I heard a loud , raspy familiar voice dictating instructions to students who had no idea where their homeroom or lockers were. It was Ms.Dabrowsky! *Oh no,* I thought to myself. *Could she really be teaching 7th grade math?* As I tried to breeze by her to find my locker, I unwillingly caught her eye.

Still tanned and wearing the same pink frosty lipstick she always did, she said, "Chantel, I almost didn't recognize you! You look so slim!"

I didn't know what to say, but for a moment I forgot that she was the teacher I once hated for spanking me in front of the class. Maybe she wasn't as bad as I thought. She noticed me. She saw the hard work. She was the first person in school to see that I changed. I smiled and told her that I had been watching my weight all summer and had been exercising more. She made a point to tell me not to get too skinny, to make sure I ate. I laughed as I headed to my locker, *is there such a thing as too skinny?* It almost felt like a challenge. I studied my schedule and put my things in my locker. I felt hopeful for this new chapter of my life.

That is, until a group of four girls walked in, all wearing the same pale-yellow hoodies with the initials BS printed on front. At first, I laughed. Who would collectively choose to brand their group with letters that stand for *bullshit*?

I guess, if you were in the seventh at my school in 1987 you would. The BS printed logo stood for the group's name, Boss Sisters. They were the badass bitches in school, aka the popular girls. They were not only the prettiest girls, but Heather, the once new girl who looked fantastic in a banana clip, was also super tough. There were rumors of her fights, and it was common knowledge that she could kick your ass. No one wanted to be on her bad side, that's for sure. Even the teachers seemed to favor her. She was confident, mature, and intimidating. Rose knew the girls in Heather's circle way more than I did, but she wasn't part of the group. We talked about how great it would be if we could get one of those sweatshirts, too.

As the weeks went by, I gradually started to insert myself in conversations around Heather and the Boss Sisters crew. I knew I had to be careful to not be a weirdo. *Fake it until you make it, Chantel.* Even though I figured out how to look the part of being socially acceptable I had no idea what to do once I was granted access to the world of girldom.

I really did feel like I killed off the old version of myself. I was amazed how much kinder people were to me now that I was thinner. First it made me mad, and then paranoid to ever become her again. Having other girls actually *choose* to strike up conversations with me was new territory. I felt awkward and vulnerable because I didn't know how to be. I was used to being the target. I was used to rejection. I was used to being invisible. Now that I wasn't, who was I?

The Birthday Fiasco

September 1987 was unfolding pretty much how I had hoped. Rose and I were hanging out and talking at lunchtime every day, we talked on the phone when we got home from school, we had sleepovers every weekend, we passed notes to each other between classes. Even though we weren't in the same classes, she was the best friend I always wanted, and we were growing closer by the day. Her bedroom was covered with posters of metal bands and 80s art. She had what seemed like every single possible beauty product on the market, which explained why her nails and skin always looked amazing. She had every hair tool imaginable, and she was so good at styling her hair with them. She taught me how to look the part of a teenager in the 80s. She was just so cool, and I loved that she did some crazy shit, too. One time she sprayed a can of Aqua Net onto her bedroom carpet and lit it on fire. Nothing more rock and roll like watching a flaming pentagram become permanently burned into your friend's bedroom carpet. She was feral, and I wanted to be just like her.

We made up dances together and performed them on my porch, always looking to impress the boys who lived down the block from me. The same boys we would regularly meet up with so we could make out with them. She introduced me to books by V.C Andrews, movies like *Dream a Little Dream*, and the iconic music of Black Sabbath. We could talk about anything. Our movie star crushes, what we wanted to be when we grew up, and even more vulnerable things that we promised to never tell a soul about. Still, there were some things I couldn't tell her. I didn't want to risk losing this friendship over something I was still so confused about.

It was easier to let her believe that what she saw when she was with me at home was all that it was. When my parents were around, they did a good job being the young and cool mom and dad. From the outside looking in, I had the nice house with the nice furniture, and all the "stuff" a kid in the 80s could ever want. No one would ever understand that I would've traded it all for a different life, to be someone else. So, I didn't tell anyone. Not even Rose.

The closest she ever got to really knowing me was the day I stole a sheet of my mom's Correctol laxatives and convinced her to take them all with me. I told her if she wanted to lose weight like I was this was a good way without having to throw up. She didn't need to lose weight, but she joined me anyway. And well, we took those laxatives about an hour before we headed on our walk to her house one day, and let's just say we learned a valuable lesson on how fast those things work if you take an entire sheet of them. About halfway to her house, both of our stomachs began to gurgle. Trying not to shit our pants, we ran as fast as we could. As we busted through the door of her house, I ran to one bathroom and she ran to another. We laughed about it for the rest of the day, even if we died a little first.

★

My 12th birthday was coming up, and I was getting to know some of Rose's other friends, so it felt like the perfect time to invite them over for a sleepover. Then Rose and I had a brilliant idea: we would invite the Boss Sisters, too. My mom was cool with it because I finally had friends. I filled out that pack of party invitations as fast as I could, and handed them out to all the girls I wanted to come. Mom was shocked when she saw that I invited ten girls and all of them ended up replying yes! Ten girls in our house?!? She was stressing about where to put us all but I reassured her that our upstairs attic was perfect. It had a bathroom and all the privacy we would need to stay up late and not bother her and my dad. I was over the moon.

The week before my party, the Boss Sisters started talking to me more. Who knew all I needed to do was just get the courage to ask them to come to a party and everything would change. I was going to become one of the Boss Sisters, and I was going to help my friends become one too! I could see us showing up in one of those yellow hoodies on Monday at school. It was going to be great! We were so close!

The Friday before my party, I raced home from school to get everything ready. On her way home from work, my mom would pick up my cake. No more Strawberry Shortcake or Cabbage Patch characters this time; just a simple, *Happy Birthday, Chantel* with pink and purple icing flowers. We would have pizza, chips, pop–all the sleepover staples. I called Rose to see what time she would be coming over because I needed her to help me with my hair and makeup. When I went to bed on Friday, I was all set, but when Saturday came, I was a nervous wreck. It was sinking in that I was going to have the most popular girls in my school at my house. *Oh my God, What will they think of my house? What will they think of my mom? What will they think of my annoying siblings? What will they think of the pizza that I order? What will they think of me?* I was snapping at my mom and siblings all morning and afternoon. I was a complete basket case until Rose arrived with her Caboodle of beauty magic.

She helped me get ready and then we sat on the couch anxiously awaiting the girls to arrive. I chose a simple look, a white button-down blouse and white baggy pants that I tight-rolled at the ankles to pair with my white Ballet Flats–*Dirty Dancing Chic.* As the girls arrived, I led each one upstairs to the attic. I knew the Boss Sisters were really into Chicago freestyle house music, so I made sure to have B96's DJ "Bad Boy Bill" playing on my boombox. My mom had picked up a strobe light that flickered enough to give anyone a seizure, but we thought it could be cool if we decided to dance. In the beginning of the night, I did a lot of running up and down stairs greeting everybody to where they needed to go. I hoped they would interact with one another even if they all didn't know each other. But by the time the last person had arrived, I saw that there were two groups of girls standing on two opposite sides of my attic. There was Rose and our small group of friends, on one side of the room, eating chips and talking. The Boss Sisters were on the opposite side of the room, where they were laughing and snickering to one another in a circle. Heather was wearing her blue Z Cavariccis with a white and blue sweatshirt. God, she looked cooler than us all. Not knowing how to handle any of this, I did my best to try to talk to everybody so it wouldn't be awkward. But it was. Even Rose was acting weird with me. When the pizza arrived, I was relieved that everyone would be downstairs where my mom could do her cool-mom thing and smooth over the uncomfortable tension I felt. We ate pizza, sang Happy Birthday, and opened gifts, and everything seemed great. I didn't feel the awkward disconnect that we had at first. It wasn't until we all headed back up to the attic when everything went south.

Once we got back upstairs everyone went back to their corners. I tried to get everyone together with the music, but the Boss Sisters just completely ignored Rose and the other girls. I had never felt so torn in my entire life. I wanted so badly to be part of this group, but I didn't like the way they were treating my friends. Even though Heather and the Boss Sisters were including me in all of their conversations, I knew what it felt like to be Rose and the others, and it was making me angry. After we got into our pajamas and set up where we were going to sleep. Heather made an announcement to everybody that it was time for me to be initiated. Initiation? I didn't know about any initiation. I was nervous about what that might mean, but on the other hand I was going to be popular and have friends. How bad could it be?

Heather squeezed all Five of the Boss Sisters along with me into the bathroom to perform this initiation. They turned up the music so no one outside of the bathroom could hear what was going on. Suddenly everything seemed to get really serious, and I had no idea what was coming. Heather unfolded a sheet of paper that had a bunch of questions on it for me to answer.

"Question 1: Have you ever kissed a boy before?"

"Yes."

"Question 2: Have you ever kissed a boy with your tongue before?"

"Yes." I didn't like where this was going.

"Question 3: How many times?"

"Three." The way they looked at me, I knew I was expected to elaborate. "There was a boy down the street from me, who I thought was cute until I kissed his big fat tongue." I trailed off. I didn't want to tell them any more. There was Jason, a boy at school that I kissed behind the rectory one day after the fall dance. And there was Matt, a boy in my neighborhood that really liked me. I didn't really like him back, but I didn't want to hurt his feelings. Even though I could add more to that list, I didn't want to tell them about the person at my grandmother's house. I didn't want to tell anyone that.

"Question 4: Have you ever watched anybody have sex on TV before?"

"Um... yes." This was getting really uncomfortable. I wanted it to stop.

"Question 5: Have you ever had full sex before?"

I looked around at all of these faces staring at me. The room was getting hotter and hotter.

. "I don't want to answer this." I opened the door without answering. I was embarrassed and I was upset that Rose was being excluded. I wanted to be out there with my friends instead of in this cramped bathroom with these five girls, answering these stupid questions that have more to do with being what my dad would call *a whore* than with being cool. I realized at that moment that I did not want to be a Boss Sister after all.

"Okay, you don't have to answer the last question," Heather said, "but we do have one more thing." She handed me a banana and told me to pretend it was a boy's penis.

I was screaming on the inside. *This is what it takes to be like all of you?* I thought as I looked at everyone while holding this banana in my hand.

"I don't want to do this." I said. I opened the door again and looked out at my friends knowing that what I was about to do would ruin our plan to become cool. I slammed the door shut, and looked Heather square in the face: "No! I won't do this. It's gross."

Heather was stunned, and didn't say anything at first. The other girls turned and looked at Heather to see how she would respond. *No one* stood up to Heather. Especially someone like me; I had spent the last few weeks always kissing her ass! I got up and left. I moved my sleeping bag and pillow next to Rose and the other girls. I told them everything that had just happened and how it wasn't worth being a part of their group.

When Heather and the other Boss Sisters finally emerged from the bathroom after a long time, they took all of their blankets and pillows and set them up on the opposite side of the attic. They made sure they would be far enough away from us so we wouldn't be able to hear what they said. I was so mad that they were choosing to be awful to us in my own house that I decided I was going to start a war. Some streamers had fallen from the ceiling, so I started rolling them up into little balls and throwing them at the enemy. The minute I threw the first ball, there was no turning back. Heather showed zero hesitation to grab anything near her and whip it right back at us. Before long, it was a full-on food fight. Chips and pretzels scattered like shrapnel, cups flew through the air, streamers and popped balloons were being whipped back-and-forth from one side of the room to the other. I realized there was no stopping this on my own. I ran downstairs in a fit of tears to tell my mom. Half asleep and furious, she came up the stairs and yelled at us all. The Boss Sisters ended up sleeping in my living room while Rose and the others stayed with me in the attic.

The Boss Sisters got up early and called their parents to come get them. Nobody said anything to me the whole morning. After everybody had finally left, Rose and I sat in the kitchen and told my mom everything that had transpired the night before. I skipped the part about the questions and the banana, but I said that they were a bunch of bullies, and it wasn't worth being part of their group. Rose and I spent the afternoon together and made a game plan for once we went back to school. We knew that the BS girls were now going to be enemy number one. We settled on sticking together first and foremost. We believed my mom when she said that eventually it would blow over. I wasn't sure how things were going to play out, but I was glad that at least I had Rose.

The next morning my stomach was in knots. With every step I took toward the school building I wanted to run the other way, but as I entered the corridor of lockers, I didn't notice anyone staring or giving me weird looks. Maybe Heather would let this one slide and just leave us alone. When the bell rang and everyone ran to their classes, I saw a group of girls coming towards me. It was them.

I tried to avoid looking their way, but a familiar voice made me look up. Rose was with them, laughing and talking as if nothing ever happened on Saturday. As if we hadn't spent Sunday planning to stick together no matter what. Unbelievable.

"Are you fucking kidding me, Rose???" I radiated anger.

Just like they do in teen movies, the whole group turned and looked at me, but I zeroed in on Rose. She turned to me, and in the most condescending tone possible, she simply said, "yup" and walked away with the rest of them, laughing.

I was beyond crushed. *This is what I get for doing the right thing*, I thought. I knew what it felt like to not have friends before, but to lose one was much worse than not ever having one at all. I never wanted to feel this hurt again.

My thoughts spiraled into a whirlwind of self-loathing and depression. I couldn't help but hear my mother's words repeating in my head, "It must be something you're doing Chantel." I surrendered to accepting that it didn't matter how much I binged and purged and starved and exercised all summer long. It didn't matter that I bleached my hair and got new glasses. It didn't matter how good of a friend I was. All the things I thought were wrong with me that I tried to fix to be accepted never mattered anyway. I would end up on the outside anyway. I distracted myself with that guy Matt from my neighborhood and just tried not to get pregnant now that my period finally came, but it couldn't erase how I felt. Nothing could. Whenever I looked into the mirror I wanted to unzip the disgusting meatsuit I was born with off my bones.

One day when the ache inside of me made me want to claw my face off, I grabbed a needle out of my mom's sewing box and began to scrape it into the top of my left wrist. Although it bled and hurt, I felt a sense of pride for not crying. I always wanted to be strong. I scraped a heart with an arrow into my skin. When it scarred up, it looked like a pink tattoo. Busia saw it when she was visiting, because I didn't bother to hide it. She seemed concerned and asked me what my mom had to say about it. I told her exactly what my mom had said: "Oh, that's cool, Chantel, did it hurt? Be careful. You can get an infection." And that was it. I used to want to feel different. Now, I didn't want to feel at all.

The Polish Mafia

After my birthday party, I spent most of 7th grade focusing on three things: Meeting new boys anywhere and everywhere, dieting and exercising, and learning to smoke cigarettes. Even though my friendship with Rose was short lived, we did so much together in those few months that I felt like I had lost a sister. I heard some rumors in school about a falling out she had with Heather and the Boss Sisters, but I refused to let myself care about it. We weren't in the same classes or circles anymore, so I wrote it off as *that's what she gets for dumping me.* I had begun to make a few school friends here and there, but I was hesitant to allow them in. I had given up on girls, but sometimes things find you even when you're not looking for them.

Instead of focusing so much on finding friends, I found a way to fill the void with a group of boys I started hanging out with in my neighborhood. Taking my siblings to the park became something I no longer hated. I'd come home from school, change out of my uniform and into something cute and typically revealing, like my white mini skirt with the zipper up the back. I'd fix my hair and put on more mascara and eyeliner just to walk around my neighborhood with the group of boys that seemed to all have a crush on me. I loved the power I felt over them. Knowing I could be who they wanted and not give it to them. Except for Matt. Even though he wasn't my type, he was persistent. I hated jock-y guys, and he always wore a Cubs Jersey and hat. He wasn't terrible looking, he was a fair, freckled, green-eyed Irish kid who treated me like a princess, and I just wasn't really interested. He looked like he could be my brother. I wanted a tall, dark and handsome guy who looked like the guys I saw driving Iroc Z's on Harlem Ave, but I couldn't tell him that because I didn't want to hurt him. And let's be honest, he kept me company those days. Even when the neighborhood girls down the street called me a slut out their front window every time I passed them on my way to hang the park he still chose to hang with me. Even when his friends called me a tease and told him that he was an idiot for liking me, he still knocked on my door every day after school.

So in between leading Matt along and flipping off the bitches that hated me down the street, I'd sit on my roof and smoke cigarettes. Picking up the habit was easy; almost everyone in my family smoked. When Rose and I hung out, we smoked a cigarette every once in a while, but not as much as I did now. My mom had recently switched to Virginia Slims, and was now buying them by the carton. I stole a pack one day, and when I realized she didn't notice, I just never quit. The first time I lit one I made the mistake of leaning my face over the stovetop burner that was set to high. Not only did I singe my Aqua Net sprayed bangs, but later in the shower I found out that I lost half of my right eyelashes too. When I was washing my face, I realized some parts of my eyelashes felt more like a man's beard stubble than my normal soft fringe. Eventually my mom figured it out and confronted me about it. Because I never confirmed or denied taking them, she said I better tell her because she'd rather have me smoke at the house openly in front of her than hang on a street corner and do it behind her back. So, I started smoking at home in the open. Her friend found it odd when I lit one up at the kitchen table one day, and my father said it wasn't a good idea for me to pick up this nasty habit, but my mom didn't see an issue with it. The only reason she regretted it was because I was too young to buy my own, and I was taking hers all the time.

It would be my smoking in the open that would eventually bring back the possibility of having girls as friends again. The Polish Mafia girls–that's what I call them, they weren't an *actual* mafia–were in most of my classes in 7th grade but it wasn't until springtime that we started hanging out. Two of the three were amazing at math, which was great because I needed all the help I could get. The other one's dry humor and pessimistic view of her dysfunctional family was all too relatable for me in a way I wasn't brave enough to talk about yet. When I mentioned to them one day at school that I smoked openly, and my mom let me, they all wanted to come over for a sleepover. The more we hung out, the more I realized that I was missing out on a whole part of myself that I wish I knew. The Polish part. They all lived in the Polonia neighborhood near our school and all three were 100% Polish and spoke it fluently. The very first time I hung out with them, I didn't even know that there was an area of Chicago that was like living in another country and it was just a block from the school I had been going to since I was six. On Belmont and Milwaukee in Chicago is where every deli, bakery, and retail store in the neighborhood was named something with way too many consonants in a row for me to pronounce. Even though my dad was 100% Polish, the closest I ever got to speaking it was calling my grandparents Busia and Dza Dza and even that was wrong. Apparently, *Busia* is the Polish-English term for grandmother, and the proper name is actually *Babcia.* Busia told me once that she and Dza Dza both spoke Polish as children, but because their parents made them learn English as their first priority, by the time my father came around, the only thing Polish about them was their last name. We didn't even eat pierogis unless my mom bought them at the bakery and that didn't happen much because of all the fat shaming my father unleashed if she brought anything home from there. Regardless, becoming a part of this new community was a huge world opener for me; I enjoyed getting to know a part of who I was, even if my family didn't acknowledge it much.

Meeting these girls influenced me in so many unexpected ways. Even though I still struggled with body image and self-hate, being around these girls showed me how to just eat normally and not obsess like I had been the past couple of years. All three, though not perfect by any means, seemed to come from homes with some sort of parental structure and guidance. Someone was always around, making sure we had eaten, that we were cared for. They weren't left on their own as much as I was, and it showed. It was a little annoying to me how much they had to call their moms to let them know where they were. And big time annoying when they would all talk in Polish to each other in front of me. They were the smartest girls I had ever met, and they never seemed embarrassed to be with me like Rose had at times. With them, I didn't just feel like I had friends; I felt like I had found a tribe to belong to. Except I didn't know the language yet.

The best thing about them, apart from accepting me as I was, I mean, was that they liked the things I liked! The school was hosting their first lip sync contest, and they entered with me. We decided to perform "Shake your Love" by Debbie Gibson. I was the lead who sang Debbie's part and they were the backup singers and dancers. In the end, of course,

Heather and the Boss Sisters won 1st place with their routine, but I was still proud to have taken fourth place.

The experience even inspired us to work on starting our own band. Only one of us had any musical ability, but we had dreams, and it was fun to plan them together. The four of us roamed the city streets on our ten-speeds, met up at the mall to shop, and made out with guys that were way too old for us. We had sleepovers as often as we could–at one of these sleepovers, I tried my first can of Old-Style beer. We also orchestrated photo shoots where we got all dolled up and took pictures of each other with a disposable camera. We would drop it off at the One-Hour Photo the next day, hoping for just *one* to turn out. There were days when we went actively looking for guys in a band with long hair and for a moment, they even convinced me that I could let go of my tall dark and handsome standards for the possibility of a grungy drummer. We were goofballs, we were boy crazy, we loved hair bands, and we loved fast food. I never felt like I was in competition with them. Each one of us brought something different to the group, and for that season, my life really was amazing. Being friends with them helped me forget about Rose, and the Boss Sisters, and Matt. Ugh. Sorry Matt.

He Doesn't Look a Thing Like Jesus

My adventures with the Polish Mafia were fun and drama free–truth be told, most of my eighth grade year was pretty uneventful, but I eventually grew to miss Rose. She was the kind of friend who didn't mind just hanging at my house when I had to babysit my siblings. She actually once told me that she preferred staying with me than even being at home. When Rose and I were friends, I didn't need to go anywhere to have fun. We used to say if my kitchen table could talk, we'd be *soooo dead.*

After a year of not talking, we rekindled our friendship. I was nervous to be rejected, but I decided to bite the bullet and give her a call. All the time that had passed and the fact that she had transferred schools gave me hope that maybe we could put the past away and start over. It must have been in the stars because after her mom answered, I didn't have to hold my breath long before Rose took the call, and by the weekend, we were back together on my front porch smoking and talking about boys, sex, movies, and music. We made crank calls in the middle of the night to unsuspecting people who kept their phone number listed in the local white pages, and we talked about our dreams to move to LA one day and become models.

I still hung out with the Polish Mafia, but I needed Rose. I felt a closeness to her, that I don't believe she truly understood. She always said that she was so different from me. I guess she was right. On the surface, she had dark hair and I had light. She was thin, and I was well, struggling to stay thin. She was raised by a single mom, and most days I wished my mom was single. I really can't blame her for not understanding; when it came to the real me, I kept her in the dark. I kept everyone there. I knew that she and I were more alike than different; I just didn't know how to tell her.

Rose was never as boy crazy as I was, none of my friends were, but she was always open to dressing up and going for a walk in my neighborhood in hopes we might meet someone (we usually did). On one of these walks we saw a guy that looked like Bon Jovi. It was getting late and we were cutting through a parking lot on our way back home. When he called us over to his black El Camino, Rose wasn't interested but she rolled her eyes and begrudgingly followed me when I started in his direction anyway. When I got close enough to the car to see his face clearly, I saw that he actually *did not* look like Bon Jovi, and also that he had his dick out and was waving it around at us.

"OHMIGOD!" I screamed, turned around, and crashed into Rose, who had just caught up with me, and who was also screaming now. Frantic and screaming, we ran the rest of the way home. Look, Rose was crazy in some regards, but approaching strange men in strange places wasn't something she would do–that was all me.

I had picked up a lot of flirting skills and was always looking to put them to use. So much so that Dorothy, the old lady that lived across the street from our house, phoned my mom at work after she saw me get out of a yellow convertible one day. I met the yellow convertible guy at the mall with the Polish Mafia, and when he asked if I wanted to go get a hot dog with him, obviously I said yes. Over lunch, he casually mentioned that he was twenty-eight, and that he had been in jail for a few days. This alarmed my friends, but I still allowed him to take me home after. Who was I to judge? He was nice to me. He told me how pretty I was, and honestly it never occurred to me that someone twice my age could be an issue.

After Dorothy's tipoff, my mom called home to interrogate me about who this guy was. She said he was way too old for me and told me not to get in any cars again. I listened with a grain of salt though. She was the last person I was going to take boy advice from. Even if she chose someone who was an appropriate age and didn't have a criminal record, my father wasn't exactly a prize. Anyway, yellow convertible guy stopped coming around when I told him that my mom wasn't happy about how much older he was. It was fine though. No matter how much attention I got, I had moments where I felt gross inside about it all, and I didn't know why, or what to do about that. So I learned to ignore it.

Instead, I focused on doing what I could to maintain the physical transformation that made me acceptable. The at-home highlights my mom did had mostly grown out, but I had learned to lighten my hair on my own using Sun-In and the heat from my blow dryer. My mom had also allowed me to ditch my glasses and get contacts, so doing my make-up was even more fun for me now. My parents were still, well, my parents, so my role as built-in babysitter was still going strong. But my siblings were older now. I could lock myself in my room for hours knowing they wouldn't leave the living room television and that they would pour themselves a bowl of cereal if they got hungry. I taught them how to fend for themselves quite well, and when they got really bored, I took them to the park.

When you grow up where winter seems to swallow half the year, anything above sixty degrees feels like a celebration. So on one of those unseasonably warm spring days, Rose and I were heading to the park with my siblings when two guys that looked a little older than us rode up close to us on their BMX bikes and whistled. Being used to this ploy to grab our attention, we pretended we didn't notice. She and I exchanged a knowing smile, as the guys' chatter trailed behind us. Their whispers and cologne drifted through the air like cartoon pheromones—they smelled so good—nothing like my dad's Old Spice. As we approached the corner, the boys rode up and stopped to ask us our names.

"Damn girl, you have some pretty blue eyes! Are those real?" one of the boys asked.

I laughed and nodded. Then he stepped in closer, his bike still between his legs, in order to take a closer look. My heart raced. He was so cute!

"They aren't as pretty as mine, though." He winked at me.

His name was Jake and I was smitten.

"I have to take my brother and sister to the park" mumbled out of me. Rose looked at me like I was an idiot. She obviously didn't see what I saw.

"Can I get your number?" he asked.

"I don't have a pen and paper" I said

Rose had already made her way across the street with my siblings and Jake's friend followed her. I gave him my address and told him to drop by whenever. That my parents were rarely around.

I spent the whole next day out on my front porch, anxiously waiting for the moment Jake might ride by, but I had given up by sunset and changed into my pajamas. My dad was home and in a rare good mood, so my family was gathered in the living room watching television when there was a knock at the door.

It was Jake.

"Crap!" I rushed to change into regular clothes while my mom greeted him at the door. My dad, who was annoyed at the interruption, also got up to see who was at the door. I could hear Jake's voice through my bedroom window, as I tore my closet apart looking for something to put on.

"You can talk to Jake on the porch," my mom said with a weird smile.

I had never felt this nervous around a guy before. For some reason, though, Jake was different. I stepped outside hoping I didn't look like I had just ransacked my closet.

Jake smiled at me. "Hi."

"Hi," I replied through sheer force of will. I was frozen.

He was the cutest guy to ever be interested in me, and smelled *so good.* It was the smell I had picked up on yesterday. He wasn't shy, so thankfully he kept the conversation going until I remembered how to talk. He told me that he was seventeen and lived with his mom and grandmother, no mention of a dad. When I asked him what school he went to, he said he was going to get his G.E.D eventually.

Definitely not going to tell my parents that, I thought to myself. They'd have a harder time with that than with the 28-yr-old jailbird with the yellow convertible. Even though I wanted to know more, I didn't press for details. There was a sadness about him; I could see it in his eyes as he looked away into the streetlight. So instead, I asked him what cologne he was wearing.

"Drakkar Noir," he laughed.

We were side-by-side on the stairs when I leaned into his chest to take a deeper breath. He smiled as I looked up at him. I could feel myself falling for him immediately. Everything around me stopped. Eventually, my mom came out to say it was time to come in. Go figure. Why do they care how long I'm on our porch talking to a guy when most of the time they aren't even here and don't pay attention to what I do. But I wasn't going to push it. I wanted to see him again.

As I got up, Jake grabbed my hand and pulled me close to him. "Can I see you tomorrow?" he asked.

Melting. I was melting.

"Yes, after church."

When I went to hug him goodbye, he pulled me in and kissed me. I didn't have a second to think before my lips were pressed against his.

I think I'm in love. I floated to my room. *Wait until I tell Rose about this.*

Nothing Like I Thought

It was the last day of eighth grade. I was surprised to find myself a little sad to say goodbye to the school and the kids that made a majority of my school life miserable, but as sensitive as I've always been, I'd cry to mourn not wanting to cry. Our graduation song was the "Wind beneath our Wings" by Bette Midler and it was apparent that we as a class chose what was popular on the radio, rather than choose a song that made sense to our graduating class. If I had a choice I would have chosen something like "What a Feeling" or "Don't stop Believing." In no way would I consider anyone at my school to be "my hero" or "the wind beneath my wings." Not even the Polish Mafia girls and I liked them. I was glad to get out of there. My graduation was scheduled for Sunday morning at the church, and my mom had planned a party for me later that evening. She had booked a room at an event hall called the Party House where we had an open bar, a three-course meal, and, of course, a cake. Mom even hired Patty, the Lady DJ, for the music and entertainment.

A few weeks before, she took me to the mall for my dress, and it was truly one of the best shopping experiences I'd ever had with her. It was fun trying on all the different dresses and seeing her reaction to me in them. It was further validation that losing weight, getting contacts and going blonde was what I needed to do. Mom loved the dress I chose, and I couldn't wait for Jake to see me in it! It was black and white with spaghetti straps and cute polka dot ruffles that hit just above my knees. Aside from Jake and Rose, I invited several girls from school, and even a few past Boss Sisters, and we all had a blast getting wasted on dinner wine and dancing. The only bummer, other than looking like a sloppy, drunk mess in my pictures, was not ever hearing if Jake liked me in my dress that day. That and catching him flirting with some of the girls I had invited to my party. I never said anything about it. I didn't want to make him mad.

Jake and I had only been dating about a month, and even though there were things that were making me feel uncomfortable here and there, I found myself making excuses for him because he had a difficult home life and because I fell hard for him. I never loved anyone in my 13 years of life like I loved him. I was willing to do anything for him, and everyone knew it. Even Rose was getting annoyed with me because it was starting to change our dynamic with me doting on him hand and foot. But she didn't understand. He had been through a lot, and it said so much to me when I was his one phone call from jail the day he got caught stealing a bike. I begged my mom to help bail him out, and she did. She said she did it for me and I was so grateful for it. I think she saw what I saw in him. She also appreciated having him around to help with the heavy lifting since my dad never was. Even my baby sister loved him, and she doesn't love anybody. So I took it all to be a sign: He was "the one" for me that all the movies talked about. Even if he wasn't always nice.

It never bothered me that Jake didn't have a job or a car. I never thought twice about him using our shower or the washer and dryer in our basement for the only outfit I ever saw him wear. My dad barely noticed, and my mom didn't seem to mind. "Can't Fight This Feeling" by REO Speedwagon was our song and I was in love. I had spent my entire childhood imagining what it would feel like to fall in love with someone, and when I met Jake, my feelings were overwhelming. I looked forward to every moment with him, never anticipating where it could lead. The summer days that followed, quickly evolved from flirting and kissing, to hot and heavy make out sessions. Even though I knew I wasn't ready to go all the way with him, I didn't want to lose him, and every day it was becoming more difficult for me to tell him to stop. What originally began as a rom com meet-cute, was devolving into more and more uncomfortable interactions where I was in tears, struggling to force Jake off of me so he would stop. Sometimes he was cruel about it, and threatened to break up with me when I didn't give in. It didn't matter how far I was already allowing him to go, regardless of how I felt; it wasn't going to be enough until he had everything.

My parents had an above-ground pool put in, and I was so excited. I bought a new bathing suit and invited Rose and another girl over on the first day we opened the pool. Before we even had a chance to jump in, Jake and his friends were at the gate at the end of my yard asking if they could come swim too. Because of how things were going and the way he was making me feel almost every day he was over I was apprehensive to allow him in. I just wanted a girl's day. As I walked over to meet him at the gate, Rose followed closely behind. Jake and the guys he brought along with him were staring at us like we were pieces of meat. But that wasn't the worst of it. It was the words that immediately followed Jake's gaze that would ring in my ears every time I put on a bathing suit from that day on.

"Are you wearing a maxi pad under your suit?" he asked.

I saw everyone try to hold back a laugh. I was humiliated. I grabbed my towel from the picnic table, but before I wrapped it around myself, I looked down at my bikini area trying to understand what he was referring to.

"No, you asshole, I'm not wearing a pad. Why would you even ask?"

He ignored my question and poked his finger into my pubic bone, making the noise of the Pillsbury dough boy: "Maybe you should shave or something because it looks like you are wearing a pad."

I just stood there, frozen. Looking down, knowing that I didn't have much hair there either, I felt sick inside by his words. He blew past me with his friends and jumped in my pool without a care for how terribly he just treated me.

Rose shook her head at me clearly communicating that what just happened was so fucking wrong, but she had been warning me about him for weeks now. I ran into the house in tears. As I stared in the bathroom mirror, I sucked in my stomach as far as I could until I could see all of my ribs clearly in the mirror. *How could he say this to me? I thought he loved me.* I banged my fists repeatedly against my hip bones. Then something sunk in. I hated feeling fat. I refused to be fat. I always felt weird and gross about my body, especially that area, but now, not only was I always feeling fat everywhere else, but even there I was fat.

When I made my way to the back porch, I saw Rose, smiling and laughing as she stood on the ladder getting ready to jump in. Everyone in the pool was staring up at her. She had no fat anywhere. *If I looked like her, he wouldn't have said that to me.* I sat on my back porch, still in my swimsuit and towel, deciding that I would hide, until someone either came and talked to me or everyone left. When the door opened, and I realized it was Jake, I got up to leave. I didn't want to talk to him. I didn't even want to see him.

Jake followed me into my bedroom and shut the door. The only light in the room was coming from the neighbors dining room window next door, so I scrambled to turn my desk lamp on. Before I could, he grabbed me from behind and pressed his lips as hard as he could into my neck while restraining my arms. As he led me onto my daybed, he forced my legs apart and pressed against me. I tried to push him away, but then I thought maybe if I allowed this to happen, he would stop treating me the way he had been lately. He didn't look into my eyes, he didn't kiss me, he only focused on himself, entering me as fast and as hard as he could. Even after I repeatedly asked him to slow down, he acted like he didn't hear me. I whimpered and struggled to hold back tears as my body was used.

He pulled out, wiped himself on my white lace bedding, pulled up his pants, and left. He never once looked at me. When I stood up to get dressed, I noticed some blood on my comforter. As I carried my bedding to the basement and threw it in the washing machine, I went numb. He didn't even say goodbye.

When I returned upstairs, I looked around to see if anyone was still there.

"What happened to you?" Rose asked when she saw me.

Holding back tears, I simply said that we did it. Rose and the other girl were wide-eyed.

"Did you use protection?" she asked.

Not even thinking about it until that moment, a sinking feeling started to form in the pit of my stomach. I looked at them both with a face that answered their question without having to say a word.

Rose looked down.

"You're probably pregnant," the other girl said.

The Kitchen Stove

After a week of refusing Jake's phone calls, and praying that my period would come so I could stop worrying if I was pregnant or not, Rose and I decided that we needed some girl time. Our plan was to tan all day and swim in the evening under the moon. As soon as she got to my house, we put on our swimsuits, grabbed the suntan oil, towels, and my radio and made our way out the back door.

My mom was at the sink, washing dishes in a cloud of steam. She had evidently decided to tear the house apart to clean every square inch of it that day. She seemed irritated, and I could sense there was something going on–probably with my dad, but I didn't care enough to ask.

"We will be outside if you need us," I said, throwing my towel over my shoulder.

She shot me a bitter look. "The house is a mess, so I'm cleaning it today," she said, implying that I hadn't kept up with my chores.

"Well, I *did* clean the house this week, mom."

She didn't look up from the sink to say anything more, so I rolled my eyes and continued on out. The woman was OCD about the house, and her guilt trips typically kicked in when something was bothering her, so I knew to steer clear.

"You better watch your brother and sister when they get into the pool," she yelled.

I took a deep breath and slammed the back door as hard as I could behind me. Once again, the built-in babysitter is expected to be on duty. *Nothing I do is ever enough for her.*

I watched my siblings all week when she was at the shop with my dad and now, even when she was home, I still couldn't just be a kid. She seemed to ignore the fact that I was also one of her children, not the live-in help. She had no boundaries. She regularly told me about what was going on with the business, and she vented to me about how much of an asshole my dad was being. She could complain about him, but god forbid I say anything.

Your father... she would start. But then she would turn around and yell at me for badmouthing him as if he was some paragon of fatherhood. Please.

I overheard one of many arguments over the phone—something about a woman he was getting too friendly with. But what could I say? This wasn't new. Whether he was wooing his customers at work, encouraging and inspiring the people he bowled with, or showering a random person on the street with his kind lending hand, everyone got my father's undivided attention, respect, and love except for us. I wished my father's behavior made my mother as sick inside as Jake had made me. I was done with him. Why couldn't my mom be done with Dad's bullshit, too? Maybe she wouldn't be so irritated all the time if she wasn't pandering to his every whim.

I laid back into the plastic lawn chair, and turned on the radio. Every once in a while, my mom would appear on the back porch to have a cigarette, her face was still sour, like she resented the fact that I was outside by the pool while she was inside cleaning. I felt guilty for not helping her clean, but it's not like I was actually able to relax and have fun like a normal kid. I still had to watch my siblings, and my brother was being a total brat. He wouldn't listen to me no matter what I tried, and my mom did nothing about it. She never did anything about it.

Morning turned to afternoon, and any time I would think that *maybe* I could finally get a few minutes to just be with my friend, my brother would harass us, splash us, or do some other obnoxious thing to demand attention. He was only six, so of course he was a headache, but I was only thirteen, and I was boiling over with frustration. When his antics escalated to using a squirt gun on us while we were face down, just trying to tan our backs in peace, I lost it.

I got up from my chair, and stormed over to the ladder of the pool where he was standing. I ripped the water gun from his hand and threw it out of the pool, so of course he started to scream like a little psycho. I put my hand over his mouth, hoping my mom wouldn't hear him. The last thing I needed was to get in trouble because *he* was being a brat. In true older sibling form, I started to dunk him in the pool; maybe that would get him to shut up. Apparently, my mom heard him scream right away and came out to see what the commotion was about. Unfortunately that means she was right there and saw me give my brother a taste of his own medicine.

"Stop, Chantel! You're going to kill him!" she screamed.

I had no intention of killing him. It was just a few dunks to assert sibling dominance. I pushed him away and screamed back at her: "He's not listening to me, mom!"

I looked over at Rose for a nod of validation, and saw that my mom was already at the pool ladder, demanding that I get out of the pool. I had seen this look in her eye before.

"I'm sorry Mom, it's just that he is acting so bad today!" I reluctantly made my way towards the ladder, begging her not to hurt me.

"She's trying to drown me, mom!" My brother said.

"No, I'm not!"I snapped back, but it was too late for an explanation.

Through gritted teeth, she repeated, "get over here, Chantel."

I knew I was going to get it. I had gotten it many times before, but her face today was scarier. When I got within reach, she grabbed me by my hair and pulled me over the ladder faster than my feet could respond. She continued to drag me by my hair up the back porch stairs. I was soaking wet, slipping and sliding everywhere, trying to get my feet under me, trying to escape her.

"So you want to kill him? You want to kill your brother?"

"No, Momma, I don't! He wasn't listening to me!"

Once we were through the kitchen door, she bashed my head into the kitchen stove and only released my hair so she could square up to kick me. From the ground, I tried to block her kicks; I begged her to stop. I screamed and cried and told her how sorry I was. It didn't matter.

I don't remember what happened immediately after that. I don't know what Rose saw of this, or what she thought about it. I just know that I was never the same around my brother or sister again.

I shouldn't have gotten so angry at him, he was just a little kid. He didn't know all that I was struggling with. He didn't know that I was desperate for the chance to be a normal kid for once–even just for a few hours! And when he laughed later on to my father about me getting "spanked" for trying to drown him, I realized that he had no awareness of the gravity of what just happened to me either.

The Talk of the Neighborhood

Summer never ended up being carefree like I had hoped, but I loved to bring my boom box out onto the front porch and watch the world go by. This also was not carefree as I usually spun *what ifs* around my head the whole time. What if Jake was sorry? What if it would be better now that we already had sex, maybe he wouldn't pressure me so much? What if?

The song "Boys of Summer" by Don Henley came on the radio. Perfect. What would be next, "Cruel Summer"? And, as if right on cue, Matt showed up. I still wasn't interested, but I was sad and didn't mind the company.

"I heard Jake and you did it," he blurted out.

Clearly the rumors reached him, but this is what he chooses to start with? Not cool. "Who told you?" I asked.

"Jake did. He said that I could have you if I wanted because you are a lousy lay, and you should learn to shave better."

I felt sick. Even if Matt was mad that I didn't want to be his girlfriend, this was cruel. He must have realized that his jab went too far because the sneering look on his face melted into shame when he saw my reaction.

Navigating puberty and teenhood is universally understood to be challenging and confusing, but my *Teen Works* book never prepared me for what Jake did. And finding out that the entire neighborhood knew and discussed my pubic area was not anything I knew how to navigate. I was barely comfortable having hair in that area at all. I knew it was part of growing up, and I knew my mom had it, but she never told me I should shave it off. Was that what people did? No one ever told me. Having been touched there so many times without my permission, I already felt deeply ashamed of my body. I hated how I felt, and didn't know why; and even when I allowed myself to be touched, I still felt ashamed. Now I had to worry about appearances even there? It was too much. It was a whole new reason to hate myself.

I sank my head into my hands and exploded into tears. Matt apologized profusely and tried to comfort me. He put his arm around me, and I appreciated it at first, but the feeling of humiliation was suffocating. I got up abruptly, ran inside, and slammed the door behind me. I didn't say goodbye; I just huffed at the door for a moment before retreating into my room. I always felt safe under my comforter, but this time, when I pulled it over me, I remembered what happened on it and all I wanted was to burn that thing to ashes.

He only said it once, but when Jake told me I was beautiful, I believed him. I believed his stupid blue eyes. Now I was convinced that Jake was embarrassed of me, that he was ashamed to be with me. It wasn't about him being frustrated that I didn't give him what we wanted when he wanted it. I let him take something I wasn't ready to give, hoping he would love me, and he mocked it. He mocked me. All of my *what ifs* were useless; I would never be enough for him.

I looked in the mirror with a pit in my stomach, and I wondered if this is how my mom felt being married to my dad. He picked her apart at every opportunity. He constantly criticized her body, her hair, her clothes, what she ate–nothing she did was ever good enough for him. No matter how hard she tried. *How could I have been so stupid?* Jake was no different from the boys in middle school who bullied me, but realizing that he reminded me of my father was even worse.

SIX

Feral Freshie

★

Freshie

My mom loved high school, and high school loved her back, so she could barely contain her excitement leading up to my first day of Freshman year. Never mind the fact that the previous eight years were pretty rough for me, she went on and on about how high school was the best time of her life. Now, I had learned to take anything my mom said with a grain of salt, but what she was saying lined up with what I had always heard until she told me she was voted the mother of her class. Of all the things the teenage version of my mom could be nominated for, *mother* struck me as especially odd, but I masked with an empty smile, and I listened to her continue to gush about high school.

When she spoke about her experiences in high school, she never paused to "read the room" or consider that I might be feeling uneasy, or anxious, or anything at all. We never talked about feelings; it just wasn't worth the excruciating vulnerability it required. I hated feeling like something was wrong with me, and I hated feeling like a disappointment whenever I failed at being a perfect, sunny daughter, who didn't need anything, and just glided through the world on a rainbow. I think she tried to connect with me through shopping, and letting me wear what I wanted, and buying me makeup, but it was too late. I had learned to keep my mom at arm's length, and no amount of shopping would change that. It was safer to keep everything surface-level.

As we drove from store to store picking up school supplies, new shoes, and groceries to pack lunches I would never eat, I wanted to be hopeful that things could be better. New school, new chapter. It was an all-girls, private high school that had a reputation for not only strong college prep academics, but also college-style traditions. I knew the Polish Mafia girls would be there, but I didn't know what else to expect.

When the first day of school arrived, my house was buzzing with the sound of our local morning news, the clanging of spoons in cereal bowls, and my Bangles cassette blaring at full volume from the bathroom. I breathed in the scent of Irish Spring soap and turned the water as hot as I could stand. I needed to wash away all the thoughts of Jake and the gossip about me that I prayed wouldn't reach the girls at my new school. Singing along to "Hazy Shade of Winter," I blow dried and curled my hair. When I put on my uniform, I did what I always did before leaving for the day: I stood in front of my dresser mirror and sucked in my stomach as far in as I could. I needed to see ribs.

High school was a sea of big hair, crimped and sprayed to the high heavens. Plaid skirts everywhere were rolled up above the knee, and the smell of Exclamation! Perfume hung in the air. I was relieved to see the Polish Mafia girls huddled up in the hall, looking as lost as I did. We all knew that one of the fall traditions involved assigning us a senior "sister" who would show us the ropes of school. Not long into meeting my "sister" I learned that my worst nightmare was becoming reality: Her brother not only knew Jake, and knew what happened over the summer, but her brother dated the girl down the street from me who would shout out her window and call me a slut every time I walked to the park. *I couldn't catch a fucking break.*

Since I didn't really have anything to lose, I decided to try my luck with honesty in hopes that she would believe me. Thankfully, she did. She was a kindhearted girl who seemed to genuinely like me. It was comforting to have an older female offer encouragement and support– kinda like a real big sister. She was super positive about life, and also really fun. She invited me to a few frat parties that she went to and even though I couldn't go, because: *built-in babysitter*, I loved hearing her stories about it. High school was off to a good start, and she was a big part of that. Maybe I finally did catch a break.

Another tradition that we all knew was coming was Freshman Initiation. The "big sister" assignment was part of it, but there was more. It was a celebration of beginnings for us freshies and the first of the "lasts" for the seniors. Most of the freshman girls I asked, had barely spoken to their senior girls, so nobody knew what this initiation was going to involve. The school sanctioned events were sure to be tame, but we knew there was more headed our way *after* school. Let's be real, this day was really about establishing dominance in the school's social hierarchy; they were the queens and we were the peasants. Whether we wanted to participate in these character-building experiences or not, we believed that if we didn't, our high school lives could be hell. We heard high school horror stories, and didn't have any reason to believe we would be spared. Even though my senior sis was kind to me, I wasn't sure what could still happen.

The day before initiation, she passed me a note explaining everything that initiation would include:

September 26, 1989

1. **Exercises at Bryson Tech High School.**
   Ugh. Whyyyyy? Bryson Tech was the all-boys private "brother" school to ours that would link up with us throughout the year for events like dances, or whenever school events needed boys, I guess. I knew a part of this day was about the seniors getting a chance to build themselves up by gently humiliating us, but because most of the boys that bullied me in grammar school went there, this sounded terrible.

2. **Scavenger hunt at the prestigious Northwestern University in Evanston, Il.**
   Apparently, this college not only produced successful doctors and lawyers, but according to my "big sister", there were some really cute guys that hosted the weekly frat parties she attended.

3. **Pizza dinner at Lou Malnati's.**
   I don't know anyone from Chicago who doesn't love pizza, but this was a place outside the city that the seniors swore had the best Chicago deep dish around. I was skeptical, but it was pizza!

4. **Benny Hutch Ice Cream to end the night.**
   Sounds good! She also said something about doing "Chinese fire drills" but I had no idea what that meant, but she made it seem like a fun thing. All in all, this initiation sounded not only *survivable* but potentially fun.

When the day came, I was cautiously optimistic. My senior greeted me at my locker with a big smile; the seniors made special hats for their freshmen to wear. As she placed a ridiculously big and awkward piece of cardboard on my head, it toppled to the floor. I expected something mildly embarrassing, but what she made was really cute. She made a basketball hoop with painted cardboard and a little net, and she posed a teddy bear with a ball glued to its hand as if he was doing a slam dunk. It was hard to balance on my head as I went from class to class, but at least it was cute.

Most of the hats I saw were an array of papier-mâché and cardboard, some had various food items like ice cream cones, and others told stories with Barbie dolls. All were unique and pretty telling of the seniors who made them. Some seniors gave their freshman pacifiers and baby bottles, but generally these were all pretty harmless. The tales of seniors making the freshman hats out of old toilet seats and garbage, or gluing used maxi pads and tampons to a hat like a ruffle made for a great story, but I never saw any proof.

After school let out, we all piled into a convoy of several cars, and headed out for the destinations I was fortunate enough to know about in advance. The first stop was fortunately not as humiliating as expected. We had to push marshmallows on the ground with our noses, but by the grace of God there wasn't a boy anywhere to be seen. The scavenger hunt at Northwestern University was cool; everyone looked like they walked out of a Lacoste magazine and the campus was beautiful. I hadn't even considered college up to this point, but this made me wonder if I should.

It was a perfect, crisp fall day. We drove around with the windows rolled down and The Cure's *Disintegration* album blaring from the car's cassette player. I was grateful for my senior sis, her kindness and guidance helped me more than she knew. I soaked in the lyrics to every song so I could stretch this moment into forever.

Becoming the Bully

I never expected to like going to school, and now I did. I never expected to have friends, and now I did. I could do a pretty decent cartwheel, so I tried out for gymnastics, and to my surprise, I made the team! Turns out, the team was terrible and they let anyone join, but nevertheless, I was finding my groove in school and in life. Inevitably, though, the glowy start to freshman year began to fade a few weeks in when the workload ramped up. I had worms and fetal pigs to dissect in biology, papers to write for my English class on books I only had time to read the Cliffs Notes for, and a math teacher who was hellbent on destroying me. And then my parents informed me that we would be moving forty-five minutes west of the city, and the house they were having built would be ready for us to move in by next summer. They tried to sweeten the deal, telling me how much bigger the house was going to be, and how I could choose my own carpet color for my bedroom, and how it was going to be on its own floor away from everyone else. I didn't know how to feel. As nice as that all sounded, I didn't want to hold my breath. My parents had a habit of talking up things that didn't actually happen, so I wouldn't believe it until I could see it. I also wasn't sure about leaving everything behind...even with my evil Algebra teacher out to torture me.

After Ms. Dabrowsky spanked me in front of my entire 4th grade class for not doing my math workbook, I just wanted to live in a world without math. It never came naturally to me anyway, but Ms. Gordon made it her mission from the start to make sure that I would never learn algebra as long as I was in her class. This woman was awful. Cartoonishly round, she was like a grape with arms and legs. Her hair was cut short, and dyed black to match her soul. The only time Gordon's face wasn't a scowl was when she reveled in my humiliation. Her favorite power move was to call me to the board to solve an equation that she knew I couldn't solve, and smirk as if she was teaching me a lesson or something.

Enough was enough. One day when she inevitably called me up for my shaming, I threw the marker at the board, grabbed my books, and walked out of her class. This became a common occurrence by the second quarter, and I accepted my fate: I was going to flunk Gordon's class. My parents didn't care to check up on me because they were too caught up with my siblings, the business, and selling our house. As long as I went to school, I was golden, and making the conscious decision to flunk Algebra allowed me to focus my time and energy on other things.

Like dealing with a bogus rumor that I was talking shit about Tammy, a girl I barely knew. She had been to my house a couple of times with Rose, but we never clicked. I didn't trust her, and that was that. I didn't think about her anymore, I barely even saw Rose these days since we didn't go to school together, so why would I bother to talk shit about this Tammy? However it started, or whatever she was trying to do, I never expected this psycho to be hanging out a car window screaming obscenities and threatening to kick my ass as I was leaving school. Completely bewildered, I looked at the girls next to me and laughed. *What the hell?* The next day she was waiting for me as I arrived at school, hanging out of the same car, with the same dude, screaming the same shit. This insanity continued daily and then weekly. It was annoying and embarrassing, and it was wearing on me. Sometimes she'd drive by in the morning, sometimes in the afternoon. Sometimes both. At first, I thought Tammy was all talk; but as it kept going, I worried that her threats might not be empty. I had to deal with this somehow; I wasn't going to let this bitch ruin things for me.

"Hey, what's up with that girl screaming at you every day after school?" It was Dawn, a girl who made her way into my circle of friends, and made a point to one-up anything anyone ever said. She made up a ridiculous story of how she was related to a guy in a popular metal band that I knew was a lie. Her entire existence irritated me.

"I don't know," I replied in a huff. Her questions continued. I ignored her as much as possible, but this girl didn't take the hint. I had bigger fish to fry; I needed to be able to get home without possibly getting jumped.

After three weeks enduring Tammy's harassment on my own, I called my mom when I got home. She was at work and audibly annoyed that I had interrupted her.

"Mom, Tammy has been coming by school every day and screaming things at me, and I am afraid she's going to beat me up or send someone else to beat me up!

"How long has this been going on?"

"A few weeks."

"I never liked that girl. Well, if she does it again let me know. I gotta go."

When I told my mom later that night that I didn't want to walk to school by myself anymore, she realized that this was actually serious. She told me to give it one more week and that if it still didn't stop, she would do something about it. I took alternate ways to school to avoid her, and hoped I could dodge her after school. It worked until Friday.

As I said goodbye to my friends for the weekend, I saw Tammy circling the block. I ran into the McDonalds across the street to hide and called my mom. I waited there for over an hour to make sure it was clear before I ran home. I was a complete wreck. When my mom got home that evening she'd seen enough.

"Do you know where she lives?"

"Yes," I replied.

"Tomorrow, we are settling this." Mom was matter-of-fact. I had no idea what that meant, but I was relieved to finally have some help.

The next morning, Mom told me to get in the car–she was serious. As I directed her to Tammy's house, I asked her what she was going to say.

"You're going to fight her once and for all."

WHAT? The panic was sudden.

"I'm going to talk to her mother," Mom continued.

I really didn't want to fight this girl, but I didn't want to put up with it anymore either. Maybe having my mom there *would* help, and maybe I wouldn't actually have to fight her.

"She needs to be taught a lesson," Mom was still going.

As we pulled up in front of her house, my stomach was in knots. We both got out of the car and walked up the wooden stairs onto the front porch. My mom stepped in front of me to knock on the door.

The smell of coffee and cigarettes wafted out the door when Tammy opened it. Her siblings were watching Saturday morning cartoons.

"What are you doing here?" she asked. The look on her face made it clear that she never expected us to be on the other side of that door.

"Where is your mother?" Mom demanded.

My heart pounded in my throat as Tammy called for her mom. She looked about as scared as I did.

"Why are you harassing Chantel at school?" Mom wasn't going to wait for her mother before getting into it.

Tammy looked at her square in the face and lied: "I'm not harassing her. I don't know what you're talking about."

Her lie immediately snapped me into the moment: "You are a fucking liar! Every single day you've been screaming names at me, and threatening to kick my ass out of that guy's car!"

My voice must've carried into the house because her mother came running to see what the commotion was about. My mom recapped what Tammy had been doing for the past month, and at every turn Tammy lied, denied everything, and played dumb.

I was enraged. I stormed down the stairs, yelling that she was lying, and trying to get my mom to just leave. This wasn't going to help.

"No, you are going to hash this out. This has got to end today."

Neighbors were swarming, curious about these screaming girls, and since my mom wasn't going to relent, I leaned into my rage. Everything was a blur.

I screamed at Tammy, and taunted her: "You aren't so brave now that you're not with that guy in his car are you?"

She laughed at this, and came toward me looking smug. Before she said anything, I grabbed a fistful of her hair-sprayed bangs, and pulled her forehead into my knee as hard as I could. Still gripping her by the bangs, I flung her head back-and-forth with everything I had. We both ended up on the sidewalk, screaming and hysterical. Our moms weren't too worried about us fighting, but they came down the steps and separated us before I ripped her hair completely out of her head.

I don't remember if Tammy defended herself or hit me back, I don't remember feeling anything, really. I just saw red. My mom must have decided things were settled enough, and somehow got me into the car.

Still belligerent with rage, I screamed one last time: "Just leave me the fuck alone!"

As we drove home, I felt the window cool against my forehead.

"You showed her, Chantel; she's not going to bother you again. Sometimes there's only one way people learn."

My mom assured me that this was over. She added that she and Tammy's mom went to the same high school. Somehow, in all the chaos, they had time for small talk? I didn't care. I never wanted to see this girl again.

Word of the fight spread around school and I actually enjoyed the attention that came with it. I felt powerful. *Don't mess with me. I may cry hysterically the entire time, but people best look out!* This new confidence fueled a whole new rebellious streak. I'd run outside during passing periods to have a smoke—not allowed. I quit gymnastics. I stopped paying attention in most of my classes and only did my homework when I felt like it. I learned the front office had old, retired school uniforms in blue. I liked it better than the red ones we had, so I purposely forgot to wear my uniform and got called to the office where I was handed a detention slip and a vintage uniform that I kept and wore for the rest of the year. I wanted to be the only freshie in blue; I wanted to stand out.

My elitism was working for me until Dawn, the one-upping girl whose very existence irritated me, got herself the same vintage uniform. *Fucking copycat.* I was annoyed that she maneuvered her way into my friend group, but I could keep my distance from her. Now, people thought we were matching on purpose. *As if!*

Our choir teacher, who looked like Steve Perry from Journey, let us do whatever we wanted most of the time, so choir class became the time I would catch up with the Polish Mafia and touch up my makeup. I was getting really good at it now, and girls would ask me to share tips left and right. I loved it. Dawn always made her way over and sat right next to me when she could, but now that she was taking her obsession to a new level by copying my vintage uniform scheme, my patience was waning. On one of these days of make up and gossip days in choir, Dawn begged me to do her makeup.

I gave my friends an evil smirk and said, "Ok Dawn, I'll do your make up."

"I love the orangey brown shadow you use, Chantel! Can you put it on me?"

"Sure!" I lied. I loaded up the sponge applicator with the brightest teal I had, and packed it on her lids. Then I added blush. *Lots* of blush. *Bright* blush.

Everyone around us was chuckling, but Dawn's eyes were closed.

"Let me see!" She reached for the mirror.

"Wait! It's going to be a surprise," I said, holding back a laugh.

I carelessly smudged my Madonna-Red Lipstick all over her mouth. It looked horrible. She reached for the mirror again, but the group of us did our best to convince her that she looked great and to just wait for lunch to see the big reveal.

"Okay!" She agreed, cheerfully.

God, this girl is gullible. I thought to myself. I hoped she might leave me alone now.

When the bell rang, we gathered up our stuff to head to lunch. A girl who sat on the other side of the choir room pushed me out of her way, to get to Dawn. She must have been watching the whole time.

"Go to the bathroom and wash your face. She made you look like a clown." She had placed her hands protectively on Dawn's shoulders.

My instinct was to square up with this girl. *Who the hell does she think she is?*

She turned to me, "You're a fucking bully, you know that?" She shook her head and walked away.

She was right. What was I doing? I knew what being bullied felt like, and here I was becoming a bully, too. How fucking ugly of me.

I called Dawn that night and apologized. Other than the blue eye-shadow, she actually liked everything else I did. She asked me to teach her how to do makeup because her mom died when she was young, and she didn't have anyone to show her. I felt even worse. Even though I hated some things about my mom, I couldn't imagine being without her. Dawn still annoyed me, but I never bullied her again.

I Shouldn't Have Let Him In

The second half of my freshman year can be summed up by saying that Gordon failed me both semesters, and my parents sold our house. My life in Chicago was going to be over soon, and maybe the change was going to be good, but the house felt empty with all our things stacked up in boxes, and it was making me anxious. Not every memory here was good, but some were, and anyway, it was home. I found myself studying every corner of it now: the orange shag carpet that I had walked on a million times before, the hallway corner that I always stubbed my toe on, the TV my mom had to have because it swiveled. I took it all in, and replayed memories of sleepovers with Rose and the Polish Mafia girls. The memories of Saturdays spent with my mom, long before my siblings, before my dad's business, before…everything, really.

Dad's business was now located out by where the new house was built, and sometimes Mom brought my siblings with her when she would make the drive out of the city to bring my dad dinner. Usually she would do this on Fridays, and I was grateful, because this freed me up to spend time with my friends. Finally! After all the years of feeling like a left-out loser, I had friends to have fun with. I wasn't obsessed with having a boyfriend anymore either. I felt like I was starting to figure things out, so what would happen when it was time to move? There was a sense of hope that maybe this was what my family needed. Maybe it was what I needed. I just had to get through summer school first.

On one of those Friday evenings when my mom took my siblings to visit my dad, my friends all happened to be busy. I had the house to myself, and I was content with my bologna sandwich for dinner. More importantly, I realized I had the TV to myself, and I was stoked to watch MTV in peace. I was entrenched in MTV's *Headbangers Ball* when there was a loud knock on my door. I peeked behind the curtain, out the porch window, and my stomach turned. It was Jake.

I flicked on the porch light, opened the door without a smile, and stared at him. My face clearly displayed my greeting: *What the fuck do you want?*

He said he noticed the *sold* sign out front, so I gave him the bare minimum explanation. I started to shut the door, but he stepped in to block it. Something about him was off; he looked rough.

"I just wanted to say goodbye," he said. But how he said it felt aggressive.

He might have been drunk or high or manic—I really couldn't tell, and even though I hated him for everything he had put me through, my curiosity prevented me from slamming the door on his fingers to get him to leave. Maybe he was here to apologize. Maybe he would grovel at my feet. That didn't happen. Instead, he forced his way through the door, and firmly planted his hands on my shoulders.

"I just need to talk to you for a second." He dropped his hands, and walked around the house looking at all the boxes. He looked almost sad.

Could this dickhead actually have some regret for treating me the way he did?

"I miss you," he said. His demeanor shifted, and he turned to look at me: "Don't you miss these baby blue eyes?"

I knew his game; he was trying everything that used to work on me. *Why did I let him in?*

When I went to the kitchen for a glass of water, he moved in behind me, grabbed my hand and kissed me aggressively. It took a lot of force to push him away, but I did.

"Stop, Jake, you can't do that." I wasn't sure what I felt about him, but I crossed my arms and acted unfazed. I needed to convince him (and myself) that I was totally over him. He was my first love, and I always had a hard time saying no to him, but I wasn't going to let him treat me like he had before. Something inside me was screaming: *Chantel, you're not going to fall for this again! He's a liar and a jerk!*

As he continued with his bullshit games, I realized with surprising clarity that I didn't want him in my life anymore.

"Jake, you need to leave." I was firm, and I think he could see that his ploys weren't going to work.

He tried to kiss me again, and to get away from him, I went out toward the back porch. I thought I could push him out into my yard and then get back inside, but he followed immediately behind me. I got to the landing but didn't even open the door before he cornered me and tried to kiss me again. I slid down the wall to get away from him, but now, the only place I could go was my basement. He bear-hugged me from behind, pinning my arms to my sides.

"I love you," he kept saying. "Come on, just one more time?"

I fought to pry his arms off me, but I knew the only way I was going to get him to release me was to give in. *I don't want to do this!* My inner voice was screaming again.

He loosened his grip enough to turn me to face him. He continued to kiss my neck.

"No. My parents are coming home soon," I said, trying to push his face away from me however I could. It was like he didn't hear me at all. He pulled me down to the basement floor, ignoring me.

"No! Jake, stop! Jake, let go!" I kept trying to push him off of me, but he was stronger than I was. *I can't do this again.* He pressed his body against me, pinning me down, and holding my wrists. Every time he kissed me, I turned away more. I thrashed around to try to get him off of me, but the more I fought, the more he laughed; he seemed to be aroused by it. He started sucking on my neck to give me a hickey. I yelled again and again for him to stop. He laughed, and said he wanted to leave his mark on me.

"Get the fuck off me! I screamed. "Jake, I don't want this!" I pleaded for him to stop, but it made no difference.

I fought back until I became so exhausted I couldn't move, and then, I stopped fighting. I went numb, just like I did when Aunt Beatrice's boyfriend touched me. Just like I did in JD's room. *I shouldn't have let him in.* The tile floor was cold and damp against my bare skin.

Feral, But Not Free

The summer my family moved to a suburb 45-minutes outside of Chicago, my parents were busy with the business, and the new house, and getting my siblings situated, so I spent the summer running around Chicago, completely unsupervised. I was supposed to be staying at my aunt's apartment, while I finished up some credit recovery summer school–it was clear I would fail algebra, but I ended up failing Polish, too. This arrangement meant that, for the first time ever, I was free of my built-in babysitter status, and I took full advantage. Summer school happened, but I crashed at my friends' houses more often than not, and I spent most of my time hanging out at the mall, smoking, and going to the Polonia club because they didn't card. After everything with Jake, I convinced myself it was better if I just didn't give fuck about anything. I met up with guys to pass the time, and reveled in my feral summer.

What I thought of as freedom turned out to be distraction more than anything else. As much as I tried to convince myself not to care about anything, I eventually began to look forward to being home with my family again. Turns out, sleeping on couches loses its novelty after a while. Maybe this really would be the change we all needed. Maybe we could all be different. Maybe I could finally be the girl I always wanted to be. Besides, I would be going to a public school now–no more uniforms, *and* co-ed? Sign me up! I imagined myself being like Cindy Mancini from the movie *Can't Buy Me Love*—I hoped to meet my own Ronald Miller one day.

My new school looked like it belonged in a movie. It was at the top of a hill in a small town turned sprawling suburb. The day my mom took me there for registration and a tour, I imagined scenes from the movie *Lucas*, playing out on the steps outside. I was so excited for the quintessential high school experience of pep rallies, football games, and school dances. I browsed all the tables of clubs and organizations, and decided that, in this new life of mine, I would try out for cheerleading. As if this wasn't already perfect enough, my mom and I learned the school was in the running for a reality TV series. Whether it would be selected or not wasn't a sure thing, but I had to sign a filming waiver just in case. This was enough to fill me with dreams of being discovered. It was settled: I had to look my best every day. A new house, a new school, a new life. It was becoming easier to leave Jake and my life in Chicago in the past.

I didn't know it wasn't cool to ride the school bus at first because the only time I ever took an actual school bus was when I went on a field trip in grammar school, and back then it *was* cool. Committed to my destiny of being famous, I made sure to dress for success. My first-day-of-school outfit was a crop top, with a zipper (of course), and a brand-new pair of Z Cavaricci jeans that I tight-rolled at the bottom. I chose white, pointed-toe flats, gold hoop earrings, a gold necklace, and a gold ring on every finger. My rings were all fake gold. I learned to put clear nail polish on the inside of them so they wouldn't turn my fingers green. I styled my hair to curled, scrunched, and sprayed perfection, and my makeup was flawless. Now that my siblings were older, I didn't have to worry about getting them ready, too. My focus got to be making sure I looked fabulous.

I skipped breakfast as usual, and headed to the bus stop. My neighborhood had no sidewalks, just driveway after driveway with a mailbox at the end of each one. This was new to me! Unlike in the city, where the houses were so close you could stand between them with your arms outstretched and touch both, the houses here were more spread out. I could blare my music as loud as I wanted, and when my parents got into an argument, no one would hear them screaming unless they took it outside. It was all different, and I was optimistic.

Eventually, the movie-set magic of my school wore off. It was clear that I wouldn't be part of the preppy girls, and I wouldn't be a cheerleader or in poms. I also figured out the downside of going to a co-ed school. I tried to date a few guys I met at school, but they all got so serious right away that I immediately felt smothered and anxious, so I would break it off. Because I usually met them through a friend in class, when I broke it off with them, I ended up breaking it off with that friend as well. At an all-girls school, at least if I broke up with a guy, I didn't have to look at him the next day in class, or lose a friend as collateral. This was a whole new awkwardness I hadn't experienced before.

I started my day with gym class, which was terrible for a few reasons. Getting all sweaty in a full face of makeup that I basically just applied was not ideal, and my gym teacher couldn't be bothered to pronounce my name correctly. I decided he was the inspiration for every stupid male gym teacher in movies. When I finally corrected him one day, he snidely responded that he had never met a white girl with a name like Chantel before. My dad showed up at school the next day to "have a talk with him" about the comment. I don't know what my dad said to the guy, but he never mispronounced my name again.

Maybe I should have mentioned my English teacher to my parents, too, but I never did. He was a nerdy, balding man in his forties, who made a point to comment on my clothing choices at every opportunity. At first, I thought he was just trying to connect with me, so I laughed it off when he said my skirt was a little short, or asked if my belly was cold when I wore a top that revealed it. But when he brought in a magazine to show me some Laura Ashley dresses—modest, ruffled, floral—that he thought I should wear one day, I started to think maybe he was a little weirder than I thought. I never saw him give any other girl in my class this kind of attention. When he asked if I would babysit for his family, I immediately got the ick, but I wanted to pass his class so I smiled politely and said I had enough babysitting to do at home. I don't know why I never told my mom or dad about him. It all made me feel weird, and it was bringing up things I had been trying to forget about.

I was trying to find a place here in the suburbs where it seemed like every role had already been cast. I tried to play the cool girl from Chicago, and it worked—for a while. I met a few friends in theater; we bonded over music we liked and smoking. I wasn't sure how long I could keep up this facade. There was a darkness in me that was starting to claw its way back to the surface. A couple of these new friends had talked openly to me about their struggles with depression, and even though I didn't tell them I was struggling, listening to them helped me feel less alone. I just didn't know how to say it out loud.

By New Years, things at home were messy again. My siblings and I were eagerly waiting for our parents to come home so we could go to a neighborhood party–it was a chance to make some friends maybe. When my parents finally came home at 10 pm, they were in the middle of a blowout fight, but instead of skipping the party, we all walked in with pasted-on smiles. The masks of a happy family. In just a few months, the hope I had felt about this new house and this new life was crumbling. Sure, the business was successful, but that came with more work and more stress. We walked on eggshells whenever my father was home because my mother did not want us to upset him. I hated how she catered to him. She was only ever focused on keeping him happy. It was like she was clinging to the dream she and my father had before we moved, and that pretty much meant *screw us kids.*

The more I realized that I didn't belong to a group, the more I went wherever anyone would talk to me. My obsessive dieting and exercise ramped up during this time, and so did my impulse to self-harm. One weekend, I called Rose and asked her to come stay at my house. I missed her. I needed something that felt familiar. I thought her presence might remind me who I was, but instead I watched as the few friends I had were drawn in by her charm and it reminded me of the pool incident with Jake all over again. I watched them all talking and laughing in my kitchen, goofing around with her and I was seething. Whenever she is around, I am invisible. I was jealous, and then angry. *Why does this always happen?* Before I had time to think, I jumped up on my kitchen counter, took a drag of my cigarette, and when I saw I had everyone's attention, I pressed the cherry from my cigarette into my wrist. I didn't wince. I felt nothing. I smiled as I blew the smoke out of my lips.

"What the fuck are you doing?" Rose was as shocked as the rest of them.

I didn't answer. I just turned on the faucet and let the cold water run over my new scar.

SEVEN

Cupid's Arrow

Dark Eyes

I missed the CTA. Getting anywhere in the suburbs was impossible without a car! While I still watched my siblings regularly, my parents also let me get a part time job as a telemarketer for a deck installation company. I hated it, but I needed to make my own money. I wanted to save for a car, obviously, but I wanted to be able to buy the clothes I liked without having to ask my mom for money. Whenever she took me shopping, it always came with strings; typically, that was more babysitting, or cleaning. She also would only buy it if she liked it. At least with a job I could get out of my house.

Unsurprisingly, my parents weren't around like they had promised to be after we moved, and I think my mom was feeling guilty about that. There were some extra shopping trips and carnival visits to try to make up for it. One of these excursions was a visit to the tarot card reader we always passed on the way to dad's shop. We laughed about the crystal ball neon sign in the window, I never thought one day we would actually go in. Mom only paid for one reading–hers, but before we left, the woman pulled me aside to tell me something I would never forget.

"Your mom is going to be friends with a woman one day," she began. The theatrics required a pause every so often. "This friend is not for her. She is for you."

I thought this was strange, but I was curious if there was anything more. Maybe she would say something that would actually make sense.

"She will have dark eyes and hair," she said, finally. So much for making sense.

When we got into the car my mom was dying to know what the woman had said. When I told her, she was puzzled. I was fifteen, it really didn't make any sense for me to become friends with any of her friends. We decided it was all *mish-mash* and went to dinner, not giving it another thought. I was happy to be doing something fun and silly with my mom. Since I had started working, it seemed like she was proud of me, and we were able to enjoy the times we spent hanging out, even though they didn't happen that often.

Working also gave me a sense of pride, and I was able to keep my depression at bay. So even though I wasn't the picture of healthy behavior, I was self-harming less. The cigarette burns on my wrists had scarred a little, but they healed. I was looking into what it would take to become a model or actress, and I didn't want to ruin my odds of getting picked because of preventable scars. I was solely focused on the exterior of myself. I walked through the world as if one day I could be *discovered.* Everywhere I went, I wanted to show up looking like I stepped out of *Teen* magazine.

When our neighborhood sponsored an event to promote the new activity center, they made it into quite the spectacle: balloons and popcorn, music and games, information tables and sign-ups–it was a whole thing. I tried to convince my mom that Bally Fitness would be better *and* they had tanning beds, but she already made up her mind: it was The Park District for us. She wanted to sign us kids up for karate, so she hauled us all over there. I whisper-yelled at my siblings to not act like total psychos, but when we got there, I was too distracted by the aerobics class happening in the street to care much about my siblings embarrassing me. Two women in their late 40s wearing shiny spandex and nude tights were leading a crowd of similarly spandexed women in *step-two-down-up, three-four-step-back, one-two-step-up-and-reeeeach!* There were slouch socks for days.

Step class was *the* class to do in the 90s if you were into fitness. I had a couple of VHS workout tapes my mom got me for Christmas, but I had never taken a class in person, so even though this scene was ludicrous, I was excited that my mom wanted to take a class and was going to let me come along, too. I just couldn't get over the sea of neon asses in the street. Surrounded by onlookers who were either middle-aged women, looking envious of the slim silhouettes and confidence, or the husbands of the middle-aged women who looked at these women in shiny spandex the way my dad looked at women. I hated that.

So when my mom's plan to attend the step aerobics class included my dad, too, I suppose it should have been no surprise why he would want to go. He was terrible at it. The instructor always had to correct his form, but didn't seem to mind. The whole class seemed to enjoy his antics, and he loved being the only man in the class; he turned on the charm and worked the room like a pro. He was the class entertainment, which I thought was obnoxious, but my mom seemed happy, so I tried to ignore it.

After a few weeks of attending classes, the instructor casually brought up that I should meet her son. Apparently, she and my mom had been chatting it up daily and decided we could be a good match. My mom knew that I was already kind of dating this guy named Mike, we were planning to go to Homecoming together soon, yet here she was trying to set me up with this chick's son, too.

"Do you have a picture of him?" I asked.

"I do!" She pulled out what appeared to be a new wallet-sized senior photo. "His name is Mike," she said. Her dark eyes had a sparkle to them.

I smiled. Of course it is.

If You Like What You See...

My mom was so eager for me to meet *new* Mike, which was both strange and cute. The whole ride home after class, I stared at the photo, and Mom stared at me. I thought he was cute, but I wasn't sure about his caterpillar brows.

"So?" my mom was dying to gauge my interest.

I looked at her and did what I did best: I ignored her and turned up the radio. Later, I reminded her that I was going to Homecoming with *other* Mike on Saturday. This was already ridiculous. I always had to specify which Mike I was talking about. I wasn't sure how this was going to work, or when there would be time, but she was eager to make it happen. She found out from her new aerobics-instructor-BFF that *new* Mike worked at a nearby video store, and like a teenage girl, she asked me if I wanted to go see if he was there. I had never seen my mother act so giddy about anything in my life, how could I say no.

Hot Ticket Video was no lame corporate company with dumb uniforms and plain walls. The owners really made it unique. It had a circus theme, complete with one of those old-fashioned popcorn machines. There were movie posters everywhere and televisions playing the newest releases. They had a huge adult video section that was off the side of the main room for those into that sort of thing. It was colorful, and unapologetically tacky, and really fun. Mom and I took it all in, pretending that we were there to rent a movie and not to stalk a guy to see if he was actually cute or not. We spied through the racks of VHS tapes as the guy at the front desk interacted with customers. Even though he looked about the same age as *new* Mike, he didn't really look like the picture I saw. After winding our way through the genres, stalling and hoping to see someone else work the front desk, we gave up.

I was surprised that I felt disappointed. I was starting to like this idea. In the picture I saw, *new* Mike had kind brown eyes and a nice smile, and I really liked his olive skin. *Damn. Maybe Mom got it wrong.*

We talked to the guy at the front desk; his name tag did not say *Mike*. My mom signed up for a membership and rented a video anyway. We grabbed our popcorn and checked out; the reconnaissance mission was a bust.

"Does a guy named Mike work here?" my mom blurted this out like it was a dare.

The guy looked at me.

I looked away, sure that embarrassment was fatal.

"Yeah," the guy answered cautiously. "He's usually here today, but he went home sick."

My mom and I laughed. This guy didn't have a clue, he just looked at us perplexed.

"Well, tell Mike that a girl named Chantel came by to meet him," my mom said.

I turned 17 shades of red.

"Should I give him your number or something?"

Without skipping a beat, my mom said, "Chantel, I'm sure you have something you can give him, don't you?"

Dying. I was dying. She knew I had grabbed one of my school pictures from the year before—my mom never bothered to send them out, so I had plenty—and I wrote my name and my phone number on it. I pulled the wallet print out of my purse, asked for a pen, and wrote one more thing on it: *If you like what you see, give me a call.* I drew a smiley face, and handed it to the guy behind the counter.

He laughed as he read it, "I'll get it to him."

The Tale of Two Mikes

The day after the movie store stakeout, *new* Mike called. He asked if I wanted to go out for lunch on Saturday. I told him I was going to homecoming but could squeeze it in if we got done by three. So, it was on. Saturday, October 5, 1991, my mother's birthday, the day I had homecoming with *other* Mike, my mom drove me two towns over to have lunch with *new* Mike.

I had been excited about this until I saw the weather. It was cold and rainy and I was pissed. I would have to get ready twice, and I wasn't sure if either Mike would be worth that level of effort. *Stupid rain.* My inner voice grumbled about everything that morning. *I want to live in California where it is nice all the time.* I reached for my tight black jeans that had a gold zipper in the back, a cropped T-shirt, and my black suede jacket with fringes. *Why couldn't this wait a few more weeks so I could drive myself?*

As I got ready, I was overthinking everything and questioning why I agreed to this in the first place. I did my make up as best as I could knowing that I would be just taking another shower in a few hours to get ready for the dance. I teased my bangs particularly high to compensate for my sour mood.

What if we don't hit it off? What if I can't get over his caterpillar brows? My mom came around to check on me, she had just gotten off the phone with his mom to confirm. She was positively giddy and wasn't interested in my mood. *If this doesn't go well it's going to be weird and awkward at step class, and I like taking those classes! Ugh!*

"Just relax and get dressed," Mom shouted from the hallway.

The whole drive there, I rolled my eyes at every question my mom had for me: *Are you excited? Where is he taking you for lunch?* She was so smiley, you'd think *she* was the one going on the date. Apparently, my dad also knew this plan was in action, but he didn't say much. Then again, he didn't care much about what we did anyway.

When we pulled up to the house, I noticed a cool, maroon Firebird in the driveway. My mood lifted a little. *If things worked out at least we could go places,* I thought. I figured they must be a car family since his mom drove a nice car, and the house was perfectly average. Inside was the same story, it was nice, but it was like they got this blue couch as a gift for their wedding in 1970, put it in place, and never moved again.

The moms made small talk and I waited for him to come downstairs. It felt like things should have been reversed. *Shouldn't I be coming down the stairs? Why didn't he come to me?*

When I heard footsteps coming down the stairs, I turned around and saw black gym shoes connected to skinny legs wearing light blue jeans. Then a Chicago Bulls jersey under a high school windbreaker jacket. Then I looked away quickly because I felt like an idiot. He looked better than his picture, but the awkwardness of the moment was killing me.

Thankfully, his mom broke the tension and introduced us. I looked at him and smiled. He was thin and gangly, like he hadn't yet grown into his feet or his ears yet. He had a mullet, and I thought it was cute how his ears popped out like a baby monkey. He wasn't super tall, but as long as he was taller than me, I didn't care. Plus, he could drive.

As the moms continued to talk, I watched him walk over to the dining room table and stand behind one of the high-back chairs, placing his hands on it as if to hold himself up. When he finally looked back at me, our moms still talking, I smiled at him and mouthed the word *hi*. He smiled and mouthed *hello* back. After enduring the awkwardness for a few more minutes we decided to leave, whether our moms were going to chat all day or not.

"Would Portillo's be okay for lunch?" He asked, holding the door open for me. "It's right down the street and I know you're pressed for time today."

No one had ever held the door open for me before. We waved goodbye to the moms and he led me to his car, the firebird. He opened the passenger door for me, again, a gesture I wasn't accustomed to. The car was so cool, it had white leather interior!

We stole glances at each other and smiled, and when we got to Portillo's, we ordered what everybody should order at Portillo's: a hotdog and fries and a Coke. When he asked for ketchup on his hotdog, I immediately told him that what he was doing was a travesty. Anyone from Chicago knows that hotdogs have mustard, relish, and onions. He didn't know what to say to that, so he just laughed. He was so nervous; I don't know if he realized I was just messing with him. I had to carry this thing.

I told him about growing up in Chicago, and I asked him questions. He seemed to legitimately care about everything I had to say about school, music, being Catholic–I even mentioned Jake. I didn't tell him all of it, just that he was a jerk. We spent over an hour eating and talking. The one thing I couldn't let go of the entire time was that he made me feel safe. His quiet smile made me feel that even though I was talking a mile a minute, and even though I had a date that night that I couldn't break, he didn't judge me.

As he drove me home, he kept turning the stations on the radio to get the best reception.

"What kind of music do you like?" I asked him.

"Pretty much everything. But mostly Metallica. How about you?"

"Same." I wasn't exactly lying, but they weren't my favorite.

When we got to my driveway, we sat there for a bit. Each of us trying to gauge the other's interest and figuring out what to say and what to do.

"Would you like to go out again?" he asked.

"Sure," I said. I started to open the car door to get out, but he scrambled to get around to my side to open the door for me. I stood up, put my purse on my shoulder, and looked at him: "You've got my phone number, call me!" I smiled at him and headed to my front door.

"Have a good time tonight!" He waved as he got back in his car.

"Well, how did it go?" My mom was eagerly waiting for an update when I came in, smiling from ear to ear.

"I gotta get ready for the dance," I said. I wanted to play it cool, but she could clearly see that it went well.

"All right, fine. Go get ready."

"He's nice, mom. I like him. I'll tell you about it later."

Despite being annoyed that I had to get ready twice in one day, I was excited for my school's homecoming dance. Mostly, I was excited about shopping for a dress, and getting all dolled up. We even had a limo! My date, *other* Mike, was a short guy with a nice smile. I met him at an arcade one night with a couple of my friends, and after kissing him once, I thought at the very least I'd give him the opportunity to take me to a dance.

The dress I had picked out was shiny blue, a sleeveless, one-shoulder style, with ruffles and a bow that laid perfectly at my right hip. I loved the layer of black tulle sewn under the skirt that popped out just enough to remind me of the Marilyn Monroe poster I had on my bedroom wall. I read a book about her life and loved it so much I began to collect everything that was her. She was so beautiful and so sad. I already knew how it felt to be sad, the hard part was figuring out how to be as beautiful. So as I did my makeup, I tried my best to get Marilyn Monroe perfect. I did my winged eyeliner, caked as much mascara on my blonde eyelashes as I could, and finished my look with a cherry red lipstick. My hair had mostly grown out and was red again, so I know I didn't look anything like my famous idol, but her spirit was in me the entire time I got ready.

When my date held out the wrist corsage he brought for me, I could see that his hands were shaking. It was three small roses and silver, glittered carnations, all evenly sprayed blue to match my dress. He really did go all out! He was cute, and I could tell that he was smitten, but all I could think about was my earlier date with *new* Mike.

Later, as we slow-danced to Whitney Houston's "I will always love you" and I had to keep telling him to get his hands off my ass, I knew I just wasn't into him as much as he was into me. I didn't want to crush this guy, but it wasn't going to work out.

I was grateful that he didn't go to my school, and that he didn't have a car to easily visit me either. Even though I didn't know *new* Mike that well yet, he didn't strike me as someone who only wanted to get in my pants. He didn't try to touch me once in the few hours we were together. While at first I wondered if that meant he wasn't interested, he genuinely listened to what I had to say. So as the night in my school gym went on under the disco ball, I went through the motions smiling and dancing with a guy I had no intention of seeing again.

When he called me the next day I told him that we weren't going to work. I said goodbye to this Mike in hopes that *new* Mike, the *right* Mike, would call.

The Worst Date Ever

Waiting for a guy to call is absolute torture when you A) have promised yourself you would never chase a guy again and B) really, really, *really* hope he calls. My parents let me get my own phone line in my room when we moved, and not many people had my number so if it rang, I knew the odds of it being him were high. So I listened to music and stared at the phone. I flipped through magazines and stared at the phone. I did my daily routine of situps and jumping jacks and stared at the phone. I had one of those clear phones, where you could see all of the internal tech-y shit, so there was plenty to study as I practically willed him to call.

When it finally rang, I jumped up to answer it.

"Hello?" I desperately tried to mask that I had been waiting by the phone for two days.

"Hi, is Chantel home?" Remember when phone calls started like this? He sounded different on the phone. But then again, I barely let him get a word in at Portillos.

"It's me, Mike! I have my own phone line. If it's not me, I ran away from this hell hole."

"You have your own phone line? That must be nice!" he said.

"Yeah, well, my parents sweetened the deal for me when we moved here from the city and it isn't that much more for the extra line, which I pay for anyway."

"Where do you work?"

"Baskin Robbins Ice Cream in the food court at the mall."

"Oh hey, I know a couple of guys that work at Potato Works next to you! Matt and Mitch?"

"The twins? I know them! Small world." I could hear his nerves through the coils of my phone as I waited for him to say something else. It was only a few seconds, but it felt like forever. I hate dead air. I lasted about six seconds before I caved: "So, I–"

"Wanna go out with me on Saturday?" He blurted out, cutting me off.

"Sure," I said, trying not to show all my cards. I was so freakin' excited.

"Where do you wanna go?"

Because I knew he was a suburbanite and didn't travel to the city often I thought I would put him to the test:

"Let's go to the Shedd Aquarium," I said.

"Downtown?"

"Yea, I told you I'm from Chicago and I want you to know I will *always* be a city girl."

"Okay, Shedd Aquarium it is!"

"Great!" I said. I was still trying to play it cool.

"Ok that's a day thing so I'll pick you up early then. Say 10am?"

"Perfect!"

"Great!" He said, and then came that awkward silence again.

"Okay well how about we talk later this week?"

"Yea. That sounds good."

We said goodbye and I hung up the phone and squealed and jumped up and down on my bed as if I had won tickets to see Def Leppard from the DJ on the radio. I smiled so hard my face hurt. This was beyond perfect. His mom and my mom are friends. His mom is an aerobics instructor, and I love to stay fit. He's Italian, and *I love Italians.* He has a cool car just like the cute *Italian* guys that drove up and down Harlem Ave in the city that I dreamed of dating one day. My junior year had just begun, and everything was coming together. I could see the wedding now: Big, happy family. Big, happy life. Everything I ever wanted.

Mike picked me up in a different car this time. He said his dad wasn't comfortable with him driving the Firebird to the city, so he used one of their other cars. It looked like a red box with wheels, not big enough to keep us safe, just less to lose if it crashed. The weather was terrible again. Terrible for my outfit, my hair, Mike's hair, but especially for driving. It was cold, with that special midwestern combo of rain and sleet that makes everything slippery and slushy. I did everything I could to pretend I wasn't scared as Mike drove us to the Aquarium. It took over an hour with traffic and weather, and I made small talk about my life as a city girl the whole way there. Mike concentrated on the road, so we wouldn't get in an accident, but somehow he still managed to listen to me and to seem interested.

When we finally arrived, the parking lot was full, so we had to park far away and walk back to the aquarium. I realized immediately how inappropriately I was dressed for this weather. My favorite black, suede jacket with fringe had no thermal insulation whatsoever, and I wore it over a crop top and tight jeans. The hair I had meticulously scrunched earlier that morning was toast. Ruined. Mike wasn't dressed any better though, he wore a thin, leather jacket over a black band t-shirt, and jeans. His feathered bangs became plastered to his forehead the minute he got out of the car into the cold, damp Chicago wind.

As we made our way to the front entrance of the aquarium, I tried to carry myself confidently, even though I was freaking out about my hair and makeup. I was sure that he would soon regret driving over an hour to take this monstrosity (me) on this date once he saw what the rain and snow had washed away. Since I applied mascara like my life depended on it, when my eyes teared up from the wind, I wiped them to discover they were black. *Great.* Maybe I could fix my make up when we got inside. I had a makeup bag in my purse. I had everything in my purse. It was a fake Louis Vuitton purse, stuffed to the gills in the event I decided to never return home for the rest of my life. It held my school planner, folded up notes from friends at school, two packs of cigarettes, a wallet with a few bucks in it, gum, a crayon I stole from my sister's school box, some pencils and pens, and the makeup bag I was relying on to save me.

Because I hated awkward silences, I could not walk beside him without words constantly coming from my mouth. I don't remember what I was even saying, but I know I was not paying any attention to my surroundings at all.

Just as I was convincing myself that this was somehow karma for dating two Mikes on the same day, I felt an immediate intense pain strike the top of my right foot. I lost my balance and my purse flew completely off my arm. It wasn't until I crash landed onto the pavement in front of me that I realized I must've tripped on something.

This is the worst date ever!!!

I looked up to see a bus full of people laughing at me. I didn't look at Mike. *I couldn't.* Then a taxi honked at me to get out of the way, so I scooted my butt to the curb of the circle drive, and threw my middle finger and yelled, "Blow it out your ass! Asshole!"

I sat there, wiped the wet hair out of my face, and examined my scraped up hands. When I scanned my surroundings to see if there was a possibility to salvage the wreckage of this moment, I noticed that Mike, who was now carrying my purse that had traveled halfway across the street, was doing his best to collect the various items that he thought flew out of it.

Wanting to understand what the heck just happened to me, I looked around and saw the culprit. Hiding below the dirty Chicago snow and slush was the top of a water pipe connection, sticking out of the ground just high enough to destroy my life!

As I stared at the ground, feeling completely defeated, two feet in black gym shoes entered my sight. I looked up and saw Mike holding my purse out to me, trying his damnedest not to laugh. I looked down at myself and saw the complete insanity of it all, and shook my head.

"Just fucking laugh!" I yelled.

"Are you okay?" He asked as he held out his hand to help me up. His sweet brown eyes met mine, and as he pulled me towards him, I couldn't help but smile.

"No, but I don't have a choice so I will try to be." I wiped the slushy grit from my pants.

"C'mon. Let's go get you cleaned up and look at some fish."

He never let go of my hand from that moment on.

We Are Magic

After the aquarium date, aka the worst date ever, Mike and I were inseparable. He picked me up from school every day because he got done earlier than I did. He would visit me at work so we could spend my 15-minute break together, and enjoy a scoop of ice cream on me. (I had no idea he was lactose intolerant because he just kept eating the ice cream I gave him!) He gave me sweet little cards and surprised me with flowers *just because.* We wrote each other letters, and took pictures together–I had already taped them up on my bedroom wall. I was obsessively practicing my future signature: *Chantel A. Ferraro.* I wrote it out over and over again, in every notebook I had. Around this same time, I was in my first play, *Fame.* I was so excited for him to see me on stage, and I'm sure part of my motivation for perfecting my autograph was my teenage certainty that one day I was going to make it big.

One night before bed, he called like he always did, and told me to check my mailbox. I ran outside so fast I didn't even bother to put on shoes. What I found was little, gift-wrapped box and a card:

To my love,
Happy 1 month Anniversary!
I love you!
Michael

He had the nicest handwriting of any guy I knew. He also was the first guy to ever give me a card. I stood there, barefoot in the cold, reading those words over and over. *He loves me?* When I opened the gift, I saw through tears that it was a 14k gold ring with a heart-shaped Ruby and two diamond chips on each side of it.

I burst back into the house, and found my mom folding laundry in the family room.

"Mom!" I shrieked. "He bought me a ring!" I held out my hand to show her. "A ring! Look!" I didn't wait to see how she would answer, I was fizzing with joy. "Mom, he wrote that he *loves* me. I need to call him!" I ran into my bedroom and closed the door.

I plopped down on my bed, and picked up the phone, but before dialing his number, I sat for a few moments. What was I going to say? *He loves me?* I took a deep breath and dialed.

"Hello?"

"You *love* me?" I was both genuine and dramatic about how I said this.

He giggled, "I do."

"Thank you, Mike." I admired the beautiful little ring on my finger. "No one has ever treated me this good in my life."

"You're welcome, Chantel."

"Mike?"

"Yea?"

"I don't just say *I love you* to anyone."

"Okay?" He was clearly unfazed by this. It was as if he already knew we would end up together.

"It's not that I don't like you a lot, I do. But I'm not ready to say *love* yet."

"That's okay. I still love you."

"Okay, well, I like you *a lot,* and thank you."

"I'll see you tomorrow after work?"

"Yep! I'll be there. You still want to do a little Christmas shopping?"

"Yea, I don't get paid this week, but we can window shop?"

"Sounds good! See you in the food court Chantel"!

"Ok, bye!"

With the holidays approaching, the mall was abuzz every day, not just on the weekends. Mike was waiting for me at the food court entrance with a big smile. *How did I get this lucky? He smiles at me like I am the only one in the world, and he doesn't know a fraction of who I really am.*

I made my way to him through the chaos of holiday music, screaming toddlers, tired parents, and people throwing pennies into the fountain in the middle of the mall. Kids leaned over and wished for wonderful things, while their doting parents did their best to supply the pennies and keep them from falling in. Sometimes I would flip a penny in there, too–I figured it couldn't hurt to make a wish. When I finally reached Mike, I greeted him with a hug and a soft kiss.

"You look beautiful," he said.

"I don't know about that, but I do smell like waffle cones," I said, looking down at my ice-cream-smudged khaki pants and white keds.

He laughed and grabbed my hand. "Where do you want to go first?"

"Everywhere!" I was excited to actually enjoy shopping in the mall for a change. I honestly didn't care where we went first. As we made our way in and out of the stores, we talked about how fun New Year's Eve was going to be. Mike's mom invited my family over for a game night. Mike said that it was the first time his mom ever had one.

"Well, there is one good thing about my family, and that is we love playing games!"

"Do you play them a lot?" He looked surprised to hear this.

"No, not a lot. But when we have it's been really fun. Actually, my parents haven't spent New Years with us in a few years."

"Why not?"

Mike liked my family. I wanted him to. He didn't need to know that my parents had a pattern of being a shitshow and breaking into an argument every holiday. Their relationship seemed to be getting better, and I wanted to believe it was.

"My dad works a lot," I said. I offered the simplest solution.

"Well, my dad never plays games. He doesn't even watch them. I have played sports my whole life and he's never gone to even one game."

For the first time in the two months I'd known him, his kind, brown eyes looked sad. I didn't know what to say.

"Well, he hasn't met my dad yet. Maybe they could be friends or something! My dad has employees and customers, but I don't think he has many actual friends." I had hope that our families would hit it off. I always had hope. Mike's face didn't scream positivity, but I let it go.

"Oooh, let's go see what KB toys has!"

There was a display outside of the store entrance, a bin that held battery-operated animals that barked and walked and moved. They made such an obnoxious racket! We hovered over the edge of the bin watching the craziness of them all, yapping and flipping and marching around the pen, when something magical happened. We both looked up at each other from the bin and at the exact same time. I swear to God, if Cupid existed, we got hit with his arrow simultaneously. I felt a jolt of electricity or lightning or magic.

"Did you feel that!?"

Those big brown eyes of his widened in surprise, like he couldn't believe what I was asking him. "I did."

We just stood there for a moment, hand-in-hand, staring at each other like we were in an 80s rom com, where the camera zooms out and the music gets louder. Except this wasn't a movie. The soundtrack was a noisy mall, mechanical pets and Nirvana songs coming from Sam Goody, as if they were trying to drown out Jingle Bells.

I leaned my forehead close into his. "What do you think that was?" I whispered. "It was weird, right?"

"Yeah, I have no idea," he said. "You wanna get dinner?"

Typical guy.

"Yes, but not here. I am not eating where I work."

He laughed. "I know a great place by my house, and they are open late. It's called Springdale's."

"Oh, I love that place!"

As we walked to his car, still holding hands, I began to feel like this was special, like we were *really* something. I was falling for him.

When we got to the parking lot he ran ahead of me to open the car door. He did this every single time, it wasn't just a show for our first date. He also probably ran because he was wearing his thin high school windbreaker in 30-degree weather and his little monkey ears that popped out of his mullet were so cold they were bright red. As soon as he closed the door and made his way around to the driver's side, I realized that I needed to tell him.

"Mike?"

"Yea?" He smiled at me, and started the car.

"I love you."

"You do?" His smile got even bigger.

I nodded and smiled back.

"Well, I love you, too, but you already knew that." He leaned over to me, put his hand on my face and kissed me. It was a good one.

"Wow! That was a good kiss!"

"What do you mean *that* was a good kiss?" He said, exaggerating his offense.

I didn't mean to offend him, but he was a little rusty at first. The day at the aquarium, I told him to relax. "I'm just saying. That one felt like you knew what you were doing!"

He reset himself in his seat to put the car into gear, and shook his head with a smile.

"Girl, you are something else."

He had no idea.

EIGHT

WTF, Universe?

★

Christmas '91

Christmas Eve was a cacophony of big personalities, loud laughter, and the kind of "good-natured" teasing that felt like a blood sport. Mike agreed to leave the 'burbs and accompany me for a little Christmas-in-the-city to visit my mom's side of the family. Meeting the girlfriend's extended family is one thing, but he had absolutely no idea what he was walking into. When we got there, I found a spot for Mike at the dining room table next to someone I didn't even know–he was an older man, a family friend I presumed. I figured Mike would be okay there for a few minutes while I went to get us something to drink. I figured wrong. The man asked Mike to help him with his boot, and Mike, ever the gentleman, agreed. When he reached down and gave it a tug, he didn't just get the boot. The man's prosthetic leg came away with it! Mike stood there, wide-eyed and helpless, holding a detached limb as the table erupted in roars of laughter.

I rescued Mike and ushered him into the kitchen where the women were congregated. My grandmother performed the role of matriarch, asking Mike questions and feigning interest in his responses. It didn't take him long to see through her act.

Most of the men had parked themselves in the living room, but others wandered downstairs to smoke and shoot the shit. Somehow Mike ended up being led to the basement with my father and my grandfather. This old house in the city had one of those basements that was more like a concrete bunker than a real room, with low ceilings and a permanent musty smell. This sounds ominous enough already, but it gets weirder. *Shooting the shit* was about to take on a new meaning. Someone had set up a paper target in the corner, and my grandfather, deciding this was the perfect time for some target practice, stood in the middle of the room and pulled out a handgun. No reasonable person would shoot a gun in that space, especially with all those other people in there, but this was not a crowd of reasonable people. Nobody ducked when the bullet ricocheted around the room. Instead, they laughed and cheered as if mortal danger was just another punchline. Mike stayed pretty close to me for the rest of that night. His introduction to my Chicago upbringing was just a taste of the chaos I knew.

★

The magic of Christmas morning isn't quite the same once the whole Santa Claus thing falls apart. Hearing my brother and sister barrel down the stairs to see what was waiting for them under the tree meant I only had a few minutes to hide under the covers before the madness of gift opening began. I envied their enthusiasm. I was nine when I figured out that it was all a sham, but before that, my mom did a great job creating the story of Santa for me. When I questioned how Santa could bring me presents if we didn't have a fireplace, my mom said he had "magic keys" that opened every door in the world. One year she bought one of those kitschy cardboard fireplaces from Sears, and set it up right next to the tree. She even hung my stocking on it! She always encouraged me to leave out the traditional milk and cookies, and check them in the morning. He always left one that wasn't quite finished yet. Santa was the one thing about Christmas morning that helped me disassociate from my father's melancholy demeanor around the holiday season.

Once I figured out Santa was actually my mom, my father's snide comments about how much money was spent on our gifts landed a bit differently. I hated how he would make a scene, complaining about having to put together our new toys, and chucking the box across the room when he would get frustrated. My mom tried to keep me engaged in Christmas by having me help her with the "Santa" duties for my siblings. My job was to set their presents under the tree after we finished the one tradition I think my father actually enjoyed: watching *It's a Wonderful Life*. I enjoyed helping my mom, but being an elf is hardly the same as believing in magic. Still, I could see that she was trying, and I knew this was something I would do for my own children one day.

My house became more and more alive as the sun rose. The coffee was brewing in the kitchen, and my siblings were buzzing with excitement, telling Busia and Dza Dza all about the presents they couldn't wait to open. After Dza Dza had a stroke, my parents arranged for them to move closer to us, but they were staying with us for a while until their new place was ready. We made our way to the family room to open gifts. My little brother was wearing his typical uniform: Charlie Brown underwear and socks, and nothing else. My little sister wore more clothes but her hair was always a mess. I was usually the one who nagged them about these things, instead of my mom, but this morning I felt softer towards them. My sister maneuvered around Busia to sit next to me, and when Busia finally did get to the couch, she stopped and looked around the room.

"I like the blue walls. Did your mother paint them?"

"Yeah. I think it feels like we are in a fishbowl," I replied.

"Your mother loves to decorate. She always has." Busia's comment was stated matter-of-factly, and it was true.

Whatever the reason, I began to notice that around the same time my mom was managing all the logistics of getting Busia and Dza Dza moved out by us, and coordinating Dza Dza's care, our house started getting a gradual makeover. New paint, new furniture, new comforter sets for all the bedrooms, and a closet of "goal clothes" for when she reached her goal weight. I wasn't allowed to touch these clothes.

"Are you talking about me?" My mom poked her head out from behind the staircase wall.

"Lorenda, let's go. The kids want to open their presents. Where's my son?"

"Yeah, mom, let's go! Let's go!" My siblings chanted, bouncing up and down in front of the sparkling Christmas tree.

"Let me get your father." My mom's cheesy smile said it all. It was going to be another Christmas morning where my father's mood was going to dictate everything and she was going to over-compensate for his bad attitude.

I wanted to tell her to leave him up there since he was just going to ruin it anyway, but instead, I grabbed our VHS Camcorder and got it ready to film. When my parents both finally showed up, coffee in hand, my siblings tore into their gift piles. I recorded the scene of shredded paper, and the chorus of joyful *thank yous,* and only stopped filming when my dad noticed the price tag was left on the remote control airplane my brother was showing him. This spiraled into him complaining about having to build it, and shaming my mother for spending so much. If it weren't for Busia's intervention, his tirade would have ruined the whole day.

During my father's tantrum, I decided to just open my presents on my own. I didn't care if anyone saw, I just wanted to get it over with as fast as possible, and jump in the shower to get ready to see Mike later. After my father calmed down, he actually picked up the video camera and decided he was going to film. He had to ask me how to use it, but once I got him set up, he walked around and filmed everyone opening gifts. His mood lightened; he seemed to genuinely like filming everything. Damn, if only we could have given him a video camera every year maybe he would have liked Christmas a lot better.

As I put on my new red sweater and red lipstick to go see Mike, I wondered if his Christmas mornings were anything like this. I learned later that his experience of Christmas involved meticulously decorated trees and elaborate gingerbread houses. To me, this sounded magical, like living inside of a perfect holiday movie scene, but for Mike, this was just what they always did. We didn't spend much more time talking about Christmas morning, or the chaos of Christmas Eve. We exchanged our gifts and made out for hours in Mike's car, occasionally pausing to come up for air.

"So am I going to see you for my birthday?" Mike asked me, his face covered in lipstick.

"Of course! It must suck having your birthday just after Jesus's birthday," I said.

"Yeah, kinda," he shrugged. "I always get the birthday/Christmas combo presents."

"Well, not from me. I will always make it special."

Whatever had transpired earlier in the day didn't matter anymore when we were together; it was just us, and we were in our own, steamed-up little world.

Not-So-Happy New Year

January 1992 began full of hope and new beginnings. Besides my typical resolutions of sticking to my diet plan–I was determined to look like Anna Nicole Smith in her model shoot for Guess jeans–I was in love. Not just a little in love. Like, big in love. HUGE. Plus, after my family and Mike's family spent New Year's Eve eating lobster and playing Monopoly together, everything just felt *right*.

To make up for all the money I had spent on Christmas presents, I took every Baskin Robbins shift I could. The Saturday before we all headed back to school, I had the opening shift. By 10am, the mall was just as busy as it was for all of December. It seemed as if everyone within a 100-mile radius was lined up outside the movie theater to see the highly anticipated, and star-studded Peter Pan movie, *Hook*. It had been out for a couple of weeks already, but I guess everyone was too busy Christmassing to go to the movies until now. I couldn't wait to see it myself–Robin Williams was, and will always be, my favorite actor. I've always loved his boisterous charm and childlike humor. Some of his facial features reminded me of my father, especially when he wore glasses. Too bad that's where the similarities ended. All these happy families waited in line to buy their tickets and popcorn. I watched them smile and laugh together from behind the rack of waffle cones sitting on top of the ice cream freezer. I was in for a busy lunch rush if they all decided to get ice cream after the movie.

I was restocking the cake cones, when the phone rang.

"Thank you for calling Baskin Robbins, Stratford, this is Chantel. How can I help y–?"

"Chantel, is your father there?" It was my mom; she sounded like she had been crying.

"No. Why? What's wrong?"

"Just do me a favor, if you see him, give me a call, okay?"

I told her I would, and that was that. I was confused, she never called me at work, but I did my best not to worry about what they could be fighting about *now*. As predicted, the lunch rush did its thing, and after that first showing of *Hook* let out, a steady stream of customers visited the counter. I happily made my way around the kitchen, making banana splits and milk shakes for the masses, having no idea that in the next few minutes everything would change. All the excitement, joy, and hope I had before I began to scoop this customer's ice cream disappeared as I saw my father and my siblings walking toward me. As they got closer to me, the picture came into focus, and my mother's random phone call earlier that morning began to make more sense now. Walking beside my father was Mike's mother. I knew immediately what that meant, and my stomach dropped.

Fuck. No way. Not her.

As I finished up with the customer before them, I felt sick. It was one thing for him to betray my mom, but this was a new low.

"Hello, daughter!" He chirped over the sneezeguard.

That fucking stupid fake smile. He was always performing. I didn't know which one of them to hate more, him or her. I just knew that instead of taking their order, I wanted to punch my dad in his smug, lying face, and grab a fistful of her frizzy, overly-processed, permed-to-a-crisp hair, and scrub off those horrible, pencil-thin eyebrows. But I said nothing. I scooped mint chocolate chip ice cream for each of them and tried to act normal in front of the kids that they brought along for cover.

Mike's mom must have felt me staring at them because she felt it was necessary to say how crazy it was that they happened to run into each other. *Yeah, crazy.*

I knew my father. She wasn't the first woman he cheated on my mom with, and most likely wouldn't be the last, but God damn it, why did it have to be her? *WHY*? He was going to fuck up my one chance for happiness. I could not believe this was my life.

As I watched them all sitting at a nearby table talking as the kids ate their cones, I called my mom like I said I would. I told her I saw him with my brother and sister, but when I told her that Mike's mom and siblings were there, too, the line went dead silent.

"Mom? *Mom? MOM?*"

"Sorry, I'll talk to you later, Chantel."

The rest of the day was a blur. I went through the motions of my job until I finally got a moment to call Mike at the video store.

"Hot Ticket Video, this is Mike."

"We need to talk. Your mom and my dad just showed up at my work after *coincidentally* running into each other at the movies. I served them all ice cream. Mike, this isn't good."

"What do you mean?" He had no idea.

"I mean this *isn't good.*"

"Well, can you meet me here at the Video Store? We can talk about it," he said.

"Okay. I'm on my way," I said.

"Love you, Chantel." It didn't matter what was going on, he always said it.

"Bye, Mike." I felt stupid for ever thinking things could be good. Fairytales were for children and it was time to grow up.

This Isn't Going to Work

"If our parents are having an affair, this isn't going to work," I said matter-of-factly. I was devastated, but it seemed obvious that there was no way to get around it: this was impossible.

I sat across from Mike at Springdale's, our favorite restaurant, and I realized that he really didn't get it. He needed to see the whole picture. I decided it was time to tell him everything about the life I had hoped to leave behind when I moved away from the city. The conversation lasted for hours and continued from the restaurant to his car. For the first time, the car windows were not steamed up because we were making out, it was because of how much I was crying. It was the same childlike crying that my strawberry shortcake blanket had heard when I was little.

In between the hyperventilating and the waterfall of tears, I told him about all of the hands that touched me that shouldn't have. As he sat quietly and listened, I could see a kind of disbelief in his eyes, but I kept talking. I didn't want to hear what he might say. I needed to get this out; I needed someone to hear me. I told him about Jake and everything he did to me. I told him about the kids in school and how I was bullied for my hair, my name, my weight and whatever else they decided to choose that day. I told him how much I hated myself and how I wished I could unzip my skin from my bones. How fat I felt, and that I wish I had the willpower to never eat again. I showed him the heart I carved into my arm years ago, and the cigarette burn scars on my wrists that were still pink. I told him about how much my mom hurt me that day she bashed my head against the stove, and how I hate the movie *Gremlins* because it reminds of the day she tried to kill herself, and take my father and me with her. It ached that we kids were never enough for either of my parents to change. I told him about how my father treated everyone –truly *anyone* who wasn't us–better than us, because he cared so much about how other people perceived him. I told him how he was almost never home, and when he was, it typically consisted of shaming my mother about her weight, or the money she'd spent. I told him about how my mother made us fall in line when he was around to not make his mood worse. I told him how I wished they would just get divorced. Lastly, I told him about the one affair I knew of for sure, and the other ones my mother alluded to as I got older. I told him how my life never stays the same, and how I'm always waiting for the next bad thing to happen–because it always did. I allowed myself to be vulnerable enough to tell him about what it was to really be me. I took off the ring he gave me, and I told him as I handed it back to him, the only solution for this was to break up.

Stunned by what was happening, he took his hand off my leg, tears filling his kind, brown eyes. I couldn't look at him, so I stared at the floor mat under my shoes in his Firebird.

"What do you mean we have to break up?"

"Mike, I can't do this to my mom. My dad is having an affair with your mother. This is fucked!"

"You don't know that for sure, Chantel,"

"Yes, I do. My mom told me everything. She said the reason she had an inkling that something strange was going on was because at your dinner party on New Years Eve, she noticed your mom handing the dice to my father inappropriately. Apparently, not only was she slowly pulling her touch away from my father's hand as they played the game, but your mom had also mentioned things to my mom earlier that day that only my parents talked about."

"That doesn't mean they are having an affair, Chantel."

"Mike, you don't understand. You don't know my father. That man never chooses to take us anywhere just to *be a dad.* My dad barely participates when my mom forces him to, and she's with us the whole time. My mom would've joined them to see the movie, but apparently, he insisted on taking them by himself."

"Well, my mom does a lot without my dad. I'm telling you, Chantel, my mom wouldn't do that. My parents don't even argue."

"Mike, I can't see my mom hurt like this. Your mom was her friend."

"Then how about instead of breaking up you ask my mom for yourself."

"Great. Name the day."

We agreed on the next day, and headed home. It was the quietest ride we ever had. He didn't even turn up the radio. As he drove through the snow, I leaned my head on the cold window. I didn't know what I would be walking into at home, so I tried to brace for whatever was to come. When he pulled onto the driveway and put the gear into park, he reached over to kiss me, but I was numb.

When he went to open the car door, I stopped him.

"Don't open the door for me. I'll see you tomorrow, okay?" I jumped out of the car as quickly as I could. I couldn't look at him. I just shut the door and ran into the house. I watched him drive away. *I fucking hate my life.*

It was late, but my parents weren't home yet. My siblings were not in bed, they were watching TV and eating cereal like I always did. I half-heartedly waved to them as I headed to my bedroom to get ready for bed. When my phone rang, I knew it was Mike, but I disconnected the cable instead of answering. There was nothing more to say. It wasn't going to work regardless of what his mom said tomorrow because I knew the truth: it was too good to be true.

★

As planned, Mike picked me up and drove us back to his house where he assumed his mom would be. The scent of leather and his Polo cologne filled the car. Was he making this hard on purpose? His eyes glistened with a hope I did not share for the situation we were walking into. We didn't say much to each other as he drove, but he handed me a note he had written earlier. Since we started dating, we wrote to each other almost every day when we were at school. This was the first time I didn't. My stomach was in knots. I couldn't recall anything I did that day because of how dissociated I was. I hated my father. I hated his mother and I was doing everything in my power to just keep cool because I didn't want to go to jail for this. When we pulled up, her car wasn't in the driveway. We waited in silence for a while, and I decided to read his letter since I couldn't look at him. I knew how this was going to go.

She finally showed up after Mike called her car phone to make sure she was coming home soon. She got out of her car and smiled at Mike. *What a fake!* I was steaming. My anger grew as I watched her open the trunk of her new car to grab the groceries. Mike helped her, and I walked closely behind, trying to figure out what I was going to say and how I was going to manage it without seeing red. This wasn't my first rodeo when it came to fighting, but I loved Mike enough to not hit his mom, even though I wanted to. I decided to let Mike break the ice before I confronted her. As they made small talk, I sat in their family room looking at everything around me, and I noticed how dusty everything was. From far away, the house looked decent, but I don't think there was a vacuum run over their carpet in months. I thought about the first time I saw her at that park district event, and how I should've known, even then. From the outside looking in, the woman was put together—highlighted and permed hair, tanned skin, perfect nails—but who was she behind all that? I had to know.

Mike's small talk was pissing me off. It was obvious he wasn't going to start this, so as she was placing items into the refrigerator, I just stood up and stormed into the kitchen.

"Are you having an affair with my father?" I blurted out.

Her eyes got big, but then she continued putting groceries away.

I started to cry immediately, and Mike looked like a deer in headlights. He couldn't figure out who to look at, so he just kept bouncing his eyes from me to her and back to me.

"What? Why the hell would you ask me this, Chantel? No, of course not!" She said, feigning shock, but moving nervously around the kitchen as I followed closely behind her.

"Look me in the eyes and tell me you are not having an affair with my father!"

"Chantel, I am not! Did your mother say something to you?"

"No, my father did. Why would he lie to me?" I thought I'd play her game, so I decided to lie to see if I could get the truth. Mike looked at me, knowing I was lying, but still speechless.

She kept looking at Mike.

"Look at me!" I snapped. "Tell me what is going on. Why did you sit with my father at the mall and have ice cream alone? Do you think I am stupid?"

She sighed and looked down.

"Chantel, your father expressed that he likes me, but I don't feel the same way. After the day you saw us in the mall, I told him that he needs to back off. I also told your mother that I don't want to see either of them at my classes anymore. Your father seems to be obsessed with me."

"She's fucking lying, Mike!" I lunged at her and pointed my finger at her face as Mike held me back, "Stay away from my fucking family! You're a whore!" I stormed out of the house in tears. I heard Mike yelling something to her as I made my way to his car, but everything was a blur.

It was another quiet drive home, but I calmed down a little. I needed to tell my mom what I had done.

"After everything you told me about your parents, why would you believe your dad over my mom?" Mike asked.

I couldn't believe the words that were coming from his mouth.

"Mike, we are breaking up. I believe my mother; she has no reason to make this up, and my father is disgusting. I'm standing by her."

★

After the confrontation, my dad claimed he and Mike's mother were in love, and that she lied about the affair to protect Mike and her family. The wild disrespect he had for my mom was infuriating, but the way he dismissed how this also affected *me* was a new level of cruelty.

"Do you even care about Mike and me at all?" I asked him, already knowing he didn't,

He sighed. I guess the prospect of caring about his daughter was exhausting to him. "So you're dating someone who could be your step-brother one day, it's not like you're blood relatives," he joked.

"I fucking hate you!" I screamed in his face. When he left that night, I hoped it would be for good. I felt nothing but disgust for him. My mom might have thought he looked so handsome wearing that stupid Indiana Jones hat that matched his brown leather coat, but all I saw was an ugly, selfish man who treated his family as an inconvenience. I couldn't even look at him. Instead, I stared at my mom. Her face seemed to age right before my eyes.

Alone in my room, I faced the "Mike and Chantel" memorabilia I had collected and displayed on my bedroom wall. *It had to go. All of it.* The daily notes, the photo booth strips from the arcade, the cards, the photos–everything came down. I put it all in a shoebox along with a cassette tape, a recording of Mike singing along to "Love of Lifetime" by

Firehouse. He was not a singer by any means, but he knew how much I loved music, and he felt like the song was about us, so he hit record. It felt like we had already been together for a lifetime. I loved him. I didn't want to break up with him, but I didn't want Jerry Springer chaos, and I didn't want my mom to be hurt anymore. I tried to will myself to forget I ever met Mike or his family.

Who Should I Believe?

It had been a miserable few days since breaking up with Mike. I didn't know what to do. One afternoon, I was leaving school with my friends and I saw him, waiting for me in his car. Without a word, I ditched my friends and ran to him. When he got out, I fell into his arms, sobbing. No one held me the way Mike did. I could always feel his love wrapping around me. It really was like magic. Our chemistry seemed to amplify in the few days we were apart. We spent the afternoon, and well into the evening, sitting in his car, making out and talking.

We couldn't stay broken up, but we didn't know what to do about the mess with our families. Mike's mom continued to deny everything, so his home life went on as usual. Whenever Mike would bring it up with her, she denied it all over again. It was insane; she acted as if nothing had ever happened! My home life was…a little different. My father seemed to be waiting for my mom to leave him, but she refused. She told me that she was getting strange phone calls at work–she still worked at my dad's shop–and that whenever she would pick up, the person calling would hang up immediately. She was *certain* it was Mike's mother, but she couldn't figure out why she was calling. It was driving her crazy–maybe that was the point of the calls: harassing her to the point of insanity so she would be done with him, done with it all. The first part of that goal was working. She was becoming a shell of herself. The second part of that goal was a tougher sell for reasons I couldn't fathom. I begged her to leave my father, tried to convince her that it would be okay–better even, but she wouldn't budge. I had sacrificed my own happiness to protect her, and it was pointless; she chose him anyway. She always did.

The anger I felt toward my father, toward Mike's mother, and toward my own mother was a lot to carry around. It was the catalyst of most of the arguments I had with Mike, and yet we couldn't find a reason to stay broken up. Our connection was so deep and so intertwined that neither of us understood it. We were either wrapped up in an electric, passionate makeout session or we were fighting—usually about our parents, sometimes about my alarming behaviors.

Mike already knew about many of the things I dealt with, but he didn't fully grasp the extent of it, and he didn't realize that my struggle with self-esteem and my need for control devolved into anorexia and bulimia, or that the chaos at home triggered my dangerous patterns of self-harm. I don't blame him for not understanding—who could understand this? I couldn't, and I was the one living it—but as things got worse, the sarcastic and "tough" Chicago girl attitude crumbled. I couldn't mask how fucked up my life was anymore. Not at school, and definitely not with Mike.

When we started to have sex, it got even more complicated. He knew that I had experienced some terrible things before I met him, but he didn't really understand how deep the hurt went. After we had sex for the first time and I couldn't stop crying, he realized there was something more going on with me. This was much more than the drama with our parents; my inner world was spiraling, and all the ways I used to cope with the intense feelings that would surface weren't working anymore. I contemplated killing myself daily. I resorted to slamming myself into furniture and walls to try to quiet the noise in my head. I punished my body for not being small enough, for existing at all, really. I was just desperate to feel relief, and as sick as it is, these actions momentarily made me feel better. Feeling pain was the only way I could focus on something other than the dysfunction and chaos around me. I was afraid that if I told Mike all of this, he would think I was a psychopath. Still, he held steady through so many storms, convinced that as long as we were together, nothing else mattered.

Mike's "us against the world" optimism helped me redirect my focus. Maybe he and I really *were* something special. I didn't know much, but I did know that I wouldn't forgive myself if I didn't try. We didn't tell anyone we got back together, but by spring, we were tired of secret meetings and sneaking around. Plus, he asked me to go to his senior prom, so we had to tell our parents we were back together. In another fun surprise, my parents had made the decision to stay together and make it work. Apparently, the affair was over, and it was time to play family once again. At one point, Mike's mom even had me questioning whether my father actually made it all up. I started to believe what Mike had believed this whole time: There was no way that she wanted to leave her family and that maybe it was all another cowardly move on my father's part to try to escape my mother. I didn't know what to believe anymore, but I knew I loved Mike and we didn't get a fair chance to be just "us" before everything went sideways. Maybe things could settle down and we could go back to being the Mike and Chantel who loved each other's company and didn't argue about what our parents were doing.

The day of prom, I felt like Marilyn Monroe. My dress was white lace with a strapless heart-shaped bodice, trimmed with iridescent sequins, and fitted all the way to my knee before kicking out fins of unfurled lace. I loved it. I added long, white satin gloves, a pearl choker, white satin shoes, and a garter that would be hanging from Mike's rear view mirror after prom was over to show everyone that he was taken. Mike wore a classic tux, and had his mullet cleaned up and feathered perfectly. I loved the white dress shirt against his olive skin, and the way his brown eyes sparkled, it was like a movie. Both of my parents were at home to take pictures of us and see us off. It was weird how perfect the scene was after the months we had all just endured, but that was my life. Good when it was good, and horrible when it wasn't. Nothing in between.

A Dream is a Wish

Just before the summer ended, my parents surprised my siblings and me with a trip to Disney World. Mike's parents had a timeshare, so they went there all the time, but for me and my siblings, this was special–I had never been on a plane before! It made him a little jealous that I was so excited to go, but I couldn't wait to stand in front of Cinderella's castle and wish upon a star. It's the most magical place on earth—where else could I expect all my dreams to come true? I had finally convinced my mom to enroll me in Barbizon modeling school in the fall, so I was well on my way. Maybe I would conveniently run into an agent or movie producer while on vacation, or maybe I'd be recruited by Disney to play Cinderella. As I packed, I meticulously planned each outfit so I would look my best at all times. I had been extra diligent about my diet and exercise, so I was actually looking forward to wearing a bathing suit. This didn't alleviate Mike's vacation jealousy, but he had to understand that *I wanted to be someone.*

The vacation started off better than expected. We drove to Cocoa Beach where we built sandcastles, ate lunch on a pier, and tasted the ocean for the first time. Everything felt almost normal. Then my father told my mother how good she looked in her bathing suit now and I was immediately consumed by the familiar noise. I hadn't thought about my weight or my body until his comment forcibly brought it back into focus. Of course he told her she looked beautiful *now* because she lost weight. *God, I hate him.* He was oblivious to the fact that she was thin now because of what he put her through. She starved herself to earn his approval.

The next day was Magic Kingdom, and my siblings were buzzing with excitement.

I chose my white jean shorts with the plaid ruffle trim and matching crop top and hat. I must have looked cute because the guy in the Goofy costume at the character breakfast wouldn't leave me alone.

My father hated crowds. I can't recall a single carnival he ever took us to, but here we were at Disney, during peak season, surrounded by thousands of people. It didn't take long for him to become who he always was. It started with the food prices, then the lines, then the heat. He didn't care that my little sister was desperate to see Alice in Wonderland or that my brother wanted to ride Dumbo. He wanted to leave and he made sure we all knew it.

My mom tried to manage him by pawning the kids off on me so they could "talk." The way she pandered to him made me sick. As we waited in line, I watched them on a nearby bench. I studied my mom's reactions to whatever he was saying. I could tell it was the same bullshit as always. I spent the rest of the day watching him smile and charm every stranger while we got nothing. I watched him stare at women and wait for them to look back. When they did, he'd flash that smile. I hated him. I hated my mother more for staying.

The next morning, before we headed to Epcot, my father disappeared from the hotel room for quite a while without explanation. By the time he returned, my mother was a wreck. Their arguing revealed that he had made a phone call to someone and she was pretty sure she knew who he called. As the day went on we all did our best to play family for my siblings' sake. Then, just before the fireworks, standing in a sea of people, I heard my mother say Mike's mom's name. Inside, I lost it.

Once we returned to the hotel room, I announced that I was going to the pool.

"Take your brother and sister with you," my father said.

"Why?" I whined.

"Because you shouldn't be alone."

Since when did he care? Earlier, a guy who worked at one of the gift shops had slipped me his number. He was older, cute enough, and completely unattached to everything I was living.

"I won't be," I replied, "there is someone meeting me there."

"I'm sure there is, Chantel."

"What's that supposed to mean, Dad?"

"Look at how you dress! I watch how you look at other boys. I'm not surprised, though. Mike is not strong enough for you."

"You would know, Dad. Wouldn't you?" I was enraged.

"I just call it like I see it, Chantel. If you dress like a whore, then people will only have that to believe about you."

"FUCK YOU." I sobbed and looked at my mother.

"Chantel, don't swear at your father!"

"OH MY GOD. Why the fuck are you defending him?" I screamed.

He lunged at me to cover my mouth, afraid of what other people in the hotel might think. My siblings pretended not to hear all of this. They did their best to watch cartoons like they were supposed to. I grabbed my purse in a rage and stormed out.

When I got to a payphone, I started to dial Mike's number, but stopped. I knew he wasn't going to believe me about the phone call earlier. I knew he wouldn't get it. I reached into my pocket for the Epcot guy's number instead.

He met me at the pool where we talked for a while. He told me he was 28, and said I seemed more mature than other 16-year-olds he'd met. I was desperate to escape the mess of my life, but I figured talking to someone who knew nothing about it was at least a temporary escape.

After he left, I didn't go back to the room. I spent most of the night curled up in a pool chair, under a towel, staring up at the stars I was supposed to wish on.

NINE

Senior Year

★

Barbizon, Take Me Away!

While most of the kids I went to high school with began their senior year meeting with their guidance counselors about what college they were choosing to attend, I had different plans. My father was not a fan of college; he thought I should choose a trade like he did. Although I didn't want to do *anything* or be *anything* like him, I did agree with him that college wasn't my thing. I always thought I'd be good at hair and makeup. It seemed like fun, and it could be a great way to make money between all of the auditions for my career as an actress. When I mentioned it to him, he said that hairdressers were a dime a dozen, and that it wasn't a good idea. He never gave me a better idea, but he made it clear that he didn't like mine. As if it mattered anyway. He made me keenly aware that any education I got after high school would be on me to pay for. When he traded in his first Corvette for a brand new, 40th anniversary edition, it was a gift to himself for turning 40, and for all of his hard work. I'm sure cheating on your wife and neglecting your family to do whatever you want, whenever you want, is grueling, but hell, what did I know? Go ahead, Dad, *you deserve it.*

I couldn't care about any of that anymore. My one-way ticket out of this life was all but guaranteed with a deposit my mom had paid months prior. I begged her for years to go to Barbizon modeling school, and she finally surrendered. This was the one case where my father's cheating actually helped me. Instead of leaving him, I was beginning to think she was trying to either bankrupt him or kill him. Between all the shopping and the high cholesterol meals she'd cook for him, it definitely made me wonder, but either way, I was getting out of there. My only hope was that Mike would eventually join me too. From the day we met, I told him about my dreams of moving to Hollywood, and being cast in movie roles, or shows like 90210, or hell, even a sexy music video. I could be a model like the blonde in Poison's video for "Mama's Fallen Angel." Most of the girls I knew had dreams like mine. We all wanted to be the girl that the J.

Geils band talks about in their song, "Angel in the Centerfold."

My first class at Barbizon Modeling school was scheduled every Monday from the first week of September until the spring. The tagline that was famously used in all of their marketing materials "Learn to be a model or look like one" had given me hope since I was 11, and now my dream was within reach.

I drove myself to my first class at Barbizon. I had recently been gifted my father's enormous 1973 Chevy Impala. That thing was *a tank,* pea-green with a dirty cream colored interior, and a radio that barely got two stations. It was actually stolen back when I was ten. My dad had just put new tires on it, so he was extra pissed when we got it back *without* the tires. This car was a monster, it could easily fit six or seven people on the bench seats, and maybe another five bodies piled into the trunk. It was tough to park, though, so I made sure I parked all the way in the back of the parking lot to avoid cars around me.

Barbizon was on the 3rd floor of a building where a bunch of other businesses also lived. It was not what I pictured it would look like. I thought the storefront would have a big red neon sign with pictures of all their most successful students welcoming us into the entrance. Instead, I walked into a boring, gray office reception area. There was shiny, metallic wallpaper with the Barbizon logo printed all over it, like a classified ad, but otherwise it was just an office with hallways into other offices. Still, the receptionist was well dressed and chic, so I tried to not let my first impression of the location ruin the magic that could happen. I checked in, received my lesson materials, and was guided down the hallway to a conference room. Along the walls were headshots of people who had been students there. That miniature gallery was all I needed to feel like I was on my way to fame and freedom! I was the first in my class to arrive, so while I waited, I paged through the lessons we would be covering over the next few months:

How to Dress for an Interview or Audition
Proper Etiquette
Theater Makeup vs. Print Makeup
What Color Best Suits Me
How to Walk a Runway
Diet and Exercise
Commercials and Acting

That last one was the one I was most excited for. This was *it.* The instructor made her way in, and greeted us warmly. She was stunning, tall and thin, clear blue eyes, and perfect teeth. Her long, ash blonde hair looked like Heather Locklear. After that first class, I was beaming. I saw a glimpse of a future I wanted, and I was determined not to let my parents screw it up.

My Roadmap

Barbizon was changing me. Everything I was learning there followed me into my day-to-day life. It gave me a roadmap for becoming who I wanted to be, and I stepped into it eagerly. I was obsessed with the TV show *Beverly Hills 90210,* and I mirrored the styles I saw Brenda and Kelly wearing. I stopped dying my hair at home and paid for it to be done professionally with the money I earned at Baskin Robbins. I learned how to take care of my skin properly—apparently it was important to wash my makeup off every night. Mike started working at his mother's tanning salon, which meant I could tan for free during his shifts and as long as his mom wasn't around. Maintaining my appearance was essential to my life plan, and I was militant about my commitment.

Shelby, a girl I had met in choir class, was also fitness-obsessed and in a serious relationship. Needless to say, we became fast friends. Whenever we weren't with our boyfriends, we were together. We did workout videos together and created routines for our Dance Fitness class at school. The class was new, and the instructor—a female gym teacher!—saw our interest and made us honorary teaching assistants. When we weren't breathlessly stepping ourselves thin, we talked about diets, fashion, annoying parents, the dates we went on, how we planned to marry our guys one day, and most importantly, sex. She was free-spirited and wild. She told me about a place Mike and I could go if we ever needed privacy. It charged by the hour–it was cheap, but it was private. I didn't tell her everything about my past or about my family drama, but I didn't need to. I finally found someone who understood me, and it made high school a lot less lonely. Most of the "friends" I had didn't understand my relationship with Mike, but Shelby did.

Every morning, I would stare at the growing collage of memories that I had once again displayed on my bedroom wall. My favorite addition was a hand-made card from Mike. He knew how much I loved the comic "Love is" that was printed in the daily newspaper. I would often cut out the ones that spoke to my dreams of what "Love is" to me and put them in my shoebox collection. So when I had started classes at Barbizon, Mike drew the characters and created his own version of the comic for me.

Love is…
You and Me, FOREVER.
Happy Anniversary! We are what love is all about!
Love forever,
Michael.

Looking at this every morning, helped me get through my miserable reality at home. Having Mike, my new friend Shelby, and Barbizon helped me remember that my days at home were limited, and I didn't have to run away. I just needed to finish high school.

He Was Just Drunk

Celebrating Christmas in the city with my mom's side of the family was never dull, but I was bummed Mike couldn't join me this year. The drive there involved a predictable collection of arguments: Dad having to take time off from work, my siblings bickering about who was going to get better gifts from Santa Claus. I layered on more holiday red lipstick and stared out the window, trying my best to ignore it all. A Barbizon lesson recommended having a suit to wear for interviews, so I dutifully bought a black, pinstriped blazer and pants that I paired with a men's dress shirt and tie. Because my hair was shorter and blonder, I leaned into the menswear vibe—I was in full Madonna "Express Yourself" mode, and I felt amazing. All I was missing was the pointy bra and monocle she wore in the video.

My grandparents' house was a revolving door of people: Aunts, uncles, cousins, family friends, and friends-of-friends. My grandma didn't greet me like she had the year prior, but then again, Mike wasn't with me, so she didn't have to make a good impression. As I made my rounds, greeting everyone with a hug and a *Merry Christmas*, I got responses like, "Wow, look at you!" or "Did you lose more weight?" It would have been nice for someone to just say that I looked pretty, but I began to realize that I was becoming someone different from them. They expected me to look a certain way. Girls were expected to wear dresses, so my suit was a lot for them. The stories my mom told me about how she wasn't allowed to leave the porch growing up while her brothers ran wild, started to make more sense to me now.

My grandfather was on the back porch with a few other men smoking a cigarette and talking. When I greeted him, he took a long drag of his Marlboro and as he blew it out, he looked me up and down with a weird smile.

"It's me—Chantel," I said, thinking that maybe he didn't recognize me or something.

"I know who you are," he laughed. "What I don't understand is what you are wearing! Are you a man now?" The others joined his laughter.

"Are you talking about my suit? Grandpa, Madonna wears this in her videos—it's the style now!" I laughed back, because he had no clue about fashion.

"No, it's your hair too," he continued. "You shouldn't have cut it. It doesn't look pretty, you look like a boy!"

I walked away without a response. After staring at myself in the bathroom mirror for a while, I decided that I didn't look ugly or like a boy, either. I spent the rest of the evening avoiding him, and biding my time until we could leave. We had dinner and opened gifts and I went through the motions. Some family members tried to start up conversations with me, but I didn't care. This life here in the city with these people wasn't my life anymore.

At the end of the night, I made my way to the back bedroom to grab my coat and purse. The light from the hallway was enough to illuminate the row of dolls my grandmother crocheted right next to my grandfather's collection of horror and *adult* VHS tapes. I rolled my eyes and began to put on my coat, when the door shut behind me. Then, a hand on my shoulder and a whiff of Old Style beer.

"I didn't mean to hurt your feelings," he slurred and rubbed my shoulder.

I reached for the light switch. "It's fine, Grandpa."

He gave me a look I'd never seen before, then opened his arms to hug me. It was weird but I hugged him back. He held me for an uncomfortably long time and as I tried to pull away to say goodbye, he hooked his arm behind my neck, pulled me in closer, and pressed his lips against mine. I could barely register what was happening: The smell of Old Spice cologne and beer, the roughness of his lip and chin, his tongue trying to enter my mouth—I felt something inside of me collapse.

I pushed him away and bolted out. Down the hallway, my Aunt Beatrice stopped me and asked me what was wrong—I can only imagine the look I had on my face.

"Grandpa tried to French kiss me!" I choked back tears and looked for my parents.

"He's just drunk, Chantel. He didn't mean it," she said.

What is wrong with this family? I went to the front porch and waited in the cold for my parents to gather my siblings so we could leave. I was spiraling. An avalanche of memories rushed in: Bea's boyfriend, JD, Jake, all the gross men that exposed themselves to me, the others I allowed to touch me when I was just a kid. My heartbeat pounded in my ears.

Once my siblings had fallen asleep in the car, my mother for whatever reason took notice of me.

"What's wrong Chantel?"

I started to cry immediately. I couldn't get the words out

"What happened?" She pressed.

I was afraid to tell her. This was the man she spoke so highly of. She always said she was his favorite. I knew how awful Grandma was to her. Now I was going to tell her this, and destroy the perception of who her father was. By the time I had collected myself, we had almost made it home.

"Chantel what happened?" This time it was my father asking.

"Grandpa tried to kiss me! He tried to French kiss me! He put his tongue—

"WHAT?" My mother yelled

My father pulled into our driveway and threw the gear into park. He turned to look at my mom. "Your fucking white trash family! I'm going to kill him! Everyone get out of the car!"

"No!" my mom shrieked, but we poured out of the car and slammed the doors.

I started crying hysterically. I felt ashamed. I didn't want my mom to be hurt. I didn't want to make anything worse. My siblings woke up with all the commotion and were sent straight to bed. There would be no milk and cookies for Santa this year.

It was a blur after that. My mom picked up the phone and screamed at my grandfather. My father screamed at my mom. In my head, at that moment, I told them about everyone, but I think it was too loud for them to hear me. I stood in the dining room, numb.

Hall Pass

Just before the bell rang in my second period class, my teacher startled me by aggressively tapping the desk right next to my head. I had fallen asleep. Unaware for a moment of where I even was, I popped my head up and quickly came to. As I wiped the drool that was lingering from my mouth, he handed me a small piece of paper and walked away without saying a word. It was a pass requesting me to skip my next class and meet with the school social worker. I was confused. First of all, I didn't really know what a social worker was. I had known a few kids I met up with on the smoker stairs every now and then that mentioned they met with one, but to me they needed it. They were constantly getting into trouble and skipping classes. Sure, I was guilty of skipping more than normal this year, but I thought every senior did.

As I made my way to the office, I was pissed because the only class I did like to attend, aerobics, was the one I was being called out of. As I made my way to the social workers office, my mind was spiraling about what this could be about.

I was exhausted. I wasn't eating or sleeping much since we returned to school from Christmas break and with the end of my high school life quickly approaching, I could care less about school. When the bell rang, I stood up and pushed through the aisles of kids and desks as fast as I could since the office I needed to head to was on the other side of the school. When I arrived, I signed in and sat on the hard green couch just outside of the office door. I could feel my hands begin to feel clammy as I looked around at the white painted walls surrounding me. In the three years I had been at this school, this was a room I had not been in yet. I could hear voices muffled behind the door and just as the second bell rang, when the door opened, a student I had never seen before walked out. *At least she was smiling. This can't be that bad.*

"Are you Chantel?" A kind looking man in glasses greeted me at the door.

I nodded and handed him my pass.

"Chantel, how are you doing?"

"Uh, fine?"

"How is everything at home?" He seemed kind, but I wasn't interested in missing my favorite class with Shelby to engage in small talk with a high school shrink that mainly dealt with the school druggies.

"Can you just tell me why I am here?" I said.

A little taken aback by my assertiveness, he introduced himself as the school's social worker, and told me that he called me down to meet him because of an anonymous phone call reporting that I had bruises around my pelvic bone and hip area.

I stared at the floor, racking my brain. *Who would've called. Who could've known?*

"Do you have any of these bruises they were referring to on your body?" he asked.

I paused for a minute to catch my breath then nodded.

"How did you get them?"

I didn't answer.

"Did someone do this to you? Are you in any kind of danger at home?"

"No, no, no, I did it," I choked out. "I gave them to myself." I buried my face in my hands, and sobbed.

He nudged me to unhide my face, and handed me a box of tissues. His face showed genuine compassion.

"Chantel, why would you do this to yourself?"

I didn't want to answer the question. I didn't know how to answer it without sounding crazy, but I couldn't deal with him just staring at me, waiting for an answer.

"I just do it because it feels better to hurt my body than to live at my house," I blurted out. I wiped the tears from my eyes and tried to catch my breath. "I don't know why. I just do it when I need to. Listen, no one at my house is hurting me. It's me. Just know it's me. Please don't tell my parents!"

"Chantel, we already spoke with your mother, informed her about the call, and that I was meeting with you." He paused to write a few notes.

"Oh *GOD*. What did she say?" I began to cry all over again. I didn't want her to know about this. She had been on a downward spiral since Christmas, and I didn't want to cause her any more stress.

"It's okay, Chantel. She wasn't sure what to say except she had no idea why someone would call."

I couldn't either. Maybe Shelby saw them when we were changing in the locker room? I really didn't think she would have called though. I needed to reassure him that I wasn't being abused. I went into full distract mode and started rambling about how I go to Barbizon and how happy I was to be able to pursue my dream of becoming a model or actress and how if it weren't for my parents I wouldn't be able to, but I had to stop because models have to be perfect.

"I'm not going to do it anymore," I told him. "I honestly can't! Models have to be perfect, and I can't do it anymore and I won't! I promise!"

As our meeting came to an end, he requested that I meet with him once a week for a while just to touch base.

"Whatever I have to do, I will," I said. I figured I would show up to our meetings and say the right things and it would all blow over, but over the next couple of months, I was finally able to talk about some of the things I had experienced. It was comforting to have someone tell me I wasn't crazy, that how I was feeling made sense. Even though I didn't tell him all the grizzly details of how I threw up my food, I did mention it one day. My teacher at Barbizon told me that I wasn't tall enough to be a model, but I could do commercials. I still wanted to be as thin as Kate Moss, but I tried my best to not throw up so much anymore. When he asked me why I was so adamant about being thin and perfect, I decided to tell him about the bullies in grammar school. Then I began to tell him about Jake, and how he shamed me in my bathing suit, and how he pressured me, and something in me felt like a volcano about to erupt.

I don't know why it bothered me so much to hear the social worker take my side. For every scenario I shared with him, he insisted that it was not my fault, and I insisted that it was.

"I chose Jake, and I let him in that day," I said.

"No, Chantel. No." In all of the times we met, this was as stern as he ever spoke to me. "You are not at fault for what he did. You realize this, don't you? What he did to you is serious. If you said no, and he persisted anyway, that's called *rape*."

"No! Jake didn't rape me. He didn't hit me or anything!"

"Chantel," his eyes saddened as he looked at me, "this is serious."

"Please do *not* tell my mom," I pleaded. I could tell where this was going and I needed to fix it immediately. "You said these meetings were between us. He didn't rape me!"

"Chantel—"

"He didn't!" I left the office that day and didn't return.

Dairy Queen

Mike had been spending a lot more time at my house, so he had a front-row seat to the chaos and the demise of their marriage. He saw what it did to me when my mom would get home from work, and tell me everything—the phone calls were happening again, and then he would disappear for hours. She *knew* he was with someone—I hated this. I hated my father for hurting my mother. It didn't take long for Mike to recognize how much this really affected me. I couldn't wait to graduate and get out of there.

Because my parents were usually gone, and because no one was around to tell us not to, Mike and I hung out a lot in my bedroom with the door closed. We bribed my siblings with fast food and ice cream so they wouldn't tell on us, but Mike never complained about having my siblings around all the time. It's what I loved the most about him.

One such bribery attempt happened in late spring. We loaded my siblings into the car to take them to McDonalds. I turned the radio up to purposely annoy my brother, and laughed as we cruised through town. Sitting at a red light, I noticed a familiar truck in the parking lot of the Dairy Queen. I looked again and, sure enough, the truck was my father's. Leaning into the car window was a pair of short, very tanned legs in striped shorts. I recognized them immediately.

"Mike! Is that your mom talking to my dad right now?"

He leaned in closer, squinting to see over me.

"I fucking told you, Mike!" I swerved my '73 Chevy across a few lanes of traffic to enter the parking lot. "Your mother is the whore who has been driving my mom crazy!"

I managed to dodge the kids' baseball team and their parents who were eating ice cream in the parking lot, and my siblings screaming brought me back to sanity just before I crashed into the back of my dad's truck.

"What the fuck is going on?" I screamed out the car window. Mike's mom ran and hid in the hair salon next door, and I sat there, staring at him in the rear-view mirror. *He's such a fucking coward* I thought, shaking my head. Enough is enough.

"I'm telling Mom right now, *Bob*!" I yelled to him as I peeled out of there.

The drive back to the house was one of those *tunnel vision* experiences, where the world around you disappears and only the rage exists. I'm sure Mike was processing what it all meant, trying to map out what would happen next. My siblings had seen enough family chaos to know they should just wait it out, but I forgot there was anyone else in the car with me.

I tore through the front door, hysterical and yelling for my mom.

She was in the kitchen holding a pile of mail. She turned and looked at me, confused about all the commotion.

"Mom! I just saw Dad at Dairy Queen. He was with that slut! He was with *Mike's mom!*"

She just looked at me. She wasn't surprised or upset or angry.

"Mom!!!!!"

She took a deep breath, set the mail down on the table, and said, "Chantel, I know. He was ending it with her today."

"What are you saying? You knew?!"

"Yes. He told me today that they were done for good."

Her removal from this entire situation was infuriating.

"This entire time, Mom? They have been together this *entire* time?"

After a long, quiet moment, she added, "Oh, and by the way, we won a trip to Mackinac Island." Apparently, my dad had written their story of trials and tribulation to some radio station, and *apparently* the DJ loved the story so much that they won.

Going Through the Motions

The last few weeks of senior year came and went. What should have been the best memories of my life, according to my mother, mostly felt empty. I was going through the motions, but none of it mattered to me anymore.

My parents were going full throttle on their "new beginning" as if what had happened between them just happened to them. As if my father's award-winning testimony to some stupid radio station was the "sign" they needed to get their shit together and move on without any acknowledgement that the chaos and destruction caused by their bad choices affected anyone but them. The fact that my mother knew about the affair, and then *still* chose my father infuriated me, and that rage seeped into my relationship with Mike. We were fighting constantly. As he discovered the truth about his mother, I couldn't find any compassion for him. I was angry he didn't believe me when I told him the first time, *two years ago.*

I could feel a shift in me that I didn't know how to name. The conversations I'd had with the social worker, the chaos I'd endured at home and with Mike—it was all too much to process. The light at the end of the tunnel was graduation day. *Just get to graduation*, I told myself. I could deal with the rest of my life after.

Just before my senior prom, I told Mike I wanted to go into the city and sit on the rocks by the lake. North Ave beach was special to me, and I hoped it would give me the nerve to speak honestly. I told Mike how my mom would take me there when I was little. She would pack a cooler of sandwiches and pop, and we'd stay there all day. I told him how great things were before my father's first affair. I told him that the only way for me to feel free was to get away from this place—move away—get as far away from my parents as possible. I told him that I was serious about the plans I had for myself after graduation, that I wanted to move to Los Angeles to give acting a try, that my teacher at Barbizon said I should, and that I did have talent. I told him that the dreams I had for myself could never come true here.

As I talked, I studied his face. I realized that the dreams I had were not his dreams. If I did choose to leave, he might not come with me after all. After all the talks about my depression and self-harming, the fights we had about our parents, the break ups when we couldn't agree, and the madly passionate make out sessions when we couldn't stand to be apart longer than a day, he really didn't understand the gravity of the situation. He really didn't understand the toll all of it had taken on me. If I chose him, if I stayed, not only would it mean giving up on my dreams, it would also mean continuing to carry everything we had been through, and I was tired. Whether we were destined to be together or not, the reality of our circumstances felt like something we could never recover from. The cherry on top of it all was that his eyes that night told me he thought moving to Los Angeles would be a mistake. Maybe he really didn't think I could make it after all.

Despite the doubt I saw reflected in Mike's eyes at the lake, I set my feelings aside, and we managed to enjoy ourselves at prom. In a sea of 90s black and blue prom dresses that the guys all matched, Mike's beautiful brown skin and eyes glowed in his head-to-toe white tux. For a moment, I felt like Cinderella standing beside him in my pink satin and lace dress.

The weekend after prom was graduation: I made it. I remember that I drove myself to my school, but I don't have any recollection of walking the stage or receiving my diploma. If I didn't have the diploma today, I'd almost say it never happened. I don't have a single photo of me in my cap and gown, and the only memory I have of saying goodbye to everyone I knew was simply standing there in the grass, feeling a deep sense of loss. I watched everyone hugging and enthusiastic about their future. I hugged a few of my friends, but none of it felt right. My high school life was nonexistent to me compared to what I was dealing with at home, and I couldn't relate to the joy happening around me. When I finally met up with my parents and siblings, I could barely contain the contempt I felt for them. With tears in my eyes, I allowed them to hug me, but I couldn't bring myself to hug them back.

You're in My Town Now

I spent the summer after graduation working a lot and trying to figure out what I wanted to do. My dreams of moving to California hadn't budged, but also knew I needed money and a plan. I traded my job at Baskin Robbins for a short stint at Baker's Square, where I learned that being a server was definitely not in the cards for me–the only thing I ever wanted to do in a restaurant was eat. I ended up working at Fashion Bug. My manager hated me, but I decided I could endure it long enough to buy clothes with my employee discount. Having my own money felt really good, and because I was working so much, my dad agreed to co-sign on a car loan for me. Life at home was just stable enough to be worth the free rent for as long as it lasted. Mike's family was apparently "trying" to work everything out after the affair came out into the open, but we generally avoided spending much time at either of our houses. The last thing we needed was more family drama, we were already arguing all the time as it was.

When we weren't working or arguing about something, we were partying with friends. There were epic bonfires and we got trashed pretty much every weekend. I even called Rose a few times and invited her to party with us.

By the time fall came, I decided to enroll in community college. Mike would be taking classes there, most of our friends were taking classes there, and I knew it had a good theater program, so I figured it was worth a shot. Maybe if I met the right people, everything might fall into place, and my acting career would take off — you never know. I made a few friends in my theater classes and spent time with them working through scenes, which made Mike feel jealous and threatened. Instead of recognizing or addressing that, I leaned into wanting independence, and did what I wanted, when I wanted. I knew Mike liked my hair long. I cut it short, bleached it, and got bangs. When an old friend from high school asked me to come hang out with her at the bowling alley, instead of asking Mike to join us, I asked for space.

We were young and stupid, and we did things that young and stupid people do. When Mike got a motorcycle, he would drive it over 100mph with no helmet. I thought he was crazy for driving that thing so fast (I stand by my position), but underneath my (justified) disapproval was the sting of watching him be equal parts brave and reckless when it came to driving his crotch rocket for fun. When it came to the idea of coming with me so I could chase my dreams? Not so much. Every time we argued, or I saw something that I didn't like, it was one more notch in the feeling I got from him that day we talked on the rocks by North Avenue beach.

No matter how much he loved me, no matter how many fun and beautiful moments we had together, the idea of us getting married one day fell heavily on me. I couldn't help but think about the mess with our parents' and how it all made the idea of ever being happy feel so impossibly out of reach. I was trying to figure myself out and I wanted to do it on my own.

When I finally decided that we needed to break up—for real this time, or at least for longer this time—Mike didn't take it well. He'd show up, unannounced, at school, work, or on the street where I lived, and wait for me in his car. The more he pursued me the angrier I became. I had explained to him again and again that I couldn't see how it would ever work after all that had happened. He didn't get it, and I was exhausted trying to explain it over and over again. I couldn't let it go, and honestly, I didn't want to be a part of that life anymore. If he was gone maybe I could erase the memory altogether. Eventually, after a pretty harsh phone call telling Mike that I confided in my parents, (I had not) to warn him to leave me alone. He finally backed off completely. I knew it would hurt him to be so harsh, but I needed to breathe. I needed to remember what the world was like without everything that happened.

Not long after we broke up, Rose called. I hadn't seen her or heard from her in a while. I hadn't gone to the bonfires where we partied in a while. Given the up and down pattern of our friendship, I hadn't bothered to tell her about Mike and me. Now that she had a boyfriend and her boyfriend and Mike hit it off, I figured she wouldn't be interested in my friendship. History proved to me that I was someone she didn't choose, so I saved myself the heartache.

She called because she had left some things at my house and wanted to pick them up.

I told her when she could come get them. My tone with her was aggressive. My defenses were up and ready for whatever she was going to have to say to me. But I was completely oblivious to what would transpire next.

As I sat outside, I waited and watched for Rose's car to pull up, but instead, I saw a more familiar car pull up in front, blocking my driveway. It was Mike's car. Rose got out and made her way up the driveway to me. I didn't care what the story really was, seeing them together set me off. I stormed into my house and grabbed the planner she said she needed to pick up that day. I remembered that Mike had left his omelet maker at my house, and *since they were both there,* I might as well kill two birds or whatever.

I handed the planner to Rose without a word. She smirked as she turned back around and it felt like the day she walked away from me in seventh grade. This time, I followed closely behind her, carrying Mike's omelet maker and a few other things Rose had asked for. I felt like I could crawl out of my skin, but as I saw who was in the backseat of Mike's car something in me detonated.

"Are you fucking kidding me?!?! Tammy?!?! Oh my God!" I didn't know if I should laugh or cry. I threw the rest of Rose's stuff at her.

"Fuck you, Rose!" I said. "I can't believe you!"

At the same time, Mike jumped out of the car and walked over to me.

"This is your fault," he said. "You chose this."

"So you are with her now?! Oh my God! Here's your frying pan!" I threw it down as hard as I could against the driveway and it cracked in half.

"Oh that's what you're going to do now?" Mike said.

"I'll do whatever the fuck I want, Mike!" I screamed at him. "We're not together anymore!"

Tammy got out of the car, walked up to me, and wagged her finger in my face, telling me to go back inside and calm down. Even if she was right, who the hell does she think she is? I kicked her ass before, I'll do it again. *Bitch, you're in my town now!*

"This is the trash that you're choosing to hang out with now?" I said to Mike. I screamed at them all to get off my driveway before I called the police. The neighbors came outside. My siblings came outside. Mike and Rose and Tammy got in the car and drove away.

Why did my friends always do shit like this to me? How could Mike do this to me? I spiraled until my parents came home.

"I want Mike out of my life for good!" I sobbed. "I want to forget I ever met him!"

"Do you really want to keep Mike out of your life?" My dad asked me.

Over tears and hyperventilation, I nodded.

Later that day, my dad took me to the police station to file a restraining order. A court date was scheduled for ten days later.

★

TEN

Adulting… Kinda

★

What Have I Done?

As the cops questioned me about Mike, trying to determine the threat he must have posed to me in order to justify a restraining order, I answered the best way I could: I said I needed space. I said I needed him to leave me alone. I didn't know how to say that I was suffocating, that I didn't know who I was or wanted to be. How could I explain to them that a restraining order seemed like the only solution? Or that getting Mike out of my life made it easier for my dad to pretend like he never had an affair with my boyfriend's mom. It was all too much. My eighteen-year-old mind never considered the gravity of taking legal action. I had no idea what filing a restraining order against Mike could do.

Mike never posed a threat to me. Ever. The terrible irony of the situation is that he is the only person that made me feel safe. Because my life had always been chaotic, I constantly felt like I was screaming into a void. I was desperate for it all to stop. I didn't tell my parents that I wanted Mike out of my life for good because I didn't love him, it was some teenage drama, wrapped in 18 years of pain and confusion.

During our "legal" separation, I had heard that Mike was working at some fence company and started drinking a lot more, but had not chosen to date anyone seriously. Even though his friends told him that I was an asshole and that he should move on, he didn't. I tried to date a few guys from the bowling alley, but there was never any connection like what I had with Mike. There wasn't a day I didn't think about him and regret how everything went down.

The anger and resentment I felt for my parents grew exponentially. The sight of my father made my skin crawl. Any sliver of compassion I once had for my mother was gone. I refused to walk on eggshells around them anymore. I was trying to save up enough money to move out, but getting promoted to assistant manager at Fashion Bug apparently signaled to the banks that I was deserving of a $15,000 credit limit. I opened several credit cards and maxed them out within a month. Saving any part of my $7.75 minimum wage was going to be difficult, if not impossible, at this rate.

One night, after a closing shift, I met up with some friends and one of the pseudoboyfriends at the bowling alley—this one looked like Luke Perry, and was a good distraction. Besides, he didn't mind that I was quick to pull out my rolodex of credit cards to pay for dinner. Even though I had a pager at the time, and told my parents to page me if they ever needed to get a hold of me, they refused (my dad hated the *new* technology). So I had no idea my parents were even aware of my absence until I came strolling in with "Luke Perry" who was coming over to watch a movie.

We had tried to come in quietly, but my father was standing at the top of the stairs in his pajamas.

"Where were you?" he demanded, startling us both.

"The bowling alley, why?" I snapped back. *Who does he think he is?* I thought.

"Well, you need to call us if you're going to be this late."

"I'm eighteen. I can do what I want." What I wanted to say was, *since when do I answer to you?*

"Not in my house you won't!"

"Your house?" I laughed. "Oh, because now Mom has decided to allow you to walk all over her again, I'm supposed to fall in line? After all that you put us through? Fuck you!"

I looked at "Luke Perry" and told him he better leave. As I walked him to the door, I overheard my father telling my mother they aren't going to put up with this.

When I got back to the stairs, my eyes met my mother's.

"Are you seriously going to tell me that I need to listen to this asshole now? After everything he has put us through?!" I screamed. "Are you *serious* mom?" I could hear my brother and sister open their bedroom doors to peek at all the commotion.

She looked at me flatly and said that I needed to respect my father, regardless, and that if I was going to live there, I needed to obey their rules.

"Fine! I'm moving out!" I crashed around my room, grabbing a few essentials. *I can't believe her. I cannot believe I stood by her this entire time!*

I slammed the door behind me, and heard my dad yell, "Good! The hell with you!"

I backed out of the driveway, and took off. My thoughts were racing, I could barely see the road through the tears.

I have nowhere to go.

I have no one to call.

No one understands.

I miss Mike.

#911-143

I couldn't go back home. This was it for me. After everything he did, my mom still took his side. No matter how much I was there for her, no matter how much I supported her, she chose my dad over me, over my siblings, and over herself. I was done watching it, done being a stand-in parent to my siblings, done being her therapist and her maid. I was done with it all.

That night, I drove around for a while before eventually pulling into a 7-Eleven. I was defiant, but I was also alone, afraid, and inconsolable. I stared at the payphone glowing under the neon sign. I had friends I *could* call, but the only one I wanted to talk to was Mike. I was desperate to see him so I could apologize for everything that had happened. I knew I didn't deserve it, and that he could get into more trouble if he agreed to see me, but I had to try. After going over the worst-case scenario a million times in my head, I walked to the payphone and put a few quarters in. I dialed his pager number and typed in the payphone's phone number, space, then *911-143,* our code for *Call me right away. I love you.*

I wasn't there more than five minutes before he called me back. I picked up immediately, still in tears.

"Mike, it's me!"

I could tell from the background noise that he was at a restaurant or something.

"I know it's you, Chantel. Why are you calling me?"

I felt like I had to say something crazy to get him to risk meeting up with me, so I took a deep breath, and went for it.

"Um… well, I think I'm pregnant," I said.

Mike went silent, and I began to spiral. *What the fuck did I just say?! Oh my God, I'm being that girl.*

"I moved out of my parents' house tonight and I have nowhere to go," I continued, my panic rising. I wiped my tears and my runny nose on my sleeve. "Will you please meet up with me? I need to talk to you."

Still no response, just background noise.

"Mike, I know that I don't deserve it, but I really need to talk to you. I miss you and I love you and I'm sorry. I don't know what to do anymore. I'm so sorry," I sobbed.

"Where are you? I'll be right there."

We agreed to meet at a nearby motel. Since I had maxed out all of my credit cards, and barely had any money to put gas in my car, let alone run away from everything, Mike paid for the room so I could stay there for a couple days to figure out what to do. Given the circumstances, I was grateful he showed up for me at all, and then making sure I had a temporary place to stay just further proved what I always knew was true: Mike would always have my back.

I confessed that I wasn't actually pregnant, I just felt like it was the only way he would ever agree to see me. We hashed out some of the bullshit we had assumed and heard in the weeks we were apart. For the first time in our entire relationship, we had a real, truthful conversation. We had always talked, but this was deeper, more honest. He told me that being apart, even though it was painful, allowed him to see how truly messed up his dynamic at home was. Learning the truth about his mother made him realize his family wasn't everything he thought it was. We grew up in very different environments, but they were both dysfunctional.

He was finally acknowledging and processing everything I had been trying to tell him. It was the validation I needed. I'm not crazy. I wasn't making it up. He said, in some ways, our situation felt like the beginning of an awakening, and while he wasn't suggesting we pack up and run away to California, he understood the feeling behind it. I felt seen.

We spent the whole weekend together, talking and making love. The fact that no one knew where we were, and we didn't have to worry about someone walking in on us made it all the more passionate, freeing, and beautiful. We had been intimate before, but this was different. It was a foundation of connection and trust. For the first time, not a single memory of the sexual trauma I had experienced came up. I felt truly safe in Mike's arms.

★

That weekend, I called up a friend of mine who was a little older than me and had been on her own since she graduated. I knew she had been steadily working full time for as long as I could remember, and had recently purchased her own condo. I took a chance and asked if she had an extra bedroom I could rent, or even a couch—I just needed somewhere to go until Mike and I figured out what we were going to do. Something must have been in the stars because she happened to be looking for a roommate to offset some of the costs of her condo. We agreed to $225 a month to rent the room. The only rules were that I didn't have anyone over without her permission, and that I kept it clean. Simple enough.

When I went home to gather the rest of my things, neither of my parents resisted or asked me to stay. There was no apology for how it all went down, no conversation about it at all. Nothing. They seemed a little too eager to support my decision to leave. They even helped me move my bedroom set into the condo. My mom gifted me a new comforter set, wished me the best, and said goodbye with an awkward hug. I could tell she was feeling something, but she didn't let on that it was sadness.

Court Date

Several weeks had passed since the "frying pan" incident and it was time to deal with the mess of the restraining order that I never needed and never truly wanted. We knew we were going to be together regardless of what our families felt about it, and now that I wasn't living at home, that actually felt possible to me. Mike and I figured the judge would drop the order, and we could move on from this charade. Mike kept dodging the officer who had been trying to serve him the papers, which delayed our court date a little, but we knew it was inevitable that we'd have to show up.

I had not spoken to my father since I moved out, so when he called to say he would meet me in the parking lot of the courthouse the day of the hearing, my stomach was in knots. I didn't want him to be there, but it was clear I didn't have a choice in the matter. The thought of standing there, next to my dad, seeing Mike and his dad on the other side, given everything that had unfolded, sounded like a Jerry Springer lineup. It was like my dad wanted to rub it in. He already hurt the man by having an affair with his wife, but let's heap this on, too. God, he made me sick.

As I got out of my car and headed through the covered parking lot my father greeted me the same way he always did.

"Hello daughter."

"Hi." I didn't want to look at him. I didn't want to do this. I walked a few paces ahead of him, listening to the echo of my footsteps as I told myself I just had to get through this and then I wouldn't have to talk to my dad again.

When we reached the stairs, I heard two other people. *Oh, God.* It was Mike and his dad. The last time these two men were face-to-face was when we were all playing Monopoly on New Years Eve, before the affair ruined everything. Once the truth surfaced, Mike told me his dad said if he ever ran into my dad again, there would be hell to pay. I'm not saying I *wanted* that to happen, it would have been even more of a farce, but I hated how smug he looked that day.

When Mike realized we were behind him, he gave me the sweetest smile and a wink to say that everything was going to be fine, just like we talked about. I was worried that someone might have seen the brief exchange, but it was clear that Mike wasn't worried about what could happen. His priority was letting me know we were okay.

I looked down to try to hide my smile. We were supposed to be appearing as enemies here, or at least as neutral. I couldn't let on that we had worked things out because he could get in even more trouble for being in contact with me the whole time.

When our case was called, Mike and I stood at opposite podiums. It was nerve-racking to stand there and hear the proceedings. My hands were clammy and shaking as the judge spoke, I couldn't look at anyone around me.

When the judge asked me about the events that led to the restraining order, I explained that things got dramatic that day because of who Mike was with. I explained that, yes, I was upset, and I wanted him to leave me alone because I needed space, but also that I knew with certainty Mike would never hurt me.

The judge paused as he looked down at the report and then looked back at my father and me and paused again. Then, he turned to Mike.

"How do you plead?" He asked.

"Not guilty, Your Honor."

"Why shouldn't I slap you with this restraining order?"

"Your Honor, there is no need. We have been going through a lot. I do not pose any threat to her and never have. I'm going to leave her alone."

The judge paused for a moment before he replied.

"Well, since you plan on leaving her alone anyway, it won't matter if I keep the restraining order in place for 90 more days just to make sure. It's for her safety."

The judge looked back at my father and me, rapped his gavel, and moved on to the next case.

I couldn't take my eyes off of Mike. He was looking down, stunned, and so sad. *Shit! Shit, shit, shit. This is all my fault!* I wanted to run over there and hug him and tell him I was sorry and that it was all going to be okay. Instead I sat there, frozen.

When we made our way down the courthouse steps, my father smiled, proud of himself, and said, "Well, it's done now, Chantel. You can move on with your life."

I didn't respond. When we reached the base of the steps, he spread his arms out and pulled me in for a hug that I didn't return.

"I have to go to work," I said flatly. I walked away feeling hollow and didn't look back.

Well, That Was a Mistake

Around the same time that the restraining order ended, I had begun to feel that I was overstaying my welcome at my friend's condo, and Mike had decided to work full time instead of continuing school. Within a week of talking about moving in together, we had found a place and signed a lease. A friend of ours, Steve, agreed to move in with us, too, to save on rent.

I had applied for any and all credit cards that crossed my path, and despite my meager wages and financial inexperience, I was granted hefty credit lines that I took full advantage of when cash was tight, which was always. I had no idea how credit worked and how these decisions would affect me in the future. I just knew I had an apartment to furnish.

Within a few weeks of moving in with the boys, I had the entire apartment fully furnished with new furniture. I had bought a black leather living room set with matching smoke glass tables, and a dining room set with black chairs and a smoke black glass table to match the living room. The bedroom set I bought was shiny, black lacquer with beveled mirrors on the headboard and end tables, and I had picked out two huge glass art pieces to hang on the walls to tie it all together. I was so proud of that apartment.

Mike never questioned how I was going to pay for it all, and I was determined to prove to my parents that I was better off without them, so I refused to ever ask for help or admit that I *might have* gotten myself in over my head financially. I just continuously made minimum payments and kicked it down the road. I figured I had it under control. I was working a new job taking calls for a messenger service, and I was living with my boyfriend (and Steve). This was adulthood, and I was doing it! Naturally, the next thing I decided we needed was a dog.

I'm pretty sure going to the shelter "just to look" doesn't work for anybody. Within minutes of arriving, I fell in love with a caramel-brown cocker spaniel puppy. We took her home that day and named her Ariel. *How hard could it be?* We thought. Fast-forward: very hard. We didn't think about the fact that all three of us worked full-time, and no dog would be happy stuck in a crate all day. We didn't think about the fact that apartment walls are thin and dogs bark. We didn't think about the fact that we lived on the second floor of an apartment building, and every time she would need to go out, we would have to make the trek down. It only took a few weeks before that sweet little pup became a lot more responsibility than our immaturity could handle.

To make matters worse, I unknowingly gave the apartment complex the wrong work phone number, and neither of the boys gave a phone number, so when she barked all day and the neighbors got pissed, I had no idea. One day after work, said neighbors were out on their patio landing smoking and mean mugging me as I passed by. Because I had never spoke to them before, I had no reason to their faces had to do with me, but as I opened the door and stepped into the hallway, I head someone yell, "Take care of your fucking dog!"

My mood immediately plummeted. I stormed up the steps to our apartment, where Mike and Steve were drinking beer and playing video games, completely ignoring Ariel who was pawing and barking at the balcony door to come inside. There was urine all over her crate, and a path of little wet footprints through the kitchen.

"You guys didn't care to even clean up her piss?" I let her in and slammed the screen door as hard as I could. "What the fuck guys? Do I have to do everything? Do you even realize that the dog is barking? Our neighbors are pissed!"

They looked at each other and tried, unsuccessfully, to stifle their laughter, which made me even angrier. I started to clean up the mess in the kitchen.

"Who cares what they think?" Mike said.

I stepped out of the kitchen, holding the soaked paper towels.

"I care! I'm the one they said something to!" I paused for a moment to breathe, and I noticed that Mike's eyes were glassy. He was drunk.

You're the one who wanted this dog, his face seemed to say.

I finished cleaning the mess in the kitchen, and opened the window to air it all out, when I saw Ariel pee on the dining room carpet.

"No!" I yelled. I picked her up, put her in her crate, and stomped off to my room, like a child. "You take care of her!" I screamed at the boys, as I slammed my door.

Before even catching my breath, Ariel was barking again, and the downstairs neighbors banged on the ceiling to tell us they were annoyed. Then I heard it again: "Take care of your fucking dog!"

Enraged all over again, I stomped on the floor to say, *fuck you!* This method of communication is pretty universal for apartment living, but it was never going to do anything but escalate the situation. I turned on my music and buried my head under a pillow.

After several more minutes of nonstop barking, while Mike and Steve were still deep in their video game, the doorbell rang. Mike got up to answer it, and from our bedroom, I heard a woman yelling. I jumped up and ran out. Almost immediately, the screaming and finger pointing descended into hair pulling and swinging fists in the hallway. When the rage cleared for a brief moment, I realized who I was fighting, and that I was seriously outmatched. My opponent was a large woman; I didn't stand a chance.

Freaked out, I slid down the wall and covered my head to block any more punches that came my way. She kept swinging.

Mike was drunk, but he was trying to break us apart when her husband came running up the stairs.

"What the hell is going on?" he shouted. He pulled her off of me, and they retreated downstairs as we continued to scream at each other.

Mike picked me up by the waist and pulled me back into the apartment. I still held a clump of her hair in my balled-up fist.

When the police showed up, I was hysterical. I didn't want to kick anybody's ass, but the reality was I didn't know how to handle anything. The reality was, I was too young, and I didn't know what I was doing. The reality was, the neighbors were right. We *were* terrible dog owners. I gave the police my side of the story. I admitted fault and told them I was having a really bad day. The conclusion was that even though she could charge me with battery, I could charge her with trespassing and self-defense. In the end, neither of us decided to press charges. Recognizing how this spun out of control made it clear that we were in no position to keep Ariel, so we agreed to rehome her.

Live Thru This

It had been about a year since I moved out of my parents' house, and instead of feeling empowered and free like I expected, I was reeling. I felt guilty for leaving my mother and my siblings, but they never called to see how I was. The only communication we had was when *I* would call *them.* Every time, I asked if she was upset with me, and something about her tone never told me that she wasn't.

I was obsessed with proving my independence, and I reacted poorly if I felt like someone was telling me what to do, or if I felt disrespected in some way. One morning when I was hungover and on my way to work, a group of girls cut me off in traffic and gave me the finger, so I whipped my breakfast (a Snickers bar) out the window at them. Stupid. I ended up smashing the front end of my car into a construction barricade, causing $3,000 worth of damage. That was an expensive lesson to learn.

The messenger service company I worked for was a husband and wife team who operated their business out of their home, so I had a front row seat to a lot of their family life in between answering calls. I'd laugh whenever my boss yelled at her daughter to turn the music down. I was only two years older than she was, but I already felt uncool and out-of-touch. She came downstairs wearing a white crop top, and a black pinstripe skirt with over-the-knee socks and Converse sneakers. Her heavy, black eyeliner, brown lipstick, and butterfly hair clips were both cool and cute. I admired her style, but more than that, there was something about her that I wanted to emulate. She would talk to her mom about her day at school, her friends, her struggles, and I would feel something twist in me.

One afternoon, my boss ran in and frantically turned on the TV. The cops were chasing OJ and it was making world news. Everyone else was glued to the screen, but I was more interested in what my boss's daughter was playing on her stereo upstairs. When I got the chance to ask her, I had to play it off like I knew the reference.

"The band, Hole. You know, Courtney Love? Kurt Cobain's wife? Her band," she said.

"Oh, yeah. Cool." Like I said. I had to downplay my ignorance. That day, I drove to Coconuts Music and bought the CD. I listened to the entire album, *Live Through This*, on endless repeat. The song "Doll Parts" was one of my favorites. It was the first time I heard somebody sing exactly what I was feeling on the inside, and project it like I always wished I could. Most people I knew disliked the music and called it trash, but I didn't care. The lyrics made me feel seen in ways I never thought possible.

Most of the time, I put on a brave face and pretended to have my shit together, or I partied to distract myself, but the next day, I would inevitably feel worse. I tried to tell Mike that I was struggling, and that I felt worthless, but because he never looked at life that way, his solution was to buy me a gift, or go out somewhere fun. We even took a trip to Panama City Beach, Florida, for spring break to get away from the seasonal depression of winter in Illinois, but it just made things worse. Being surrounded by swarms of partying college kids, having the time of their lives made me feel like a washed up, boring 30-year-old before my life even began. I began to question whether anything this life had to offer was ever going to be enough. The deeper I sank, the more Mike pushed. He didn't understand the darkness in my head, but he figured if he could even just get me to eat, that was better than nothing.

I hadn't been self-harming like I did in high school, but I thought about it. Every morning, I would look in the mirror before work and think to myself, *I guess this is it,* and when I'd return home, I'd sink even lower. Sometimes, when I was driving, I would have the impulse to press the pedal to the floor and just end it all. I would ruminate on all of the things in my past that I couldn't fix, and how impossible everything felt.

On one of my visits to the house, my sister told me our parents were almost never home, and when they were, my father was getting on her about her weight, and that my mom was mad at her because she was messy and hid her food under her bed. The sadness in my sister's eyes was like looking into my own. I felt responsible for her pain and powerless to fix it.

I stopped bothering to do my makeup and my hair everyday. Then I stopped dressing up at all. When a coworker noticed and brought up a counseling center she knew of, I broke down. I scheduled two sessions and then quit. I didn't feel like telling my story to a paid stranger would do any good.

Later, Mike and our roommate were doing what they always did: beer and video games. I left them on the couch, and went into my room, took off my clothes, lit a cigarette, and stared at my body in just my bra and underwear. I sat down on the floor with Mike's charcoal set and paper, and let Courtney Love say what I didn't know how to.

I stared up at the black and white print of Marilyn Monroe that Mike had put his fist through during an argument one day. *She's in a better place now.* I thought to myself. I sketched Marilyn. I sketched myself. I lit cigarette after cigarette, and sketched whatever came up as I sang along and felt the words.

ELEVEN

A Purpose Found

Never Saw That Line Before

I had taken pregnancy tests before. Truth be told, Mike joked about how we should buy stock in EPT because we bought so many of those pee sticks. I freaked out every month because I knew my eating and smoking habits could make my birth control less effective, but every time, I would welcome my period a couple hours after seeing the negative results. So this time when my period was late *again*, I followed the routine: Freak out. Pharmacy. Pee stick. I always waited the full ten minutes to make sure the result was negative before I threw it in the trash and went on with my life.

This time, however, the moment my urine seeped past the first line, it glowed. *Wait, I've never seen that line before.* I grabbed the instructions, and stared at the result window in disbelief.

After a few moments, I heard the front door open. It was Mike. I pulled up my pants and went out to meet him, but I didn't know what to say. I told him earlier that day that I was going to buy a test, but he didn't think twice about it because it was just part of the drill.

He detected my awkwardness immediately.

"What's going on?"

I took his hand and led into the bathroom. He was confused, kind of half-smiling because I was kind of half-smiling.

"Will you just look?" I insisted.

When he saw it, he looked at me before he picked it up. I raised my brows and with my eyes instructed him to pick it up. I watched him hold and try to make sense of what he was looking at. His beautiful olive skin began to appear greener and paler. I had never seen him look that way before. Fear rose up from the pit of my stomach.

"I'm not getting rid of it. I'm keeping it whether you want to stay with me or not!" My defensiveness was immediate. He was still green with shock when I threw myself onto the bed in explosive tears.

"Wait! Hold on!" He followed me. "Why would you think that I wouldn't stay?"

"I don't know! You look weird right now and I'm just letting you know what I'm going to do. I won't change my mind." The confidence and clarity I felt in that moment was something I hadn't experienced before. I felt a sense of purpose.

"Mike, I want this. I get it if you don't."

"Of course I want it, Chantel." He seemed shocked that I would suggest raising a baby alone. "You didn't give me a minute to process what it meant."

"I'm sorry."

"Don't be sorry. I love you."

After a couple days went by and we began to absorb how much our life was going to change, I decided to call my mom. When I told her, there wasn't a pause. No questions about what I was going to do or how we were going to make it work. There was no mention of the fact that I was now carrying a child that would forever bond her to the woman her husband had an affair with. There was just a simple, gleeful statement.

"I'm going to be a nana!"

It was the first time in years I had heard so much warmth and positivity in her voice. I felt love in her voice. I hung up the phone and ran to the bathroom mirror, pulled up my t-shirt and placed my hand on my belly.

"I know you don't know it yet but it's because of you I am never going to give up," I whispered. Every dream I felt I had lost, every idea of who I should become one day disappeared. I felt a deep sense of responsibility to this little person growing inside of me. I felt it was a boy, but only time would tell.

My first prenatal visit happened to be the day before a family wedding. Despite having made it clear to both of our families that we were going to be together regardless of what they thought, not everyone was excited about seeing us together. So, given the drama of the previous few years, we decided to only tell his parents and immediate family. Everyone else would have to wait until I was farther along.

It was a beautiful wedding, everything I dreamed of having one day. Mike and I danced and laughed, and had a great time celebrating the newlyweds. For a crowd who knew I was the daughter of the man who essentially destroyed the family, everyone was really kind to me. At one point, I sat back and looked around, thinking *this is going to be my family now*. I started surrendering to the idea that maybe this *can* work.

As we said our goodbyes, Mike thought there was one particular guest we could share our happy news with. But instead of offering congratulations, this person's wide, tipsy smile faded.

"He's going to be a bastard, huh?"

I took a deep breath and walked away without saying a word. I had often heard my father and Dza Dza use that term as an insult, but I didn't realize it had some contextual meaning. Even so, I was humiliated.

Mike did his best to console me and apologize.

"Chantel, Fuck them! Who cares what they think!?"

He Put a Ring on It

Near the end of my first trimester, my morning sickness finally began to subside. Toast and orange juice were the only things I had been able to stomach in order to choke down that horse pill prenatal vitamin every day. Being responsible for my baby's growth and development replaced my previous obsession with my weight and eating. For the first time since I was maybe twelve years old, I was eating normally.

Just before Christmas, my mom took me shopping for some things for the baby. I had mentioned to her that I wanted to decorate the baby's room in a Winnie the Pooh theme, so she bought the baby a huge stuffed Winnie the Pooh, and wall décor for a nursery we didn't have yet. I was seeing a side of her I forgot existed. She was trying and for the first time in a long time, I felt special to her. She also bought me a book, *What to Expect When You're Expecting.* It was the first book I was interested in reading that wasn't about a celebrity. Although her intentions were to help me, it ended up being a book that she regretted buying for me altogether. What was supposed to be a mother-daughter date turned into another shopping disaster (like most of middle school). While we were having lunch, I opened the book and skimmed the pages telling me what stage of development my baby was in, and then I saw a note about a section that I should not read unless I had a reason to. Obviously I turned to it immediately. The section was a caution about cats and toxoplasmosis. I had a cat! I cleaned the litter box! The paranoia set in and our lunch went from: *yay, a baby!* to: *OMG my baby is going to be born without a head!* Of course this was how our time together would go.

On Christmas day, instead of driving home from the party we were at, Mike asked if I wanted to go down to the city and look at the Chicago Christmas tree. This was something I loved to do every year, but because I was exhausted, I was reluctant. Mike promised me we didn't have to get out of the car, so I agreed. It was snowing heavily and the roads were just as bad as they were the day we went to the Shedd Aquarium on our first date. I just closed my eyes and prayed we'd make it. When we finally got into the city, Mike, the one who has a memory of direction like no one else I knew, seemed to be lost.

"Um, do you know where you're going?"

"Yeah…" The way he said it wasn't very convincing.

"But the tree isn't this way!" I argued.

"I know, I just want to show you something first."

When we came to a stop, everything was blanketed in snow, but the sign said we were at North Ave Beach.

"What are we doing?" I asked.

"Let's go for a walk," Mike said.

"You're kidding, right?" Pregnant, and not in the mood to walk in the middle of the snowstorm, I reminded him that he said we wouldn't have to get out of the car.

Frustrated with my response, he asked again. He almost convinced me, and then a police officer shined his brights into our car and pulled up behind us.

"Damn it!"

"Mike, it'll be okay."

As the police officer approached our car, Mike was concerned about the past restraining order situation rearing its head, but I couldn't help but think about how many times this has happened to us. We always found places to park the car and make out, and more than a few times an officer would tap on the window, shine their flashlight in, and tell us to get dressed and go home. It made me smile. This time, the officer just told us we couldn't park there.

We drove around for a while longer, looking for someplace to park, blocked by huge snow drifts at every turn. Finally, Mike gave up and pulled over. He got out of the car, walked around to my side and opened my door. He didn't ask me to get out, but he knelt down in six inches of snow, and reached into his pocket.

"Would you marry me, Chantel?"

I covered my face and started crying instantly. "Yes of course, Yes!" I couldn't even see the ring through all the tears.

He shivered and leaned in to hug me, dropping a pile of snow onto my lap.

I kissed him and asked why he first brought us to North Ave Beach. A snow plow was headed our way, so we needed to move. Now that I could see again, I stared at my ring as Mike maneuvered the car through the snow. He explained that he wanted to propose to me in the spot where I told him I wanted to run away from it all. The night on the rocks, when I said I wanted to move to Los Angeles and get out of this place. He wanted me to see that my life could be good here, with him, if I gave it a chance. If I gave *us* a chance.

Is That My Son?

I had smoked since I was twelve, but the minute I found out I was pregnant, I quit cold turkey. By the time I hit my final semester, I could no longer tolerate smoke at all. Unfortunately, every single person in the office smoked, and they smoked all. day. long. I was grateful for the family who gave me the job to begin with, but I couldn't breathe and I was tired of smelling like an ashtray. They rarely opened the windows in that office and I was suffocating. So, I decided to quit that, too.

My father had an opening for a starting position and offered Mike a salary that would allow me to work part time or not at all until the baby came. Despite the multiple reasons why Mike shouldn't have accepted the position, we needed the money. My father never bothered to call me or try to talk to me to salvage any semblance of a relationship, but I think this was his way of trying to repair all that he had done.

My mom even rented a hall and threw us a baby shower and invited *everyone*, including Mike's side of the family—even his mother, too. She bought me a pink and blue maternity dress and a necklace with Winnie the Pooh on it. We had a cake and got everything we registered for and more. She showed me that our two families could put all of their feelings aside for the first time, and I was grateful.

★

It was a hot June, and my due date came and went. Even though I tried to keep busy, I was swollen, lonely, and miserable. The sweet moments of my second semester where I could easily clean the house and sing Mariah Carey's "Always Be My Baby" at the top of my lungs hoping my growing boy (I was *sure* it was a boy) could hear and feel how wanted he was. Some of our friends from high school would come around to visit every once in a while, but not having much in common with us now we were beginning to realize how much our lives were changing.

Up until this point I hadn't cared about my weight like I did all the years before. But when I had to go to the doctor every week that last month and the scale moved 3-5lbs *a week*, I was beside myself. I stopped leaving the house. My nose didn't even look the same! I had taken it as a source of pride that the only stretch marks I had were on my lower belly. That all changed by the time my due date came and went. The doctor said it was typical for first time moms to go overdue, and that he would allow me to carry up to two weeks before they would consider an induction. I felt like an ogre.

Knowing how uncomfortable I was, and how depressed I was becoming, Mike thought it would be a good idea for me to get out of the house. Every day, when he got home from work, we went on an evening walk. That was great until we ran into his friend's mom, who saw me and didn't take a second to pause before running her mouth.

"Wow! I didn't even recognize you! You've gained so much weight!"

I cried the entire way home, and told Mike I wasn't leaving the house again until this baby was out of me. He didn't argue. She was an asshole for saying that to me, but I felt like I didn't look like myself anymore. My legs no longer had a shape. They were so swollen my shoes barely fit.

The two weeks went by, and I finally went into labor the day before I was scheduled to be induced. Mike and I checked into the hospital, and called everyone to let them know. My mom was excited, and told Mike to call her when the baby was born. We never thought about asking anyone to be there with us that day. Mike and I had each other.

After 12 hours of labor and pushing in all ways possible, the baby's heart rate fell and I was rushed into surgery. There wasn't even time for Mike to get scrubbed in. A mask went over my face and a nurse counted down *three...two...* and I was out.

When I came to, I was in the recovery room, trying to remember why I was there to begin with. As the fog cleared, I turned to look at the nurse who was fixing my IV.

"Congratulations, you're a mom," she said.

"What is it?" I asked.

"It's a boy!"

I knew it! I smiled and asked how much he weighed.

"9 lbs. 2 oz," she said.

Thank God, I thought. *That's 10 pounds off my body.*

She told me that he was just fine and would be in my room soon. I assumed that Mike was in the operating room with me, but I found out later that he met our son for the first time in the hallway outside of the delivery room. When they rushed me into surgery for the emergency C-section, no one informed him what to do next. So, he stood in that hall waiting, not knowing what to do until a nurse came out with one of those clear baby beds with a baby in it. As she passed him, Mike stopped her.

"Hey, is that my baby?" He asked.

"Are you Mr. Ferraro?"

"Yes, I am."

"Then, yes, this is your son!"

You Are the Inspiration

It turns out that being baptized, receiving all the sacraments, and attending Catholic school for nine years of my life was not enough for any of the Catholic churches in our area to give us the okay to baptize our son without becoming parishioners. Mike and I were not quite sure where we wanted to plant our flag when it came to religion in general, but parents on both sides made it clear to us that we needed to baptize our baby boy as soon as possible in case something happened to him. My father said if he happened to die, without being baptized, he would not go straight to heaven. He might not go straight to hell, but ending up in the no-man's land of purgatory didn't sound great. I never felt right about that belief, but as a new mom, who never loved anything like I loved my son, the pressure was on to get a priest to pour that water on his head.

Mike and I had talked about finding a church anyway, so we made some calls, and visited a dozen churches, and eventually we did find one that agreed to save my son's soul without requiring a full commitment of attendance from us. With that handled, our families returned their attention to the fact that we still weren't married. The process of visiting all those churches gave us the impression that they were more interested in membership numbers and money than anything about faith, so Mike and I decided we didn't want to get married in a church.

It would have been nice to wait a year and not walk down the aisle with an extra sixty-seven pounds of baby weight, but we could only endure the family pressure for so long.

We decided Michael Jr. should have officially committed parents, so we agreed to make it happen sooner rather than later. Since my parents had thrown us a baby shower just a few months before, it was clear that we were on our own to pay for our wedding. We didn't have any extra money to spend, but we also wanted something a little better than a quick courthouse nuptial, so I booked a little event space in the city Mike grew up in. Because it was on such short notice, they didn't have our actual anniversary date available, but they did have the day before: Friday October 4th. For $250, we got to rent the space for two hours the day before our sixth anniversary.

It was an old building, but I liked the vibe. The wooden floors creaked under every step, and the dusty silk plants and flowers that were draped around the windows had strings of white Christmas lights for ambiance. If you wanted music, you had to bring your own. If you needed an officiant, they could provide one for you for an additional fee. The aisle was narrow, and had a white runner that led to a white, wicker arch with a windchime hanging from the center of it. The wicker arch was most definitely acquired from an estate sale, where I'm confident it once resided outside. Why else would it have a wind chime dangling from it? My wedding day was clearly not going to be anything close to the dream I had growing up, but it was what we could afford. With the past family drama and having a new baby, we just wanted to get it over with. We made a pact that if we made it to ten years, we would renew our vows and have the kind of wedding I always wanted.

Two weeks before the wedding, my mom and I went shopping for a wedding dress. Michael was three months old now, and I had lost some weight since he was born, but my body still felt like mashed potatoes. I didn't want to hate my body after creating the most perfect beautiful human being I had ever seen in my life, but I was only 20, and I was convinced that I would never wear a bathing suit again. I had so many bright red stretch marks on my belly, hips, and thighs that I looked like Freddy Krueger had slashed me up in a nightmare—apparently cocoa butter doesn't prevent everyone from getting stretchmarks after all. I was less than enthusiastic about the whole thing, but my mom insisted.

Our first stop was a chain bridal store whose whole sales pitch was that anyone can buy a wedding dress off the rack. The saleswoman watched me carefully as I pushed Michael in his stroller through rows of satin and lace gowns. She didn't bother to hide her condescending attitude, insisting that we not touch anything. I just wanted to go home, but my mom was determined to at least find a white dress. There was a JC Penney in the same mall, and they happened to have a small bridal department. The dresses they carried were just what I was looking for, and they even had my size. I chose a simple white lace dress with a few pearls sewn onto the bodice, and we found a little suit for Michael to wear. Mike wasn't part of our shopping adventure, but he found a brown suit and tie—on clearance at Structure, actually. It was a little big on him, but he still looked handsome in it.

Our wedding day arrived like most October mornings in Illinois, clear and brisk. I got up, fed the baby, took a shower, and turned on the television, just like any other day. I didn't expect this wedding day to be anything I dreamed of, but I didn't expect to be completely alone the whole day either.

I found out last minute that my father had some big-time clients coming to visit his shop that afternoon, and apparently that visit required both of my parents and Mike to be there. No big deal, just both of the bride's parents and the groom busy working the afternoon of the wedding.

It was so shitty of my father to do this. He really couldn't reschedule the visit for another day? I told Mike that the minute he could find another place to work, I wanted him too. I didn't care how much my father was paying him, I didn't want the same work-before-everything-else attitude for us. I didn't want my father to have any influence over our lives.

Getting ready by myself was another way this day wasn't at all what I envisioned. Nobody thought that *maybe* I'd want something to feel special that day, *maybe* it would be nice to have some company, or someone to help me with the baby while I got ready. It would have been nice to have someone to talk about what I was thinking and feeling as I headed into this next chapter of my life. Instead I had my lonely reflection in the mirror.

I tried to convince myself *it's really not that big of a deal anyway.* Before I allowed it to really upset me, I got my son dressed. He in his little tux was the only thing that could pull me out of my head. He was just big enough to prop up on our couch in between the two back cushions. He really was the cutest baby I had ever seen. While most brides pose with their bridesmaids before the event, I had my son. Just us. As he smiled and cooed it made my heart melt. My father's words to me that he had never seen a good looking "Polish-Italian" didn't hold up. Mike and I really did make a beautiful baby.

I had a friend coming to drive the baby and me to the event space, so I gave her a quick call and asked her to pick up a few disposable cameras since a photographer was not in our budget. When she arrived, I stood in the closet door mirror and directed her to shoot a picture of me applying my red lipstick.

When I was a little girl, I loved looking at my mom's wedding photos, and photos of brides getting ready. They're iconic, really: Applying lipstick, putting on a necklace, sometimes the bride's mother is helping her, sometimes a sister, sometimes a best friend. I love those photos. *Maybe next time,* I thought, as I stood in the mirror alone.

When I arrived at the venue, my friend held the baby so I could practice walking down the aisle a few times with my flowers and white satin heels. I was surprised by how cute everything looked. They added white bows on each pew and the white Christmas lights glowed. The officiant was an old man who had a kind voice and an outfit to make him look legit. We didn't invite many guests, but I was grateful for the friends who showed up.

Before the ceremony began, my mom scooped up the baby, making a point to show that she would take care of him during the ceremony. I think maybe she liked the idea of rubbing it in Mike's mom's face, as if holding Michael was the final trophy. It signaled the illusion that the affair was ancient history, that everything was great now. Mike's mom probably didn't even notice—her attention was on her new, younger beau.

My father breezed in just in time to walk me down the aisle. I was trying to stay hidden while also trying to signal instructions to my brother, who was responsible for pressing play on the boom box when it was time. We chose the beginning of the song "You Are the Inspiration" by Chicago for my processional. Once I heard the music, I didn't care about who was or wasn't there anymore. This was about us. Under the windchime, Mike gazed back at me with those kind, brown eyes that had always felt like safety.

TWELVE

Everything is Wonderful

★

Well, That Didn't Last Long

I always knew I wanted to be a mom. Still, I settled into motherhood surprisingly well considering it was light years away from the California dream of being an actress/model. The stretchmarks clawed into my skin were a daily reminder that it was time to let that dream die. I had prepared myself to lose the baby weight. I had not prepared myself for this new category of body-shame. I resolved to focus on what was in front of me: A sweet little man who had his daddy's eyes and my smile. He was my world, and even though I didn't have a clear picture of what mothering a son might be, I had learned plenty about what I was not going to do. No one would raise him but me—that was a non-negotiable, and Mike understood why.

Shortly after the wedding, my dad gave Mike a raise, which derailed the plan for him to find a different job. The higher wage allowed us to move into a larger apartment with a pool, so we said we'd give it just a little more time. Then my dad started talking about giving us his business one day, and the money clouded our judgment just enough for us to think that maybe this could work if we did things differently than my father had.

Every morning when Mike went to work, I'd put Michael Jr. in his highchair and make him his favorite breakfast, eggs and toast with jelly. He did a great job feeding himself (and the kitchen floor). I loved watching his little fingers do their best to pick up the pieces of the scrambled eggs; I didn't mind cleaning up the mess he made. I memorized all the nursery songs and committed myself to becoming the mom I always wanted to be. Our everyday TV lineup was Blue's Clues and Sesame Street, and going to the laundromat was our weekly field trip. I kept our apartment spotless and made dinner for Mike every day when he got home. The routine I created for us was the most consistent one I ever had in my life.

I was determined to reach my pre-baby weight, so I did my exercise videos while Michael napped, and I even bought one of those plastic sauna suits to wear over my clothes to sweat off as much water weight as I could. Our apartment being on the third floor also helped. Hauling a baby, groceries, and laundry up three flights of stairs was a regular bonus workout. Nothing was going to stop me from reaching my goal.

As much as I adored being a stay-at-home mom, sometimes it got lonely. Desperate for adult interaction, I would often bring Michael to my father's shop to visit my mom and Mike. She loved seeing the baby and I loved watching her be his nana. I wondered if she was that way with me when I was a baby, before everything went crazy. I could only visit Mike for a few minutes and steal a kiss, because my father was still my father and he made it clear that Mike was there to work, and I shouldn't distract him with Michael. Whenever I would get upset about it, my mom would remind me how much money Mike was earning, so I bit my tongue.

When I began to see a change in Mike that was all too familiar, I chalked it up to him assuming the nature of a tool and die worker. It wasn't until one afternoon when he came home early that I realized the reason his mood was shifting wasn't about the work at all. It was about my father.

"I need to tell you something," Mike said. He sat down at our kitchen table looking defeated.

"Okay?" I didn't like where this was headed.

"Your father fired me today."

"What? Why?"

Mike was reluctant to tell me what had been going on because I was finally in a good place with my mom and he wanted to protect me, but he told me that my father had discovered AOL chatrooms and had been using them to meet other women online. Apparently he had become so consumed with this that he was skipping our Friday night bowling league to hang out online chatting with random women, instead of working late like he said he was.

"So why did he fire you?" I asked.

"Because I told your mom what I saw. Your dad hasn't changed, and I told your mom she needs to leave him for good this time."

I didn't know what to say at first, but then I did what I always do. I called my mom. And like always, the conversation was useless. She was "handling" it. Thankful Michael was taking a nap, my mind raced and I went into panic mode. My family was falling apart again, and I didn't know how to fix it. How the hell would we pay rent? Mike reassured me he would find a job but that wasn't the point. I was furious that we trusted this man again.

"I knew it, Mike. We sold our soul to the devil himself taking his money. We should've never allowed him to convince us that this family could ever be a family."

I Don't Want To Be This Way

My father did eventually reach out to Mike to give him his position back, but we decided that enough was enough. We didn't want his business or any part of that life. I got a part-time job at Coconuts Record Store, but it didn't pay much and I'd heard about an opportunity to be a cocktail waitress at a nearby dance club where I could earn a lot more, and still be at home with Michael all day. Getting married young and already being a mom at 21, I hadn't experienced the bar scene at all, so there was something appealing about it. Mike never liked the idea but knew he couldn't convince me not to. Besides, we needed to bring in money. The job was short-lived because the promised wages weren't worth the repeated assault on my dignity. The uniform of Daisy Dukes and a very tight top put us on display, and I soon discovered we servers had no protection from the drunk, disgusting men who felt entitled to ogle and grope us when we walked by. After one of those creeps took advantage of my barely-there shorts and the bouncer did nothing, I quit on the spot. Enough was enough.

Eventually Mike got a job working for *his* family's business. Regardless of whose son he was, the starting pay there was just barely over minimum wage. After searching the classifieds for weeks, I finally found a full-time job that allowed me to bring Michael with me because I was terrified to leave him. A local daycare was looking for a cook and a bus driver. The job didn't pay much, but the incentive was I only had to pay $25 a week for Michael's care, and I could see him all day long. I had no experience in the field other than being a daycare kid myself, but working a job where my son could join me was enough motivation for me to figure it out. The new jobs were helping us make ends meet, but we wanted to buy a home eventually, and with no savings, terrible credit, and no degrees, that just wasn't in our near future. We had to figure something out and find a way to save money.

Following the discovery of my father's new, AOL-powered cheating, my parents' marriage was in shambles again. I forced myself to keep my distance from them because I needed stability. I didn't want to get sucked into the drama that felt inescapable. I had my own little family to take care of, but it killed me to see my siblings neglected so badly. I worried about them. My sister had lost a ton of weight playing basketball for school, and she told me she was having Slurpees for dinner most nights. I feared she was following in my footsteps when it came to her eating and restriction patterns. She also told me that my brother was being bullied really badly in school, but refused to burden my parents with it. Since my parents had become so unreliable, it mainly fell to my siblings to check in on Busia and Dza Dza, and make sure Busia hadn't set the kitchen on fire trying to light her cigarette in the stove burners.

They lived just two houses away from my parents now. The whole point of living that close was so they could be cared for, but that wasn't happening how it should have. Dza Dza never fully recovered from his stroke and Busia was going blind and showing signs of dementia. Knowing that they needed help and we needed a place to live, Mike and I came up with the idea to move in with them. It would be difficult to go from having our own space to sharing a single room for all three of us, but it would be temporary. Dza Dza wasn't super excited about it but Busia didn't hesitate to welcome us in. She was lonely, and she loved Michael jr, and needed someone to take her to doctor visits and grocery shopping. The arrangement solved several problems: we could save up for a house, we could make sure Busia and Dza Dza had what they needed, and I liked that I would be around to help my siblings. It was just a year. We could do it.

Busia's decline was heartbreaking to witness. She was taking walks down the street and forgetting how to get home, and she would have me take her to appointments with multiple optometrists just to have each one of them tell her the macular degeneration was incurable. The stress of it all didn't take long to catch up with me, and I coped with it the way I always had: I restricted. I binged and purged. I was using some new diet drops, too. I wasn't managing well. Working full time, caring for Busia and Dza Dza, and trying to be a good mom, while having a front row seat to the chaos at home—it was difficult to watch the demise of my family, even if it wasn't my problem anymore.

My father was blatantly flaunting his behavior, no longer sleeping at home, and came and went as he pleased at work. My mom would cry to me and say how she was done with it all, but then wouldn't take action. I got the feeling that she was still holding on to hope, and it was driving me insane. Realtors were coming by to show the house, and it was always a mess. Dirty underwear on the bathroom floor, dishes piled in the sink—no one could be bothered to even tidy it up. Potential buyers would walk into the house and find my siblings watching TV because they weren't warned about visitors dropping by.

After a long talk with my sister about how things were going, I called my mom at work and asked her to stop by Busia's house to fill me in on what was happening. I was steaming. I couldn't understand how she could neglect my siblings so blatantly. When she got there, Busia was in the kitchen smoking a cigarette, and Dza Dza was watching television in his bedroom. Mike had taken Michael to pick up some take out for us. I noticed that she was in a particularly good mood, which I thought was odd. As the conversation went on, I realized why. My father had said something to her that had her considering working it out again.

"What the fuck is wrong with you?!" I screamed. "Can't you see what this is doing to everyone? I know you can't see what it's doing to you, but do you at all care about the kids? They are not okay!"

She then pointed her finger at me and told me to watch my mouth and that I didn't have a say in her life.

"Are you fucking kidding me?" I exploded on her. "I don't have a say?! I don't know if you know this because you're a delusional bitch, but I am the only one who should have a say!"

I don't know if it was the lack of food, the diet drops I was using, or all the years of taking this, but something in me snapped.

She raised her hand to slap me and I grabbed her wrist.

"Don't you fucking touch me! You will never touch me again, you hear me?" I pushed her away and went to my bedroom. I broke. Screaming at the top of my lungs in hysterics, I slammed my fists into the bed. "Why are you like this? Why can't you just fucking see?"

She had followed me into my room, and Busia came in to see what all the commotion was about. I saw my mom raise her hand to slap me again, as if hurting me was going to calm me down. The exact moment I lifted my foot to push my mom away, Busia stepped in between, and my foot landed on her instead, slamming her into the wall.

"Look what you have done, Chantel!" My mom wasted no time before hurling guilt and shame at me. She helped Busia out of the room as I spiraled.

Oh god, what have I done? Why am I like this? I cried and cried and cried. I was so ashamed of myself. *How could I have hurt Busia? I don't want to be this way. I don't like who I am around my mother. I can't live around this anymore.*

When Mike got back, I told him we needed to move, and within two weeks, we had found a house to rent.

Cat's in the Cradle

I carried an incredible amount of guilt for what happened with Busia, but I also felt the weight of leaving her and Dza Dza after they so generously allowed us to stay with them for as long as we had, rent free. It felt heavy leaving my siblings as well, knowing that they were not being properly cared for. Especially with the hardest years of school still ahead of them: high school.

My sister and I had grown closer since she wasn't the same pain-in-the-butt baby that I had to hide behind a cereal box from. She loved being around Michael Jr. and I loved watching them play. She was brave about experimenting with her style, and I admired how she embraced her dark side in her fashion. One time I brought over a disposable camera and we had a little photo shoot. It's one of my favorite memories with her. I was far from perfect and there was so much I hadn't even begun to figure out, but I wanted to be there for her. As I began to see the struggles she was facing, something in me shifted. I wanted to protect her.

When it came to my brother, we butted heads more. I tried to help, but it always ended up as an argument. He seemed to disagree with anything I had to say about our parents, or the house, or the business, or Busia and Dza Dza just because *I* said it. I felt like he just refused to accept the reality we were facing, and his allegiance to my father was mind-boggling. Even when he reaped the destruction of what my parents sowed, he would still find a way to minimize it or write it off. My father was still everything to him and what little he actually saw of him was somehow enough to make believe he was some kind of hero.

Months after Mike and I moved, the house finally sold. What was once our family home, my parents' American Dream, was crumbling around my brother and sister without explanation or sympathy. My father's once-successful business was in collapse, and my mother was dissociating from it all. Moving day was only a couple weeks away and she hadn't lined anything up, so even from a distance, even in my frustration and anger, I felt responsible for making sure my mom and my siblings had somewhere to go. I ended up finding them a nice town home in a great school district. The rent was a little out of my mom's price range, but she said she would make it work.

Just before moving day, I was at the house to help with packing when my father stopped by. Apparently, he was in the neighborhood visiting Busia and Dza Dza. He looked around, visited with my brother, said hello to my sister, and then he paused. Some kind of realization hit him that day, but I think the regret I saw cross his face had more to do with losing a house that felt like an achievement than anything else. He looked at Michael Jr. who was propped up on my hip, and then he looked at me.

"What?" I snapped.

"How is your mother?"

"How do you think she is, Dad?" His guilt may have been weighing on him, but still this man couldn't give a shit about us, even if he tried.

"Listen, Dad, she *will be* fine. But you need to leave. For good. She doesn't know she can do it alone because you keep coming back. Go!"

"Okay."

I heard a finality in his *okay* and I began to cry as he walked out the door.

I turned back to the task of packing and noticed a box of CDs. The Harry Chapin single, "Cat's in the Cradle," caught my eye. It was my father's favorite song. I grabbed the CD and ran out to his truck before he drove away.

"Here," I said, handing it to him. "Isn't this your favorite song?"

He looked at me without response as I turned and went back into the house.

★

When my mother's family showed up on moving day to help load everything into the truck, they were overwhelmed by how much still wasn't packed, and directed their questions about this to *me,* instead of my mother, who had been avoiding everything she possibly could. Then I noticed they were taking things from the house and loading them into their own cars instead of the truck. My mother shrugged it off.

"They can have it," she said.

I understood she was grieving the loss of her marriage and her house, but I wasn't about to let them take my family's memories away because my mother didn't care anymore. I directed Mike to grab all of our family pictures, and my mother's record collection—I wanted to hold on to what reminded me of my childhood, even if it was shattered.

New House, New Everything

Our first home was a rental, a tiny old ranch built in the 60s, with three bedrooms, one bathroom, and a narrow kitchen, where my arms could cook on the stove top and wash dishes in the sink across from it if I wanted to. Mike was convinced that landlords couldn't care less about people's stories, but at the walkthrough, I decided to be completely honest about our situation. I warned him that we had terrible credit but were working hard on changing our lives. I explained to him that Mike and I had been together since we were teenagers, that we had come from chaotic families, and that we were trying to break free from it all and make things stable for our son. I pleaded with him to give us a chance.

I was on pins and needles for days, trying to focus on my work at the daycare, and praying that my vulnerability with a stranger wasn't in vain, and that this kind, middle eastern man would take our word that we were responsible enough to pay on time. It took about a week, but to our surprise, he called and told us that we were approved! He told Mike that he, too, had children and he would do the same for them. He expected us to keep our end of the bargain and to never be late on payments. We made him a promise, and signed the lease the next day.

My job at the daycare was going well. Washing dishes for hours and preparing lunch for seventy littles wasn't glamorous, but it was teaching me structure and routine in a way I had never experienced. Eventually, I was trained to oversee some of the classes to relieve teachers for breaks and assist as needed. I loved playing with the kids and seeing their little minds learn foundational childhood skills. When the director asked me if I would ever consider going back to school so that I could lead my own preschool class one day, I said I would. The only problem was that I didn't have the money. She told me they would pay for my certification as long as I met certain requirements, so I decided to do it.

Mike was also prompted into a better paying position at his family's company, and he was so proud of me for taking this new path. Being away from the mess of my parents and focusing on us was paying off in so many ways. We were thriving and felt hopeful. I still talked to my sister often, and I was glad to provide a place for her to come by on the weekends to get away from the chaos. She told me about my mom's dating experiences with men she met online and it reinforced my decision to keep my distance for a while. A door was opening for me and I didn't want to screw it up.

The child development classes I was taking were not only helping me become an early childhood teacher, they were helping me become a better mom, and they were helping me realize that my own childhood experiences had become part of my brain wiring and were still affecting me. Memories began to surface, and things that I hadn't ever thought about were opening up and needed healing. One morning, on the way to work, I heard the song "Wonderful" by Everclear, and even though it was on the regular radio rotation, something about it hit me differently at that moment. It was naming everything I had felt as a child and was still feeling as an adult, but didn't know how to process.

When I was first placed in a classroom on my own, I didn't want to instruct the kids, I dove into their play with them. Every time I chose an activity that Mean Miss Monika wouldn't allow me to participate in, a little part of myself healed. Every time a child needed to go to the bathroom during naptime, I didn't question if they really had to, or shame them for having an accident. I knew how that felt and I made it my mission to never be the memory Miss Monika was to me. Even though I was an adult, a wife, and a mom, I approached the children with a childlike demeanor myself. I decorated my room in all kinds of colors and themes. I wanted it to feel approachable and safe with a splash of sunshine. Part of me was re-growing up with them, and most telling, I found myself worth growing. I showed up in the brightest clothing I had. I did my hair and wore a full face of makeup just because it was fun. This led to face-painting gigs and doing wedding makeup for some of the other teachers. My life was starting to make sense, and my eating disorder behaviors completely dissolved.

After our landlord renewed our lease with a Rent-to-Own agreement, Mike and I decided it was time to try to have another baby. Michael would be starting Kindergarten in the fall, and because we had started our family so young, we wanted to have all of our children before I turned 30. I got off the pill, and within a few months I was pregnant. We were so excited and didn't hesitate to tell everybody the minute we found out, but one night just as I hit the four-month mark, I noticed blood on my underwear. I called my doctor and went in for an ultrasound the next day. There was no heartbeat.

That moment was absolutely devastating. A few teachers at the day-care were also pregnant, and having to show up every day knowing my baby died inside of me while theirs was growing strong became more than I could bear. I grew more and more depressed, and just couldn't be the sunny Miss Chantel I was before. Even though working at that preschool/daycare was the best job I had ever had, it felt like it was the right time for a change.

Two months later, I was pregnant again. But this time, Mike and I kept the news to ourselves. From the moment I found out, I was a par-anoid wreck. Constantly checking to see if I was bleeding or suffering through bad headaches because I didn't want to take anything that might hurt the baby. It didn't help that I now worried about Michael when he was at school. Columbine introduced a whole new fear. Having a five-year-old come home to tell you about where to go in a lock down was more than a little unnerving. I was happy about being pregnant again, but something was slipping.

I decided it was time to reach out to my mom again, or maybe I just wanted a more familiar kind of stress than not knowing if the baby inside of me was going to survive this time, but whatever the real reason, I started calling my mom sometimes when the phone lines at work were dead. I had found a job answering calls for an HVAC company—it was simple and I wouldn't mind leaving it when the time came. I knew my dad had moved to Arizona with his new wife after Dza Dza died, and he took Busia with him. My sister had kept me updated on my mom's internet dating escapades and she was so fed up with it, she decided to move to Arizona to live with my dad for a while. Maybe he wouldn't be so awful now, she reasoned. Anything was better than staying with my mom at that time.

I learned that my mom was moving again. Turns out, even working two jobs wasn't enough for her to afford the town house I helped her get when my dad left, and she passive aggressively blamed me for finding it. *Of course,* I thought.

After I hung up the phone, a woman at work noticed I was visibly upset. She asked me to join her for lunch and asked me something I hadn't had a female ask me in years.

"How are you doing?" she asked.

I kind of laughed and realized that I didn't know where to begin. "How am I doing? Well, do you have a year to spare?"

She didn't get the joke.

"I'm fine," I continued. "Crazy, but fine." I didn't want to get into it with her.

She just looked at me in a motherly sort of way, and asked:"Do you go to church?"

"I used to."

"Why don't you go anymore?"

"Because all they care about is money, and most of them are hypocrites like my father."

"Aw hun, I'm sorry to hear that. I just wanted to let you know that a new church is starting up at a nearby high school and my husband and I are church elders. We are starting a weekly Bible study at our home if you and your husband are interested. The church has a great kid's program and—"

I cut her off.

"The church is in a high school?" Sorry, but that sounds a little 'Waco' weird," I said.

She laughed.

"I know it might to many traditional Catholics, but I promise you it is not. The church doesn't have the money for a building yet, but we have a great pastor. He's about your age and I think it might resonate with you and your family."

I didn't want to be rude, so I told her I would talk to my husband about it.

"Even if you aren't comfortable with the church, please feel free to come by our home on Thursdays at 6pm," she said. "We always have dinner before we start our study."

I went home that day and mentioned it to Mike. It all sounded weird to me, but I felt myself unraveling. Maybe a little God in our life could help.

Wait, I'm Having a Girl?

Leading up to the ultrasound, I assumed my anxiety was the aftermath of having a miscarriage, but when I heard *it's a girl* I knew instantly that my fear was bigger than wanting a healthy baby. I was already worried sick about every phase of her life. Mike was an amazing father, but the thought of raising a daughter filled me with terror. The childhood memories I had tried to suppress felt like they were about to break through like the Kool-Aid man. The bullies at school, dance, teachers who made me feel unworthy, the boys—oh my God, the boys—and men?! What if a family member touches her… no, I was never going to let that happen. I rarely left Michael with anyone and worried about his safety constantly, but having experienced sexual abuse, I was adamant that no one else was ever going to watch her. Ever.

The life I envisioned for her was different from what I had. I would be there to comfort her if she had bullies. I wouldn't let her quit. I would never let her father make her feel small. My mom and I were in a better place than we had been for a long time, but I was determined to create a different kind of mother-daughter relationship with my girl.

And then there was Michael. Mike and I wanted him to know how special he was and how special it was to be a big brother. I made sure to tell him all about her as she grew in my belly. We told him how much we loved him and how much we loved her. No favorites. Mike and I decided we wanted to spoil him a little before his sister came and changed everything, so we made use of the Disney timeshare Mike's family still had. We were grateful to be able to use it, because otherwise, a trip like this would not have been possible.

We arrived at Disney's Boardwalk hotel on September 9, 2001, and had tickets for Magic Kingdom the next day. It was the first time I had been there since the whole debacle with my dad when I was 16. We soaked in the experience as a family of three, and talked about what it was going to be like when our baby girl joined us. I dreamt of what she would look like even though my little boy with daddy's big, beautiful, brown eyes provided a clear example. *Could she have red hair like me?* I wondered. If the old wives' tale was true, then she was definitely going to be beautiful because she stole every sliver of beauty from me during those nine months. I knew my nose would return to normal, and the swelling would deflate eventually, I just wished I wasn't such an ugly pregnant person. My skin was red, my face was swollen, and my hair was dry, but I was happy. This was a small sacrifice to make to have her and I wanted to meet her so badly.

The morning of September 11, 2001, we were just getting up when I turned on the news. From the hotel's jacuzzi tub (a day of walking was not great for pregnancy sciatica), I learned that a plane had struck the World Trade Center. I yelled to Mike to come check it out, and watched as another plane crashed into the building on live TV. *Oh my God, what is going on?* I hoisted myself out of the tub and sat on the bed in my towel. We sat, wide-eyed and solemn, watching the news unfold throughout the day. Disney was closed for the first time in many years, and we, too, felt the widespread fear and devastation that rippled through the country. It was clear that our world was changed forever.

We cut our trip short, but since I was too afraid to fly, we rented a car and drove home. We had the radio set to the news for the entire 18-hour drive, afraid that we might be attacked again, afraid that we might get stranded somewhere, afraid that more awful things were in store. The heightened fear and uncertainty was agonizing. And so was spending 18 hours in a car with the baby mashing my sciatic nerve.

The way I saw the world was shifting. Columbine was horrific. September 11th was horrific. I didn't know how to deal with a world that felt so impossibly scary. I went back to work for a few weeks after the trip, but my paranoia intensified every day, and the depression was creeping over me; I couldn't shake it. By November, I was eight months pregnant and stopped working. I drowned myself in painting fairies and mermaids on the walls of the nursery and watched the show, *A Baby Story,* on TLC every day.

Hello, Daughter: A Christmas Miracle

I was nesting like crazy, and decorating for Christmas. Michael was at the fun age where he was anticipating Santa, so he loved it when Mike found us one of those cardboard fireplaces for hanging up our stockings–the same kind I had as a child. Even though our tiny home didn't have many windows, there wasn't a single one that wasn't dressed in garland and colorful Christmas lights. I was so excited to experience Christmas with a new baby in my arms.

One afternoon, I was washing dishes (we didn't have a dishwasher) and had my favorite show playing on the television. Typically, I would just have it playing in the background and would only stop and watch it when delivery time arrived. I was so excited to have my daughter naturally. Because so much time had passed since my c-section with Michael, my OBGYN said a natural birth was possible, and watching other women do something I had not yet experienced was fascinating to me. This particular episode stopped me in my tracks, though. I had watched so many episodes of this show, many involving complications, difficult labors, miscarriages, but for whatever reason this episode nudged me to pay attention in a way I can't quite explain.

The couple the show was documenting had been nervous to deliver their babies because they had previously lost two babies to a bacterial infection called group B strep. After the episode, I immediately went to my computer and logged in to AOL. I was part of a baby forum that I would check daily, and connect with other pregnant women. The episode bothered me so much I posted a question asking if anyone had heard of group B strep and if so, what their doctor did about it. Almost immediately, my post blew up. To my surprise, every one of the comments were women who not only knew of it, but who were due around the same time as I was, and were already tested for it. I learned it was a simple test, a swab taken in the vaginal canal. If the test was positive, the doctor would order an antibiotic to administer through an IV. A simple but potentially live-saving test. I was encouraged to call my doctor and ask to have it done since I still had time. I had a check up the next day, so I made sure to bring my concern about this to his attention. When I did, he said the test was not required and can often be wrong, so he never required it unless they had it for previous deliveries. Being young and naïve, I didn't press for it. I trusted his decision even though I felt uneasy.

He asked me if I was interested in scheduling an induction a little bit early since my first delivery with Michael was difficult, in part, because he was so big. I was immediately on board; the sciatica pain was becoming unbearable, and I couldn't wait to bring her home for Christmas. I even asked my mom if she wanted to be in the delivery room with us this time around since she didn't make it to the first one. She said she had to work but would come by after, since I wasn't being induced until the early evening anyway.

When the day came, everything was so calm, unlike the first time around. We checked in, went over all the doctor's details with me, and got into a hospital gown. Just as the nurse was about to hook me up to the Pitocin IV, a dark feeling settled in. I grabbed her hand and told her I hadn't been tested for group B strep and wondered if it was a problem. She gave me a concerned look, but said that it had its problems with inconsistency and reassured me that if the doctor didn't feel I needed it, not to worry about it. Once the Pitocin kicked in, it didn't take long before the contractions started, and they came on *strong*. I opted for the epidural as soon as I could, because even though I watched multiple women do this without drugs, I realized quickly that I was not like them, and I did not feel bad about it. By the time my mom arrived at the hospital, she and Mike laughed about how calm I was. The drugs had kicked in. The pain I was experiencing pre-epidural was long gone. Even as the labor intensified, my mother marveled at how I felt nothing when she suffered so terribly with all of her pregnancies, and prided herself on being drug free. Well, not me.

A couple of hours before I began to push, my daughter's heart rate became a little harder to track. So, they did a fetal scalp electrode where they attach a thin wire just under the baby's scalp to monitor her heart clearly. I was uneasy about it, but once again, I trusted the doctors. When the time came for me to push, Mike stood by my side as he held my leg and a nurse held the other. I had some trouble in the beginning because the epidural really numbed me out and I couldn't feel anything. My mother, visibly uncomfortable with the situation, stood about six feet from the doctor as she watched the moment take place without me screaming and crying in agony. As I pushed the final time, I started to cry and Mike rubbed my head and kissed me. They lifted her up to show me she was, indeed, a girl. I was shaking from the cocktail of meds and hormones, so they didn't hand her to me right away. This upset me but I wasn't given a choice, they just whisked her away to clean her up. I didn't get that magical bonding moment I was looking forward to. I wouldn't get to hold her at all for two excruciating days.

I asked Mike to go make sure she was alright because her cry wasn't a cry. It was a whimper. He didn't want to leave my side, but I demanded it. As he walked over to the flat infant warmer, I watched him intently as he watched the nurses suction her nose and mouth. I couldn't care less about what the doctor was saying to me about sewing me up. As Mike made his way back to me smiling, I could only focus on what I wasn't hearing.

"Mike, she's not crying normally." My face must have shown my worry.

A nurse that overheard me said she had a lot of fluid they were working on clearing out, but after they had her cleaned up, they would bring her to my room.

"What are you naming her?" The doctor asked, as a distraction.

The worry still hadn't lifted, but Mike and I looked at each other, and in unison said, "her name is Lily. Lily Angelina."

The doctor told us it was common for babies who ingest a lot of fluids to sound this way. He told us not to worry. The doctor left, and the room got eerily quiet. Eventually, I was taken to my recovery room, where my mom congratulated me, and kissed my head before leaving. Mike also left to relieve my sister who was staying with Michael. I fell asleep for a while and woke to a nurse changing my IV.

"Are you nursing?" She asked.

I nodded..

"Well, then let's get your baby girl to you!"

I smiled as I struggled to push myself up. *I have a baby girl now,* I thought. I couldn't wait to meet her.

About twenty minutes later, the nurse returned looking serious. "Unfortunately, we are not able to bring her to you right now, but would you like to go see her?"

My heart sank.

"I knew it! I knew something was wrong! Yes, please take me to her."

The nurse got me into a wheelchair, and explained that Lily was having a difficult time breathing and that her coloring wasn't right.

As we entered the nursery, a new doctor was standing over her. When he finished up, he let me know that they needed to monitor her a while. Something about a shunt that should close, and that it was not doing what it was supposed to be doing. In a flurry of panic and tears, I told the doctor that I hadn't been tested for group B strep and I just *knew* that something was wrong. Then I really started to cry. He reassured me that they would be testing her for everything and treating her for everything. From a wheelchair, I watched as my hour-old infant, my sweet baby girl, was poked and prodded. She was purplish-blue, and so tiny, hooked up to all those monitors and tubes. I was beside myself, sure that the helplessness I felt would crush me.

The nurses in the unit felt it was best to bring me back to my room, a shared room. The mom on the other side of the curtain had given birth to a healthy baby boy who was right there in the room with her. I listened to them and overheard a nurse directing her on the best ways to breastfeed. I lay there, staring, my mind in a million different places.

God, why? What have I done? Why her? It's because she's a girl, isn't it? You must not think I deserve a girl. What am I going to tell Michael if something happens? He is so looking forward to being a big brother. I cannot lose her. God, you can't take her away from me. God, if you take her from us, you're going to have to take me, too, because I cannot live if anything happens to her. I sobbed quietly and prayed, desperate for a miracle.

I called Mike to tell him what was going on, but I could barely communicate what the doctors had told me through the tears. Shocked and scared, he headed back to the hospital right away. When he arrived, I fell apart.

"I told you, Mike! I told you that I felt something was wrong! I knew something was wrong! Why didn't anybody listen to me? I knew her cry wasn't right."

I didn't care if the woman on the other side of the curtain heard me anymore. It was visiting hours, and she welcomed a steady stream of visitors bringing her balloons and flowers, while Mike and I feared the worst and tried to process what was happening with our baby. Mike updated our friends and family, but no one knew what to say. No one called us. No one visited.

Lily had her first spinal tap to check for infection when she was just hours old. She had constant IVs, she was jaundiced, we had no idea what would happen. Really, what could anyone do or say? My brother was in the service, and was stationed in another state. My mom decided to hang back until she heard something, and besides, she had to work. My sister was helping us by being with Michael, so she couldn't come visit. Despite the difficult past with my father, Mike had called him and told him what was happening, and apparently, he wanted to come see us. I hadn't seen him since he moved to Arizona a few years ago. If there was ever a time I needed comfort and family support, this was it. We needed someone to show up for us. Anyone.

A few of Mike's family members started trickling in to see us, and one of them happened to be sitting next to me when my father arrived. When he walked into the room, instead of greeting me, he immediately started up a conversation with my visitor about how beautiful she looked. As always, everybody else came first. In my worst moment as a woman and mother, he had to make sure that a pretty girl felt special, a pretty girl who wasn't me. Mike saw it and tried to distract me. He held my hand and I just stared until my father finally greeted me.

"Hello, daughter," he said. He was the same as always.

I kept wishing he was the kind of dad who would hold me while I sobbed into his chest, but he wasn't. Mike took him to see Lily through the nursery window, and relayed all the details to him so that I didn't have to. A bit later, I was able to bring him with me into the nursery so he could see Lily up close. The tape holding her IV in place looked so tight and she kept crying and crying. I asked the nurses to retape it, but they wrote me off and ignored my request. My dad noticed it too, and when I told him that they ignored me, he caused a fuss and insisted that they fix it right away. I was grateful to him for that.

I was discharged the next day, but Lily had to remain in the hospital. Her blood culture confirmed she had sepsis caused by group B strep. Most babies with this diagnosis die within the first day. I didn't know what to do. I didn't want to leave her side, but I knew I had to see Michael Jr. too. It was Christmas time and he didn't understand what was happening.

During the following days, Mike and I spent most of our time driving to and from the hospital. I was exhausted and hanging on by a thread. Whatever milk production I had, dried up. Lily was being fed with a tube, and for days, no one could tell me if she was going to live.

The day after Christmas, we were headed once again to the hospital. Our route took us past a church whose sign I had seen every day. This time, as we drove by, I yelled at Mike to stop.

"Why?" He must have thought I was losing it.

"Mike, pull over! I need to go to that church right now!"

"What!?"

"The church. I'm going in!"

As he pulled into the parking lot, I opened the door and got out before he could even put the car in park. I walked up to the door and pulled. It was locked. *Figures.* I sat down near the door and cried. I was at my wits' end.

A man who must've heard me pull on the door came out with a sandwich in his hand, still chewing the last bite he took.

"Can I help you?" he asked

I looked up at him through drowning eyes. "I was just looking for a place to pray. My daughter is sick and in the hospital, next door. I thought this was maybe like Catholic churches, where I could kneel and light a candle or something."

He excused himself as he went back in to drop his sandwich and came back out and sat next to me.

"Can I pray over you?" He asked.

Having never been asked this before, I just nodded.

He put his hand on my shoulder as he prayed out loud, pleading that God would heal my daughter and my heart.

I thanked him for his kindness.

"When she is better, you should bring her by," he said.

"Oh, I don't know about that, we still don't know if she will be... I hope so." I looked at the sign again. *Living Hope* it read. Hope was all I had.

"Trust God," he said. "I look forward to seeing you and your family one day."

I nodded and went back to the car.

"What was that about?" Mike asked.

"That guy prayed for me. For us. All of us." He seemed so certain she was going to get better, and on day ten she was. Miraculously, she was.

Postpartum Spiraling

Jesus and antibiotics saved my daughter, but I had a difficult time accepting it fully. No matter how much Mike reassured me that she was okay, I was angry that he didn't believe me the first time when I said her cry wasn't normal. I was angry with the doctor who said the test was inconsistent and not worth ordering ahead of time. I was angry with the nurses who treated me like a problem when all I wanted was someone to help me understand what was happening. I was angry with my mother who didn't come back to the hospital because she had to work. I was angry that I felt like I could never go to her for help. Even though my father showed up, and even though he got the nurses to do what I asked, I was angry that he still managed to make me feel second-rate. Mostly, though, I was terrified of what could still happen.

When Lily was discharged, they told me it was possible for a late-onset GBS infection to occur. If I suspected anything, I was instructed to bring her to the hospital immediately. I asked how I would know if she was in serious condition, and the hundred different scenarios they gave me could either be life-threatening or a common virus. Not exactly helpful. As Mike buckled her baby seat into our car, I did my best not to think about the worst.

I stared at her the entire drive home. *My peanut. You have gone through so much.* No one could convince me that I wasn't going to lose her. They said she was better, but for how long? How could they be sure? I blamed myself. I was sure that I just didn't deserve her. *What was it with me and girls, God?* My heart was bracing for loss.

The first few months of her life, I insisted on controlling everything I could. It was the only way I felt I could keep her safe. We barely went anywhere and we had very few visitors because I was terrified that she could catch something. Since she spent her first days on a feeding tube, it took some time for her to be a good eater so I obsessed over her feeding schedule. I obsessed over her sleep schedule. I obsessed over her changing schedule. I obsessed over everything. Even though Mike had taken some time off from work to help, I didn't trust him to take care of her properly. I didn't want him feeding her and I definitely didn't want him changing her. I didn't want *anyone else* to touch her. I didn't tell him my fears about this, I just always did it myself. I made it clear that the best way he could help was to make sure Michael was tended to.

When he went back to work, I was actually relieved. I didn't need him barking at me about how I was getting a little overboard with everything. I didn't need his judgment and lack of understanding. What I needed was structure and space to figure it out on my own. I felt a disgust toward him that I never had before. When he reassured me that everything would be fine, I felt dismissed, not comforted. He never carried a baby or miscarried a baby like I had. He didn't gain weight, or suffer with sciatica. He couldn't understand the physical experience of it all. He didn't have the intuition I had that something was wrong. He wrote off my fears, and told me to trust the doctors, and then he wasn't there when I learned why they couldn't bring her to me. I was alone. I was always alone when things went south. Of course he couldn't understand that anxiety became my new normal.

Because I was so paranoid about Lily getting sick, the only time I went outside was when I drove Michael to and from school. The anxiety and restlessness made me irritable, but I didn't want to leave the house, and because I felt responsible for being a carrier of that disgusting bacteria, I found myself washing my hands until they cracked and bled. I scrubbed the house top to bottom and kept it so clean that I forgot that our home was a place to live. Michael, being just a kindergartener, struggled to understand why his mama got so upset about any crumbs on the floor or his toys laying around too long. But I could only keep my anxiety at bay if I knew the house was clean and kept a certain way, if Lily's bottle was made a certain way, and if I was overseeing everything to make sure it was done a certain way. My way.

For months, I let control mask everything else I was feeling. Everything that was under the surface and that I didn't know how to face. Unsurprisingly, the iron-grip I had on my household extended to my body, my weight, and my food intake as well. I took over-the-counter appetite suppressants and when I felt I over ate, I took laxatives. I was obsessed with the celebrity mothers in the magazines and wanted to look as great as they did post-partum. After about six months, I was getting there.

By the time she was eight months old, I started to relax a little. Other than an issue with acid reflux that resulted in months of us changing her puke laden outfits multiple times a day, she was growing into a healthy, chunky baby girl. Ironically, she stopped puking after it was diagnosed. Go figure. I eased up on the hand washing and house cleaning, and returned to living a somewhat normal life. I started going out again and took them everywhere with me. We went to parks, and we went to stores. We even stopped by Mike's office one day to surprise him for lunch.

He was doing well at work and had been promoted recently, so he was working with a lot of new people that I hadn't met. Especially women I hadn't met. The day I dropped by his office, there was a thin, pretty blonde sitting across from him at his desk, casually laughing and talking to him as if they really knew each other well. As soon as I walked in, he straightened up and she turned around.

"Hey, babe, this is Ashley," he said.

I didn't respond. I looked at her, shook my head and booked it out of the building. *I knew it. They are all the fucking same.* I told myself. Her glasses were the same exact style as the ones he suggested that I should get just a week earlier.

"Chantel!" Mike chased behind me to the parking lot in his dress pants and tie.

"Fuck off, Mike."

"What is going on?"

"You know exactly what is going on!"

"No, I don't. You didn't even give me a chance to introduce her."

"Oh, the girl with the same fucking glasses you told me to get."

"What?"

"Fuck you, Mike."

"I don't know what you're talking about!"

"Oh, you know *exactly* what I'm talking about."

"Chantel, you are overreacting again."

"Again? Oh, that's rich. We're done!" I screamed at him. I slammed my car door shut and drove away.

We argued about that for weeks. It didn't matter how Mike tried to explain it, I was certain he was no better than my father. So, I retaliated the best way I knew how: I spent a ton of money. I bought workout equipment, clothes, and toys for the kids without any concern for maxing out a credit card that we had worked so hard to pay. Plus, I was restricting my food more than ever, so I was also doing all this starving. That's not a great foundation for rational thinking.

The paranoia that Mike could be cheating on me settled in deeper every time he dismissed my overreacting as *being crazy*. During one of our many phone arguments, Michael heard me screaming at Mike and ran to the doorway of the laundry room where I was standing.

"Mama, are you okay?"

I saw myself in that moment and everything in me deflated.

"Yes, baby. I'm okay. Go back to the living room."

I hung up on Mike and sat on the couch and cried like I hadn't cried in years. My sweet Michael sat next to me and rubbed my arm.

I didn't want my little boy to feel like he had to take care of me, but I didn't know how to shut down the all-consuming thoughts racing through my mind.

My brother happened to be in town and happened to stop by that afternoon. I'm told he found me lying on the couch, humming to myself. He called Mike and told him I didn't look alright. He held the phone up to my ear.

"Chantel, grow up! Take care of our fucking kids. What's the matter with you?!"

This snapped me out of it, but I still didn't have the energy to move. I'm grateful my brother hung around and played with the kids until Mike got home.

When my brother left, Mike asked me what was happening to us, what was happening to me?

"I think we need to separate for a while," I said.

"No way! We are not separating, Chantel. Something is very wrong with how you are seeing things."

"You think?! Mike, have you been living in the same house with me all these years? Did it ever occur to you that I AM NOT OKAY?"

"What is going on, Chantel?"

"I don't know. I DON'T KNOW! I just need to go somewhere else, anywhere else."

We went to bed with these issues unresolved and it stayed that way for months. We did the best we could to parent our kids and hold our marriage together, but we only knew so much. Neither of us had the support we needed, nor the vulnerability to ask for it.

I loved being a mom, and wanted to be a mom. I loved Mike, and wanted us to be happy. I didn't know what was wrong with me, I just knew I didn't feel right. Something bigger than me, deeper than even I could recognize had been winding around me for years, and after Lily's birth, it became harder to ignore. It took everything I had in me to make sure I didn't fuck up the kids with what I was trying to manage, and the loneliness that came with this felt absolutely crushing at times. Survival mode was all I knew.

My mom had distanced herself from visiting and calling, because she was dating someone new again, and it angered me that even her role as a Nana to my children seemed less important than some guy. The few friends I did have, remained at arm's length. I never felt comfortable telling them what was really going on. Rose came back into my life briefly when I heard that she had gotten married and started a family. She knew a lot about me, but I couldn't even let her in far enough to reveal the full truth. I refused to show anything less than a highly controlled facade. I felt I had something to prove. I wanted to show everyone that we made it; that all the pain of our families' chaos wasn't in vain; that we were soulmates. Admitting to anyone that we needed help felt like an open invitation for a steady stream of *I told you so* comments and I wasn't going to allow it. But real life, marriage, and motherhood started to unravel, and I felt more alone and isolated than ever. I was breaking.

California

When my father told me that Busia's health was declining rapidly, I knew I had to go see her. Dza Dza had passed a while back, and I didn't say goodbye to him. I didn't want that to happen with Busia. I knew it could be a mistake staying with him, but the plane tickets were all I could afford, and I was desperate to get away. Mike was not happy about it, but he didn't stand in my way. He just warned me of the obvious: seeing my father could make things worse.

My dad and his new wife, Beverly, had recently moved from Arizona to California. He thought of himself as a nomad now, untethered from both the company he built and the family he had, and wherever he went, Busia went, too. I didn't know his wife, but my sister lived with them for about a year, and she told me I would like her. I was also hopeful that she would be a good buffer in case my visit stirred up any conflict, old or new.

The two weeks we spent there couldn't heal a lifetime of how his choices affected me, and I could still spot his old patterns, but he was a little different now. Beverly worked in the medical industry and encouraged him to change some things about his diet and caffeine consumption, and I could see a change in his demeanor. Whether it was her influence or the California sunshine, he seemed to be a bit calmer and more present.

The trip to California actually turned out to be the best thing I did for myself. Beverly took me and the kids to see the places I had always heard about like Santa Monica Pier and Hollywood Blvd, but the best day was when she took the kids and me to the beach. It was the first time Michael had dipped his toes in the ocean. It was the first time Lily had felt the sand. It was the first time I experienced a moment of true joy and peace since she was born. As we walked out to the water, she took some of the most beautiful pictures I ever had with my children. Usually I was the one behind the camera. If I wanted a photo of me and my kids, I would have to ask someone to take it. The fact that she just did it meant a lot to me. She welcomed me and the kids with open arms. She treated me like a daughter, and her kindness made me feel loved in a way I so desperately needed.

At the end of the trip, we went to visit Busia. She was in a beautiful facility and seemed to have a lot of friends around her. Michael soaked up all the attention from the elderly residents who seemed to miss the company of children. When Busia saw Lily in the stroller, she called her Chantel. She remembered me, just not as the person I was now. As we reintroduced ourselves, she was so happy to have us there. It was heart-breaking and healing to see her, talk to her, and hug her one last time.

THIRTEEN

The Last Straw

★

Crazy's Lookin' Good Today

Since 1992, Mike and I had made it an annual tradition to go to Six Flags Fright Fest around our anniversary and my birthday. We never cared about having to wait in the long lines of favorite roller-coasters, even when the thermometer barely hit fifty degrees. When we were teenagers, he would wrap his arms around me and I would take his cold hands in mine and tuck them under my sweatshirt to warm them up. There was never a day I didn't want his hands in mine. We loved this tradition and kept it up even as we became parents. It was a reminder for us to have fun.

This year, I asked my brother to join us. He was in town, and I thought it would be a nice break from his military life and a good way to spend some time together. Fortunately, my mom was willing to watch Michael and Lily for us because it was my birthday. I often avoided asking her to watch the kids because the response I usually got was "I'm working," or "I'm busy," which made it feel like we were pretty low on her priority list.

As we hopped out of the car, eager for rollercoasters and fun, my brother grabbed a wrinkled up old jacket out of his trunk and put it on.

"Don't you have any other jackets to wear?" I snapped.

He looked at me, puzzled. The jacket had our father's company logo on it.

"Seriously, why are you wearing that? It's *so old.*"

"Um, because I want to?"

Mike saw where this was going and stepped in to redirect the focus. He grabbed my hand and pulled me along, leading us all into the amusement park.

My brother and I had different childhood experiences, but he knew I held a lot of anger and resentment toward our father. I hated what that jacket represented, and besides, it looked terrible. I thought he might at least understand how much it irked me, and how it was pretty much the last thing I wanted to see on my birthday, but instead, he doubled down and rubbed it in my face. All day, standing in line, that jacket mocked me. He didn't care that it triggered me and brought up everything I had fought so hard to suppress. Every interaction we had that day escalated to an argument. I was so mean to him at one point, even Mike told me to back off. I just couldn't swallow my anger anymore. By the end of the day, I told him I hated him and we rode home in silence.

Completely unaware of how disastrous the day had been, my mom had Michael greet us at the door. It was sweet; he was so excited to show me the cake they made together. I didn't know how to explain that I wasn't in the mood to celebrate. When we sat down to eat it, my mom asked about our day and my brother and I almost immediately erupted into an argument. I told my mom that I couldn't believe how disrespectful he was to wear that stupid coat on my birthday, knowing damn well how difficult things had been with Dad.

"What's the big deal, Chantel?" she said.

With sudden clarity, I realized that it wasn't just Mike who thought I was always over reacting. The way my mom dismissed my feelings at that moment crystallized 28 years of feeling invisible and unworthy.

"What's the big deal, Mom? Are you serious?" I lost my mind. "I would think after all Dad has done to you, by now, you would see where I'm coming from!"

"Chantel, your brother is only home for a brief time. Is this really worth it?"

Lily was already asleep and Mike knew I didn't want Michael to be around this much yelling and tension, so as soon as he saw the signs, he brought Michael to his room and tucked him into bed.

"How can you stand up for this man who screwed us all over? How can you enable your son to support him? Hasn't he hurt you enough? Hasn't he done enough damage?" I felt something break loose and I didn't hold it back. "Do you have any idea what I have been going through? Do you even care? I know you have your job, your boyfriends, and your *me time*, Mom, but why is it that you always seem to forget about me? You do know I went through it all too, right? You pulled me down with you!"

I walked into the kitchen, grabbed a knife from the drawer, and held the blade to my throat. "Should I kill myself, Mom? Should I fuck up my kids like you and Dad did?" Mike tried to wrestle it away from me. "Do you remember when you did this? Do you remember what I saw?"

My mother stood there wide-eyed. I can't be sure whether or not she recognized the moment I was referring to, but she was visibly worried. The moments that followed were a blur, but by time she and my brother left, I had collapsed into a heap on the floor. Mike pleaded with me to get up, but I couldn't move. He alternated between desperate pleas and tough love. He didn't want our children to witness any more screaming and crying, but I was frozen. I barely registered what was happening around me. I traced the cool tiles, square after square, because it was the only sane thing I could do.

When the phone rang, most of the conversation was muffled, but just before Mike slammed the phone down, I heard him say, "This is your fault, Lorenda! It always has been."

I could hear my daughter, who wasn't quite two yet, jibber-jabbering as Mike tried to keep her from seeing me in this state.

"Your mother called the police, Chantel!" He yelled to me from the hallway. "You need to get up off the fucking floor right now!"

I wanted to tell him that I needed him now more than ever, but I was drowning in shame and self-pity. I convinced myself I didn't deserve him. I didn't deserve my kids. And after what had just happened, I didn't deserve grace either. I deserved the cold, unforgiving tile floor. I wanted to disappear.

I heard my son's little footsteps run down the hallway, into the living room, and turn towards the kitchen. *Oh God, Michael's up.*

"What's wrong with you, mom?" The question was innocent. He was understandably confused why his mother was lying on the kitchen floor.

I couldn't look at him. I rolled onto my stomach and hid my face in my arms.

"Are you happy now? The police are here!"

"No, Mike! I'm sorry!" I started to bawl. *It's over.* I thought. *There's no going back. I can't undo this.*

With our daughter in his arms, and our son at his side, Mike opened the door. As soon as I heard the radio crackle and the policemen speak to dispatch, I stood up and tearfully made my way into the living room before they decided to look for me.

In a firm voice, one of the two officers said, "Chantel, your mom called and said you were going to hurt yourself. Can you talk to us please?"

I sank into the couch.

"Chantel, just tell them you are alright!" Mike pleaded.

I wasn't alright. I didn't say anything.

"Chantel, can you talk to me please?" The officer asked a bit louder this time.

"Okay," I sniffled. I was trying to calm myself. I didn't want to look at him, so I looked the other way and saw the flashing lights from the police cars out our front door window along with an ambulance. "Oh my God." I dropped my head into my hands and cried harder.

"Chantel, talk to me." He said again.

My eyes were so swollen I could barely open them.

"Can you tell me what happened?"

I nodded as I looked at my little family, staring at me through the window with fear and concern. The other police officer had brought them outside to talk with them while the officer I wasn't responding to stayed with me.

"She took his side again," I sobbed.

"Who took whose side?" he asked.

"My mother. She took his side." She has always taken his side.

The officer didn't ask anything more, and Mike and the kids stepped back into the house. Michael ran up to me and sweetly put his hand on mine.

"Don't cry mom," he said. His hands were so cold from standing outside in his pajamas and bare feet.

I took his hands in mine to warm them up. *I promised I'd never do this.* I thought, as I looked into his big brown eyes and let him know I was going to be okay.

Because I didn't resist, they let me say my goodbyes and then they walked me to the ambulance and strapped me down to the gurney like a psychopath. As the EMS guy strapped the last one, I could see Mike and the kids standing in the door watching this, and I panicked: This was not who I was or wanted to be.

"I don't want to die! I'm just sad! I have just been so sad! I don't know why!" I begged them to let me go. "I'm sorry!" I said it over and over.

They told me to calm down and slammed the ambulance door.

I'm going to change. I promise.

★

The lady at the intake desk informed me that the floor I should be admitted to, the second floor, didn't have enough beds. She apologized for the inconvenience and told me that I would be put on the third floor for the night instead.

Not knowing what the third floor consisted of, but reasoning that it couldn't be good if the lady felt the need to apologize for it, I felt uneasy. When the elevator doors opened, I understood her apology. I may not have been able to see what everything looked like very clearly, but there was plenty to hear. Some patients were milling about talking to themselves in very animated ways, and some were sitting and rocking violently back and forth, watching or not watching TV. Enveloped in a haze of cigarette smoke was what looked like a conference room. Evidently it was the smoking room.

The third floor was for patients with aggressive mental and behavior disorders. I begged the front desk nurse to let me call my husband. I frantically tried to convince her that I was not at all depressed or suicidal anymore; I just wanted to go home. She didn't budge. I tried to explain that I couldn't see; I just needed my glasses. She reassured me that I could make that call tomorrow, and told me that I just needed a good night of sleep. It was hopeless. I slid down the wall with my head in my hands. I just kept crying. I'd calm myself for a moment and then start crying again. One of the nurses handed me a cup with a little pill that was supposed to help me calm down. *Happy 28th birthday!* I thought. *You get to spend it in the psych ward! Bottoms up!*

I was given a pillow and blanket, and some comfy socks with grippy, anti-slip treads, and led down the hall to my room for the night. *Oh, Jesus.* I had a roommate. A large woman with long fiery-red hair was in the bed closest to the door. She was not happy to have been interrupted, and as I tried to get comfortable on the lumpy, thin mattress on the bed next to the window, I could hear her begin to spiral. She sat straight up in a huff, threw off her sheet and blanket, and got out of bed. I held my breath, certain she was going to try to kill me.

She paced back-and-forth in the room, repeatedly saying, "Why is she crying? Why is she crying?" She seemed to be speaking to someone else about me, but there were just the two of us in the room. Frozen in terror and misery, I watched her pace back and forth, muttering, her wild hair lit by moonlight. Time doesn't really exist in places like these, but after it was clear that she wasn't calming down, but also wasn't lunging for me, I got up and went to the front desk.

"Hi, listen, I don't belong here!" A compelling opening line from someone placed on a 72-hour hold, I'm sure. "Please let me out. I can take care of my kids. I can take care of myself. I promise I will not do anything to myself or anyone," I continued, but the nurses just steered me back to my room. "I just had a bad night. Please!"

The more upset I got, the more the nurses felt threatened by me. They warned that they would have to sedate me if I didn't cooperate. Hopeless and scared, I returned to my assigned room, and opened the door carefully to peek in. The woman had put herself back in bed and appeared to be asleep. As quietly as I could, I covered myself with the hospital blanket and cried myself to sleep.

The next morning, I woke up with the worst headache I had ever felt in my life. My vision was already blurry, but my eyes were practically swollen shut from my endless crying. Fortunately, I could see that my roommate was already gone. *I have to get out of here.*

As I waited at the front desk to see what I had to do to get discharged from this looney bin, a man with dark skin, an Afro, and a big smile walked towards me, vibing to whatever he heard on the other side of his headphones. I had nothing in me to smile back at him; I just continued to look forward. When he got closer, he slowed down and leaned against the counter right next to me. Now I could hear his music blaring. He was still smiling, and I was still ignoring him.

When I finally looked over at him, he began to hum, *"Mm, Mm, Mm,* crazy's looking good today!"

All I could do was laugh. This man broke me open, and there in the psych ward, face all puffy, I laughed! If there was anything that could shake me out of my hopeless, depressive state, it was this. While I'm certain I didn't actually look good, his comment brought me back to life. I saw the scene for what it was: I was a crazy woman in a crazy place. I was there because I needed help; maybe not the same level of help that those around me needed, but I did need help, and I was determined to do whatever I needed to do to make things better. My kids needed me.

Three Big Things Before the Big 3-0

The day I was discharged, Mike was parked at the entrance of the hospital. Before I got in the car, I looked at Lily, smiling from her carseat. I could hear that Mike was playing the Celine Dion album, *A New Day Has Come*. It was our go-to music for calming Lily. As we drove home, I couldn't help but feel immense guilt for what had transpired just two days before. I thought about how afraid Michael must have been to see his mom in that state. I thought about how frustrated Mike was, unable to fix what he couldn't understand. I thought about how my brother was home visiting for just a short while before he would be deployed to Afghanistan, and how even though we didn't agree on much when it came to our parents, he didn't deserve a day of harassment over a stupid jacket. And finally, I thought about why it hurt me so much that my mother couldn't seem to understand me.

What I had realized during my forced 72-hour hold was that the postpartum depression and anxiety I experienced after Lily's birth were amplified because of the traumatic circumstances. I knew they had always been there, but I recognized that the intensity was stronger and I had become more reactive. My darkness was affecting more than just me, and I refused to let that continue; something needed to change. I had to get better for Mike and for my children. I needed to follow what the doctor said: Go to therapy, take the meds, and become the best mom and wife for my family that I could be.

Since my mother was a significant trigger for me, I decided to cut her out of my life until I learned how to control my emotions when I was around her. There was no conversation or phone call, there was just no more trying. I also began to distance myself from Rose, whom I had only recently reconnected with. As much as I wanted that friendship, I realized that her experience of my family and the reality that I lived weren't ever going to match. I never told her everything; I didn't know how. I only knew that it was a recurring source of pain and frustration, and I was supposed to be implementing boundaries, so I did. Imperfectly.

The first time I went to therapy, I was frustrated. I hated starting from the beginning with someone who would look at the clock every now and again, and scribble down some secret notes about how hopeless I was. Inevitably I would be in the middle of describing a traumatic experience, and be told *time's up*, as if I could just turn off the faucet of emotion and go home, make dinner, and carry on like everything is fine. It felt impossible, but I tried to remain optimistic about the process. The medication I was prescribed eventually seemed helpful, or at least, it helped me quit smoking, which I had tried to do for years. As a way to remember what it was like to be in the land of the living, outside of my stay-at-home-mommy world, I got a part-time job at Target. It gave me a reason to get dressed, put on my makeup, and talk to people again. When someone told me I looked like I belonged at a make-up counter, a small part of me came alive again. Maybe I hadn't completely lost myself, after all.

After a few months of therapy, I was learning how to control my intrusive thoughts better. I was no longer struggling with cleaning the house constantly or fearing that Lily was going to get sick again. I still got on the scale every day, and it still impacted how I chose to eat that day, but I was closer to being honest with my therapist about it. The anti-depressant I was on made it hard for me to eat at all some days, but it was a small victory to no longer feel the need to purge my food every time I did eat.

I felt that God had a huge role in Lily's recovery, and Mike agreed to start going to church with me. We returned to the church where that kind pastor prayed over me when Lily was in the hospital, and we were welcomed with open arms into a new kind of family. It was a community rooted in common beliefs, something a life of attending Catholic school never gave me. We found ourselves reading the Bible and actually applying it to our everyday life. We were witnessing the fruits of it play out firsthand. Even though I had to talk him into it at first, Mike ended up teaching me more about Jesus than I ever expected. We learned how to communicate better, how to show up for each other, our family, and other people out of love and compassion. We were learning who we wanted to be, and we enjoyed watching our son grow up in church. He loved learning and singing about Jesus. It felt like things were falling into place.

Mike and I made a promise to each other: by the time I turned thirty we would own the home that we would raise our family in; we would be done having kids at whatever number we were at, and then we would plan our ten-year wedding renewal.

The director of the daycare I used to work at came through my checkout lane at Target one day, and shortly after, she called to offer me my job back. With that added income, we would be able to afford a bigger house. Before long, we found it. It had everything I had dreamed of for our family: Four bedrooms, 2.5 baths, a nice big yard, and it was on a cul-de-sac! As a city kid, who never got to know many neighbors growing up, I was excited for my kids to live near other young families like us.

I was so desperate to move into the new house, but we had to sell the current house first. After it sat on the market for four months without a single bite, I asked everyone at church to pray about it, and I was even willing to buy into an old wives' tale I had read about online. Apparently if you bury a St. Joseph statue in the front yard of the house you are trying to sell and pray over it, it will bring potential buyers. Mike thought I was nuts, but he didn't argue. He knew I wouldn't let it go without giving it a try. So, I did it. Except, I didn't just buy one statue, I bought three. I explained to Mike that I read three different stories about how and where to place it and because I wanted to cover all of our bases, I needed to do it that way. He was skeptical as always, but a week after I planted those statues, we sold the house! What made the whole story crazier, was the family who bought it was moving from Bethlehem, Pennsylvania. We couldn't ignore the irony of it, and I took every opportunity I found to rub it in.

The day we moved into the new house, I took Lily and Michael by the hand and had them lie on the empty living room floor with me. They thought I was crazy as I stared and smiled at the ceiling, but I just wanted them to take in the moment with me before Mike and his friends began to move everything in. The dream for our family was becoming a reality. After all the ups and downs, bad credit, and family drama, we were finally feeling proud of how far we had come. Box one: *check*.

It ended up being a little over a year before my mom picked up the phone to call me. She expressed more emotion than I was used to. She said she missed us and asked if she could see the kids. I told her how Michael was in a play at church and how Lily preferred playing with pots and pans over all the toys I had bought for her. We laughed as we caught up, and even though I learned that things were still chaotic for my mother (she had moved back to the city and was living with my grandparents), I was in a different place now. I really felt like it was the right time to forgive and move on. My therapist was worried, and warned me that even though I was doing the work that I needed to be healthy, my mother was still the same person. She instructed me to uphold my boundaries with her, but I was optimistic. My mom had called *me* this time. She never did that, so I felt she had to be changing in some way. Besides, I didn't see how holding boundaries went along with what I was learning at church. My understanding of forgiveness and what the Bible teaches about *turning the other cheek* and such was still new. I was a little baby Christian, according to my church. I was hopeful that I could repair our complicated relationship, and if that worked out, maybe I could figure out a way to get there with my father too.

It only took a month for me to have the house unpacked and decorated like we lived there our entire life. I had so much fun finally being able to hang pictures on the walls knowing it was my house now and not a rental. Mike and I had moved so many times that we knew more than anything the real wealth in our life wasn't money, it was stability, and not moving every year was a big step in that direction.

My mother and I still had work to do, but she was showing up in ways she hadn't before. She was choosing to make herself available to me and the kids more than I ever expected. It wasn't perfect, but she was trying. My father was even making an effort, largely because Beverly encouraged him to call me one in a while. I knew there was a lot of work to do if we were to ever have a real relationship, but as long as our phone conversations were light and only occasional, I could hang up from our calls without feeling terrible, and at the time, that was enough for me. I told myself that as long as my parents didn't hurt my children in any way, I could let go of the past. They just had to show me they cared enough to try.

This new experiment with allowing my parents back into my life coincided with our insurance coverage of my therapy sessions running out. If I wanted to keep going, it would cut into our necessities, so I stopped. I figured I had already learned the tools I needed, and now I had the internet if I wanted to learn more. I would be fine. I convinced myself that I was healed as much as I ever would be.

Myspace, Motherhood, & Makeup

From the moment I discovered I could have an internet page where I could represent myself with my own style, a chosen song, and I could post what I was thinking about, I was hooked. Myspace opened up a new world to me. I was connecting with women my age who were also young mothers like me, but there was a particular account of a woman my age who appeared to be killing it in life, specifically in a way I wanted for myself. She lived in southern California, she was gorgeous, a talented makeup artist-turned-photographer who specialized in themed photoshoots. Her images of women of all shapes and sizes dressed up like 50s pin-up models and fairies were incredible. From makeup and hair, to styling, to the photography and the editing, she did it all *and* she was a mom of three as well. I admired her work and her bubbly presence.

Like me, she didn't have a degree or formal schooling, but she had the will and the talent to do what she wanted to do, and she made it happen. My father's negative attitude about anything art related rolled into my mind any time I thought about going to cosmetology school or working in makeup, but this stranger on the internet was challenging everything I had been told, and seeing her accomplishments made me believe that maybe I could do it, too. I was already doing face-painting for parties and doing makeup for friends' weddings, and even though I knew nothing about using social media to create a brand, I knew I could learn. Every day after working at the preschool, I logged in to Myspace to see what my favorite account posted. I watched her videos, studied her photos, and began to play around with different styles of makeup. I was determined.

When October arrived, we went all out decorating the new house for Halloween, and we decided to host a costume party. It was part housewarming, part birthday celebration, all Halloween. We invited everyone we knew, and had a great turnout. I put my makeup skills to use for our costumes: Michael was a dead ninja, Lily was a teeny snow white, Mike dressed up as the comic book villain, Bullseye, and I chose to be a fairy, like the ones my favorite Myspace creator photographed. The party was a success! More than that, though, we genuinely had a great time. Dressing up and doing fun makeup brought me back to a part of myself I missed. I felt so beautiful in my blue fairy costume and long blonde wig. I felt carefree and fun. Apparently, the allure of my fairy magic was irresistible, because six weeks later I found out I was pregnant. Mike really did like how I looked in those fairy wings! I knew I wanted another baby so it was a welcome surprise. Box 2: *check*.

Knowing that this pregnancy was going to be my last, I wanted it to be my best. I felt more prepared this time around, and I didn't want to gain as much weight as I had with the other two. I decided I was going to be really strict about how and what I ate so that it wouldn't take me as long as it did with the other two to feel normal again. I knew that I could lose the weight, but gaining almost seventy pounds with the first two pregnancies was a battle, and I figured I could avoid it if I really stayed consistent with my diet and didn't gain extra weight.

Having that focus on my diet and switching doctors gave me a peace of mind I didn't have during my other pregnancies. I felt instantly at ease to find out that not only did my new doctor routinely require the group B test, but she told me right away that it would be better for me to have a scheduled c-section to lower the risk of transferring it to this baby since I was considered a carrier. The relief I felt was immense. Noah was born in July, and just like his big brother and sister, he had his daddy's kind, brown eyes. He made our family feel complete.

Unlike with the other two, I was able to nurse Noah. When I had Michael, nursing never crossed my mind. My mom said she couldn't nurse us when we were babies, so I just assumed I should bottle feed him. By the time Lily came around, I had a little more knowledge of how good it could be for the baby, but the trauma of her first weeks of life dried me up immediately. When Noah latched on so easily, I lamented not having experienced that with my other two babies. I didn't realize how grounding nursing could be for me. Being the source of nourishment and survival for my child was an incredible feeling. Knowing he would be my last, I treasured those first precious early months at home with him in a way I didn't know how to before.

It was a beautiful time. No chaos. No drama. But the best thing about this time was being able to share it with Michael and Lily. Michael was the best big brother and helped whenever he could. And Lily, who was just three at the time, marveled at how mama's boobs made milk. I made sure to tell her that one day, if she wanted, she could do it, too. She was always watching, always curious. I loved that I was home when Michael got off the bus, and I could go to Lily's first dance classes. If it wasn't for Mike working so hard for all of us, I wouldn't have been able to be the mom I wanted to be. We really had become a good team. How could I be anything but grateful? There was one more box to check before I turned 30.

The fall after Noah was born, it felt like the right time to start planning our wedding renewal. We didn't really have the money for it, but we stuck to our goal and decided we would make it happen no matter what, and we wanted to do it right. All of it mattered to me: The cake, the dress, the DJ, the photographer, and a beautiful venue to invite all of our friends and family. And the best part was all of our children would all be in the wedding photos with us.

We booked a venue that we could afford, and we had one year to plan and save for it. I asked my sister to be my maid of honor, and brought her with me to shop for a dress. We went to a real bridal salon where they served me wine and treated me like a princess. It was a far cry from the mall experience I had ten years before. I tried on several gowns and ended up choosing the first dress I tried on. It was a beautiful, strapless Maggie Sottero design that made me want to cry when I saw myself in the three-way mirror. It was perfect. As the lady at the bridal salon took my measurements, I asked her about alterations, and informed her that I would be losing weight before the event.

I hadn't gained nearly as much weight with this pregnancy as I did with the others, but I was determined to look my very best. I got serious about looking fit. I joined Weight Watchers and I went to the gym six days a week. Noah was old enough to be in their nursery room now, so every morning after I dropped Michael and Lily off at school, I started taking some crazy hard spin classes and lifting weights. At this rate, it didn't take long to shed the baby weight, and people around me noticed. All of the compliments felt great and inspired me to keep pushing myself. Because I was working out hard, and not eating a lot, I took appetite suppressants so I wouldn't binge. I really didn't want to do that anymore.

I was a mom of three, I reminded myself. *Moms don't do that.*

The spring before our renewal, I took a part time job at a department store makeup counter. We needed the extra money for the wedding, and I figured I could learn new tricks and practice on customers as I learned how to build my business as a makeup artist. Mike was fully on board with my new endeavor, and even bought me an airbrush sprayer to show his support. All my Barbizon training paid off; I was a natural at working the counter, and before long, I was getting side gigs where I was paid really well to do makeup for all types of events.

Because life was so full and busy, and because my mom had a new boyfriend, I hadn't seen her in a few months. We had talked here and there about what she was going to wear for the wedding or about what was happening in the kids' lives but we hadn't seen each other. A few weeks before the renewal, she stopped by the mall department store to introduce me to the person she was seeing, her date for the wedding. When she saw me, her jaw dropped.

"My God, Chantel, you look so beautiful. You're so thin! And your hair reminds me of when I was in high school."

I didn't know what to say. I just felt my face blush as I introduced myself to the man standing next to her who must have been wondering if she forgot why they had come.

"Wow, you really look good, Chantel."

"Um… thanks, Mom. Did I not look good before?"

"You have always been beautiful, but I can tell you must be happy."

I didn't know what to say or think. Here was a really nice compliment from my mom, something I had never heard quite like this, yet instead of feeling good, it felt like pressure.

As I cleaned up my counter and stared in the mirror at my face that was visibly thinner than it had been in years, I resolved to keep it up.

There is no going back, ever. I need to stay this way.

Wedding 2.0

I sent out the invitations in late August. I knew it was a few months earlier than most would choose to send, but I wanted everyone to be there. I found the perfect ones: weathered paper with torn edges, a path leading to a fairytale castle. It was like an announcement to everyone we knew that we really could live happily ever after.

Three weeks before the wedding, I was frustrated with the lack of responses. *How hard is it for people to reply yes or no, and send it back in a self-addressed stamped envelope that I provided?* My ranting was driving Mike nuts, but it was mostly his side of the family who hadn't replied, so I asked him to do the follow-ups. It turns out, many people didn't understand what we were actually doing. They asked why we were having *another* wedding. Even though not everyone knew the full story of our relationship, and our parents' poor choices, surely they recognized that there was an undeserved black cloud over us when we got married ten years ago, and surely they could understand wanting to celebrate a milestone. Well, a lot of them didn't even attend our first wedding, and I couldn't help but assume their lack of response this time was confirmation that they held me responsible for the demise of Mike's family. Maybe they never accepted us at all. Maybe they never considered me a part of their family at all. Even my father wavered about whether or not he would attend. Granted, that was revealed only *after* I told him I was going to have Michael walk me down the aisle. I was trying to have the kind of wedding I always dreamed of. I wanted a day that felt special, a day that was about us and about our love, a day that wasn't overshadowed by other people, and everyone was telling us to just *get over* it already. My dad insisted it was a waste of money, and maybe it was, but we were committed to our wedding 2.0, and we were going to have our moment no matter what people thought.

Leading up to the big day, I had restricted my food intake so much that I easily got lightheaded. It felt like a small price to pay for perfection, and anyway, it was only for a little while longer. I went out to run some last-minute wedding errands, and probably would have fainted if it wasn't for a nearby mall bench. I got dizzy all of a sudden, and my heart was racing so fast that I thought I was having a heart attack. Thankfully it subsided after a few minutes and I decided to get some water. It scared me, but I chalked it up to stress. *It's okay. I'm okay,* I told myself. *It will all be worth it when we stand there, in front of everyone, and show them how happy we are.*

★

November 17th was a chilly, cloudy day. The trees had dropped all their gorgeous, fall leaves, but I was glad it wasn't raining or snowing like many November days in Illinois. Mike and the boys were getting ready at home, while Lily and I got ready at a nearby hotel with my mom and my sister. We had salon appointments for hair and nails, and everything we'd need for pre-wedding pampering. I was really looking forward to it since we didn't get those moments together the first time around. When my mom arrived, I immediately sensed her mood. Maybe she was nervous to see my father, but even after I reassured her that his wife wouldn't be coming, the mood had already settled in. My sister saw what was happening and stepped in. To this day, I'm grateful for that redirect. She helped my mom with her makeup as I got Lily into her little purple dress so she could practice her walk. She was so excited to toss her flower petals as she walked, and my little four-year-old perfectionist demanded a lesson.

I peeked in to see if my mom would be ready by the time the photographer arrived, so she could help me get into my dress. For a moment, I watched as my sister applied blush and bronzer, and then my mom saw me watching and sighed.

"You are so lucky, Chantel. Look, you're getting everything you always wanted. Look how everything turned out for you." Her tone seemed almost envious. I couldn't tell if she was genuinely happy for me or not.

"Yeah, it's been a long-time coming, Mom, but Mike and I are paying for all of this so I wouldn't say we are lucky. What we are is doers! We told you ten years ago we would renew our vows. I don't know why everyone is so surprised."

I didn't want to get worked up, but I stormed away in a huff, and then I caught a glimpse of myself in the mirror. My collar bones were as defined as they had ever been, and I felt a sense of accomplishment and pride about being as thin as I was.

When the florist and the photographer arrived, we learned that the loose petals had been left behind, and Lily was devastated that now she just had a basket of regular flowers to carry, not petals to toss. We all attempted to console her but it was time to get this show on the road.

I don't know what I expected my mom's reaction to be when I got into my dress, but what I got wasn't it. She did say I looked beautiful, but it was followed by a rushed comment about her having to get dressed because the photographer was already there. The photos I had in my mind of my mother and me, and maybe Lily with us, slipped away. That just wasn't the relationship we had, and I was starting to accept that I couldn't force it to be. As the photographer captured a few shots of Lily and my sister, I smiled. I was grateful for both of them, and they looked beautiful in their purple dresses.

My reflective moment was short-lived because the photographer was rigid about the timeline. While Lily burst through the doors to show her dad and brothers her fancy dress, I had my sister walk in before me so she could orchestrate a "first look" moment with Mike. Our lives were anything but traditional, but I still wanted to have that moment. When I got the cue to walk in, I saw my three handsome boys in their tuxes, all smiling at me. I could see that Mike had been a little stressed from wrangling our freshly walking one-year-old, who didn't look where he was going, and put everything in his mouth, and wasn't interested in following wedding day decorum. But Mike's exasperation melted into a smile, and those kind, brown eyes that I loved told me that I was beautiful, and that however things went, it was okay because we were together.

The venue for the ceremony and reception had an Old World, Italian vibe, with a grand staircase and marble floor. I peeked in to see how everything looked before I was whisked away to the Bridal suite so no guests would see me. I honestly wasn't sure how many people would come since we hadn't received nearly as many responses as we expected, but by the time our officiant came to get me, I noticed that we had a packed house. I was relieved and happy and nervous all at once.

When the music started, the officiant walked in with Mike and Noah to take their place. Then, my sister practically raced down that aisle as fast as she could. I'm surprised she didn't slip. When it was Lily's turn, she took her time. Everyone smiled and *awwed* at her as she made her way to her spot, smiling ear to ear. Michael was waiting with me for our sign to go, when I heard a familiar voice.

"Hello, Daughter!"

"Um, hi Dad."

"Hi, Grandpa!"

"Glad you made it, Dad, but I'm about to walk down the aisle. Get in there!"

Just as the doors opened for Michael and me, he and my aunt scooted in and found a seat. I wanted to be pissed, but my dad was being who he always was. It confirmed that my choice to have Michael next to me was the right one. As we made our way to the front where Mike was standing with Noah, and Lily was peering around a chair, I smiled seeing all the friends and family who showed up for us. We did it. We made a promise that we would do it and we followed through.

Our vows went smoothly and they were meaningful to us, but Noah actually stole the show. The only way forward was to just let go and let him do what he wanted. The photographer got a great shot of him standing in the middle of the aisle right in the middle of our vows. He was in his own little world.

We were announced as being recommitted and married once again and then we made our way to the reception. I didn't give my parents more than a passing thought most of the night because I was too busy explaining to people why Mike and I chose a skeleton couple in wedding attire as our cake topper. Clearly it symbolized "til death due us part," but apparently, people thought it was dark. We thought it was *us*.

Just before the dinner, my father grabbed my hand. I felt a piece of paper in it and pulled away to see what it was.

"Sorry, I didn't have time to get a card."

It was a hundred dollar bill crumpled into a ball.

"Can I get a dance with you later?"

"Sure, Dad."

During dinner, we played a slideshow that we had worked on for months. The crowd roared in laughter and conversation at certain photos that popped up. Not everyone knew the whole story. Actually, almost no one knew the whole story, but we felt celebrated and supported. The song we chose for our first dance was "My Best Friend" by Tim Mcgraw and Faith Hill. Not because it was "our song," but because it was the truth of who we were becoming.

I Can't Fix Me

I woke to the smell of coffee. Mike had left a cup of coffee on my bedside table before he left for work. *God, I married a great guy.* I picked up the mug for a sip, and looked out the window. *God, I hate living in this state.* January was gloomy. Cold. Depressing.

"We need sun!" I grumbled as I climbed out of bed. I popped two appetite suppressants and two laxatives out of the shiny foil packages I had hidden in my underwear drawer. I washed them down with coffee and headed to the bathroom, hoping Noah wasn't awake yet. I needed the caffeine to kick in soon.

I stared at my collarbones in the mirror and thought about how many times since the wedding renewal I heard the words *you look so good now.* If anyone actually knew what it took for me to maintain this, I wonder if they would still say it.

I heard the screeching and calamity of the cartoons Michael was watching downstairs, and I could hear Lily rummaging through her things on the other side of my bathroom wall. Whatever she was searching for, she was determined to find it. *Please, God, I need energy.* Life was busy. I didn't have time to be as tired as I was.

Everything Mike and I set out to accomplish, we did. We owned our own home, we created our family of five, we showed them all. Check, check, and check. It was done. Our marriage was the best it had ever been. Mike supported my desire to build a career in makeup and photography and helped me invest in whatever I needed to make it happen. Everything I was convinced would make me happy had been checked off the list, and yet…

"Michael! Lily! Did you eat?" I called down to them as I opened Noah's door.

"Yes," they responded in unison.

Noah was standing up with his chin on the crib rail. He greeted me with his arms outstretched and a huge smile that was just for me, his mom. I cherished those moments. *I'm going to get it together*, I told myself.

This is my reason.

I didn't want to accept that what I was doing to myself would eventually kill me. Even if I believed I had it under control, I knew the truth was much darker.

By the time everyone was dressed and ready for the day, the caffeine from both the diet pills and coffee had kicked in. My heart raced.

"Got your lunches?"

"Yes, Mom!"

On the short drive to school and back, my stomach was in knots. *I need to stop taking those pills.* I set Noah up in his highchair with a scrambled egg and was shaking so bad, I had to eat something. *I hate this. I hate feeling like this.* I put a slice of bread into the toaster. *I need to fix this.*

After a few bites of toast and water, I physically felt better, but then I was upset I had given in to the toast. The gym was close by, and the girls who worked in the gym nursery loved Noah, so I didn't feel guilty leaving him there while I spent my morning in spin class, then on the treadmill, and finally, the elliptical. Before picking him up, I weighed myself in the women's locker room. I was obsessed with staying close to 140 pounds, a weight I had not been since I was in high school. That might seem heavy in relation to the models and actresses on television, but on my frame it equated to being a size six. Being any bigger than that was simply not an option in my mind. I put on a few pounds since the wedding renewal and over the Christmas season, so I had been trying to do everything I could to lose it. The scale read 148. That weight was unacceptable.

Noah was sleepy when I picked him up from the nursery, so I knew the car ride home would be a quiet one. The minute I placed him in the car seat he closed his eyes and was out. I contemplated stopping at every fast-food restaurant I passed, and then beat myself up for it.

Chantel don't be a dumbass; you just worked your ass off.

When we got home, I laid Noah in his crib. I stared at his sweet face as I removed his coat and hat. I ran my fingers over the dimples of his little knuckles. *My last baby.* I just wanted to hold these moments forever, and wished I could do it without punishing myself in the process.

I left him sleeping peacefully and went to take a shower. Thankfully, the shakes had stopped, but the thoughts were loud. I stepped on the scale. *Maybe mine would say something different than the gym's.* It didn't.

As I patted myself dry, I fixated on my imperfections like I had since I was eleven. *If I could just get rid of this.* I pulled on the loose skin of my belly, then sucked it in as far as I could. *I hate these fucking stretchmarks.* I pounded my hip bones. *Disgusting.*

My mom was right, I am lucky. I'm lucky that Mike still loves me like this. I wrapped the towel around my body and checked on Noah once more.

I remembered the day this all began when I was little. It was a way to focus on something I could control. It felt like survival. But I knew better now, I just didn't know how to let it go.

I felt woozy again and stood in front of the refrigerator, staring at the leftover lasagna.

I really wanted to eat it, but I pulled out a carton of eggs instead. After frying them up on the stove, I sat down at the table and ate the eggs as fast as I could. Still hungry, I pulled out a jar of peanut butter, a package of saltine crackers, a bag of potato chips from the pantry, and a container of cottage cheese. I turned on the television and flipped through the channels as I mindlessly stuffed myself until everything I had pulled out was completely devoured. I sat in the fullness for a split second before berating myself for what I had done. *This is why you can't lose weight!* I felt disgusting.

I knew what I needed to do, what I had always done when I got like this. I filled up a tall glass of water and headed for the bathroom. As I placed the glass on the sink, I looked at myself in the mirror. *This is the last time.*

I lifted the toilet seat, and wiped off the little-boy-pee from the rim of the bowl.

Gross, I thought, and then, I caught myself. *Really, Chantel? That's gross? What about what you are doing?*

I washed my hands and chugged the glass of water as fast as I could. It was a ritual I had done for twenty years. I left the water running in the sink to drown out the noise that followed as I shoved my fingers down my throat violently until my body heaved up the food I binged. It didn't take long before I purged it out of me. I washed my scratched-up hands and looked at my swollen face. *You are too fucking old to be doing this! Have some fucking willpower, would you?*

I could hear Noah. He was learning to climb out of his crib, so I had to get to him before he tried. I wiped my mouth with a towel and ran up the stairs to his room.

"Hi Mama's lil' guy! I'll be right there. Mama needs to brush her teeth and then we will go get Lily and Michael, okay?"

He smiled.

I felt like a piece of shit. As much as I wanted to stop, I didn't. On days I worked, I restricted. On days I didn't work, I went to the gym and always ended up binging and purging.

The calmer my life was with Mike and the kids, the worse my eating disorder became. I had no reason to be doing what I was doing. I was chasing something I could never reach, and I didn't know how to stop.

My routine continued like this for months. Skip breakfast, take kids to school, workout, binge during Noah's nap, feel like a loser, purge everything, feel like an even bigger loser, repeat. I had sold myself the lie that I could beat it on my own. I was wrong. If I didn't stop, my heart would.

During a naptime binge-purge cycle, I scarfed an entire leftover pot of spaghetti. I didn't warm it up and I didn't stop until the bowl was scraped clean. I filled my glass of water and started toward the bathroom when I was interrupted by a little voice.

"Mama!" Noah was up early from his nap.

Shit! I have to get this out of me. Shit. Shit. Shit.

I ran upstairs to get his pack and play, and turned on *Sesame Street.*

"Look, Noah. Elmo!" I said. I could feel the food digesting. "Mama has to go potty, okay? I'll be right back."

He seemed interested in the distraction, so I raced to the bathroom. There was no time for the ritual of shaming myself in the mirror, I skipped right to the water. I chugged it and purged as as fast as I could. I purged and purged yet I still didn't feel like I could get it all up. My throat paid the price for my urgency.

Blood. Shit.

Exhausted, I paused for a moment to listen for Noah. Sitting on the floor next to the toilet, staring at my scratched-up knuckles, speckled with vomit, I realized that my baby boy had climbed out of his pack and play. I was flooded with shame seeing his little fingers reach through the space between the floor and the door. I scrunched down as low as I could, pressed my swollen cheek onto the cold, bathroom floor, and saw a big, brown eye staring back at me. He was lying on the other side of the door trying to see what his mama was doing.

I hated myself, *the only girl on the floor.*

"Noah, what are you doing, silly boy?"

"Ma-Ma-Ma-Ma"

As I pushed myself up from the floor, my heart started beating weirdly, like a flutter. It scared me. I flushed the toilet, wiped my hand on my pants and opened the door. I didn't want to leave Noah alone for one more second. He walked in, smiling and reaching for me to pick him up.

"Hold on, baby. Mama needs to wash her hands." I pumped the soap, and looked into the mirror. *What is wrong with me?* I picked up my baby and walked into the living room, defeated. *Sesame Street* was still playing on the television. Feeling dizzy and strange, I called Mike at work.

"I need you to come home," I said.

"Why?"

"I just need you to come home now. My heart feels weird and I think I need to go to the hospital."

On his way home he picked up the other two kids from school. They had no idea anything was wrong, thank God. They got their snacks and turned on the TV. Mike looked around the corner and saw me on the stairs, guarding so Noah wouldn't fall. Before he made his way up to me, Noah came rushing out to greet him. Mike looked at me concerned, but didn't say anything. He just air-lifted Noah over to his siblings. After the kids were settled, he sat down on the stairs with me.

"Babe, what's going on?"

"I can't fix me."

"What do you mean, you can't fix you?"

"I need to go to the doctor; something is wrong with me. My heart feels really weird."

"Ok. When did it start?"

I didn't want to tell him.

"Chantel, what is wrong?"

"I'm a fucking mess, Mike! That's what's wrong. I'm bulimic and I can't stop and I don't know why. I need help."

"What do you mean you're bulimic? You told me—"

"I lied. I fucking lied," I sobbed. "I need help."

He sat next to me in silence for a moment, and then hugged me. Neither of us knew what was ahead, but we knew that we'd navigate the next step together.

Can We Climb This Mountain?

My head was pounding as I sat in a hospital gown with my cold, bare feet dangling from the doctor's exam table. I could hear Mike on the other side of the door, talking to my sister on the phone.

"Do you think it would be possible for you to switch your work schedule to evenings for a few weeks?" he asked.

I always prided myself on being able to do things on my own. I hated this. I hated needing anyone. The beige walls that surrounded me didn't offer any distractions either. Maybe if there was one picture somewhere in this room for me to stare at, I could disassociate from all the feelings of guilt that threatened to smother me as I continued to listen. As he explained how out of control things had gotten for me, I wondered if he was finally seeing me for who I really was. From the moment he said he loved me 16 years ago, he really believed that his love alone would be enough to fix me. I still have the notes that he wrote to me in high school expressing how worried he was about me. How, if only I could see what he sees when he looks at me. I wonder what he sees now all these years later. A 31-year-old mother to his three children wearing nothing more than a sheet with strings, waiting for a doctor to clear her so she could enroll in an eating disorder program where the average age of the patients was under 23. I guess I never could see what he saw and now it was going to cost us all to help me try to figure out why.

When the doctor finally came in, Mike followed immediately behind him. The doctor's interaction with us was brief and serious. My cardiac arrhythmia (irregular heartbeat, chest pains) and shortness of breath was due to my low potassium levels and an imbalance in my electrolytes from the vomiting. My throat and esophagus were both severely irritated and swollen and I also was extremely dehydrated. Even though my BMI was normal, considering how long I had been doing this, he made it very clear that this was something that could have grave effects on my health later.

He then wished me luck, shook Mike's hand and just before he reached for the door to leave, he turned back and said, "if she doesn't get help soon, instead of finding her crying on the stairs when you come home from work, you might find her dead. Bulimia is a serious disorder that does a lot of damage to different parts of the body that can go unseen for years until it's too late. If she's had this for a long time, maybe it's time to really figure out why."

As soon as the door shut behind him I jumped down to get dressed. I was ready to get out of there.

"I don't want to die, Mike. I love you, and I love our kids. I won't do this again. I promise."

"Well, just finish getting dressed, okay?"

I could hear it in his voice. I could see it in his face. He was starting to understand what we were up against.

"I'm going to change, Mike. I have to."

Without saying anything, he put his arm around my waist and guided us both to the admissions desk. The woman we gave our insurance information to handed my card back to me along with a folder that had all of the information on the hospital's eating disorder program. She went over the paperwork I needed to fill out that asked me questions like: "In the past three months, how often have I…"

1. Gone on binges
2. Made myself sick (vomited)
3. Used laxatives or diuretics to control my weight
4. Exercised to lose or control my weight

As I filled out the paperwork, she let us know that if I decided to enroll, I could start the following Monday.

The outpatient program was twelve hours a day for a minimum of four weeks. I looked at Mike in fear and panic, knowing how much this was going to put more of a burden on us and our family. Last but not least, the lady mentioned that our insurance covers some of this program, but it was going to still cost $3000 out of our own pocket.

I felt like the wind got knocked out of me. I couldn't even look at Mike. I knew that we didn't have that kind of money readily available, and we didn't have anybody to ask, either.

"Do you have a payment plan?" Mike asked. He knew I was avoiding eye contact so he put his hand on my lap to get my attention. "We can borrow from my 401k," he said to me.

I stopped filling out the paperwork and looked at him.

"You can do that?"

"We have to." He patted my thigh to reassure me. "I want you to get better."

I recognized something in those kind, brown eyes that I had not seen before: He saw the monster too. He knew it was bigger than him and we needed to learn how to fight it together.

The song "When we were young" by the Killers came on the radio as we drove home. For weeks I had been singing it at the top of my lungs whenever it was played, but not being in much of a singing mood, I just sat quietly and listened to the lyrics.

Today Is the Day

"What's a blind weigh in?" I asked the woman at the front desk as she handed me a folder of essentials, like a map of the building, my schedule, and lots of papers that I needed to fill out before the day was done. Then, with a big smile of bright pink lipstick, she let me know that Ms. G was the woman I would see next. She was just a hop, skip, and a jump down the hall, and she would explain everything.

Her upbeat welcome was unexpected. I couldn't imagine cheerfully welcoming people who were purposely starving, puking, drinking, and drugging themselves to death every day. Yet here she was, smiling like the beige walls and mass-produced motivational prints that surrounded her exuded pure sunshine.

Everywhere I looked, there was another beige wall with another generic picture of a bridge or a droplet of water with a caption that said something like, "Don't give up!"

At the end of a windowless hall, I came upon a line of young women waiting quietly. I checked the room number to confirm that this was my stop and yep, it was. When it was my turn to enter, I was greeted by a short, stout woman with strong features and bare skin. Not a stitch of makeup whatsoever. Her shoulder length black hair and grey roots were one haircut away from being a full silver sister. Her long nose, thick eyebrows, and small, squinty eyes reminded me of an illustration from one of my favorite childhood books, *The Witch on Hissing Hill.* I hadn't thought of that book in a long time and it made me smile.

She had me stand in front of the scale. No friendly introduction, just right down to business.

"This office will be open every morning until 8:15," she said. "You will stop here first to see me before anything else. Turn around, and step on the scale."

"You mean, step on…backwards?"

"Yes, ma'am."

"But I won't get to see wh—"

"That's the point." Her reply was sharp but not unkind.

I did as I was told, and she began to introduce herself as she filled out my chart. Then, with her clipboard and pen held close to her chest, she finally glanced at the number on the scale and wrote it down. It felt like I was standing on it forever. I could not make out the numbers she wrote down.

"From now on," she continued, "your weight will not be discussed with you. The only ones who will have access to that information will be your clinical director, your case manager, and your psychiatrist. You will be meeting with them often as you go through the recovery process."

What the fuck? I need to get out of here, I thought.

"Do you have any questions for me so far?"

"Nope, not at this time." I grabbed my packet and walked out.

From the speakers mounted to the ceiling, I heard the song lyrics, *"I ran"* by A Flock of Seagulls. The irony.

"Head to the cafeteria for breakfast! Check your meal plan for more information on what your choices are!" she called out to me as I kept walking.

I took a deep breath. *I'm not eating breakfast, but I will definitely grab a cup of coffee.* I was only 45 minutes in, and I already wanted to quit. Being told what to do, having everything managed and planned and controlled by others did not sit well with me. Besides, I felt so awkward being there at my age. It was like being the new girl in school, but being a decade older than everybody else.

As I stopped to grab the hospital map out of my folder, a few girls from Ms. G's blind weigh-in line were headed my way. I dug through my purse pretending to look for something until they passed by, and then discretely followed behind them from a distance. None of them spoke to each other on the walk there, but behind the double doors of the cafeteria was a roar of chatter and utensils clicking. The girls went left as I stood at the entrance unsure where to go. Being in a busy cafeteria reminded me of high school, too. Holding my purse and information packet like a shield, I maneuvered through the chaos looking for any kind of direction. I thought maybe I'd find a sign saying, "Pukers and Starvers sit here," but no luck. The only signs I found were the ones in red: exit. *Maybe that is my sign.* I thought.

Eventually I noticed that people did seem to sit in groups according to whatever brought them there, and then I saw Ms. G. She waved me over to our table and I found a spot that hadn't already been claimed by a purse or a draped sweater.

"For each meal, you'll need a protein, a fiber, some fruit, and something to drink," Ms. G explained. "In the ED program, caffeine is usually restricted, but you can talk to your dietitian about it. When you get into the line, just hand this card over to the server and they will fill your plate for you. When you have gotten your items, return back to me so I can check your tray."

The humiliation continues. I thought to myself, but I nodded and made my way to the serving line. When asked for my meal plan, I handed over the card as I was instructed, and I learned what my options were. I pointed to the overcooked scrambled eggs, which he scooped onto my plate alongside half a bagel and a banana. As I grabbed a bottle of water and headed back to the table, I noticed that the once-empty seats had filled up, and that our table, unlike the others, had a more consistent demographic: almost all of us in the ED program were young women.

I sat down and forced myself to shovel some food into my mouth as I took stock of my surroundings. There were a few gals who appeared comfortable; they chatted and ate their breakfast. Some were aloof and acted as if the plate in front of them didn't exist. There was one who moved her food around to form an intricate shape on her plate, and there were still others who meticulously separated their food so none of it was touching. Then there was me. *Even in my fucked-up-ness I don't fit in.* I could pass for a Chatty Cathy, but I was old enough to be their mom, or at least an aunt, or a much older sister. The women who were my age were all sitting at the other tables. *Why couldn't I be an alcoholic or addicted to Xanax instead?* I sighed and swallowed another mouthful of rubbery eggs. *What could I possibly have in common with these kids,* I thought.

To avoid conversation, I opened the information packet and read the program guidelines:

1. Patients are expected to follow the nutritional plans given.
Ugh, check.

2. No side conversations about food, eating, weight or appearance during meals.

My mother would be kicked out immediately.

3. Please try to avoid comparing yourself to others.

Too late. I'm the oldest one here.

4. Avoid drinking large quantities of liquids—especially water.

Ah, they know about that.

5. Both breakfast and lunch would be 45 minutes long.

What the hell was I going to do for these ungodly long mealtimes?

The packet said the long meal times were intended to provide us with support and practice new coping skills, and learn to manage our emotions around food, but *forty-five ever-loving minutes?* I closed the packet, looked around at the table, and then, I saw it. A sign, like a beacon of hope for my desperation: *RESTROOMS.*

The moment I stood up with my tray, Ms. G called out to stop me.

I turned around, feeling very silly. *Was I in trouble?* It felt the same as when I got caught throwing a bunch of crinkled up paper balls out the open windows of my science class in 8th grade because I was bored.

"We will all be able to discard our trash as a group and will head to the restroom after," she explained.

"We go to the restroom *as a group?*" I asked. I didn't need clarification. I needed to pass judgement. My mounting frustration needed a release valve or I was going to lose it.

"Yes, we do. But if you really have to go now, I will call for someone to accompany you."

Oh. My. God. What? I am not a child! The tantrum my inner child, I mean inner *voice*, was threatening to have was dangerously close to the surface.

I dropped my purse off my shoulder and plopped back down at the end of the table in a huff. I'm sure my face didn't hide how spectacularly annoyed I was.

Sitting near me was a girl I hadn't paid much attention to until this moment. She arrived late to breakfast with one of those IV stands on wheels trailing behind her. The bag hanging from the stand looked like it was a feeding tube. It reminded me of the one my daughter Lily had in her nose for the first ten days of her life. She looked fragile, but kind. Her face was pretty.

"I'm Sadie," she said with a genuine smile. Her round, dark eyes somehow sparkled even in that terrible, fluorescent cafeteria lighting.

"I'm Chantel." I managed a half-smile back at her.

"The first day is the hardest," she said. Then, she laughed. "Actually, every day is hard. But you'll get used to it. The things that bother you right now will be the least of your troubles."

She looked barely 20 years old and yet these few words showed the hard-won wisdom she has gained.

Ms. G made her rounds to check each of our trays and then dismissed us to the restroom (as a group). I walked with Sadie.

"I know I need to be here," I told her. "I just didn't expect it to be like this."

The reason we went as a group was that Ms. G checked the unflushed toilet after each

of us went.

Could everyone here be bulimic? What if we had to poo? It just keeps getting worse! Everything about this was deeply uncomfortable. I wanted to cry. I washed my hands and wondered if someone was going to check that, too.

Ms. G was holding the door for us to leave, and she leaned in towards me.

"It's really brave for you to be here. I hope you know that."

I looked at her and choked up. Brave was the furthest thing from how I felt.

"I'm glad you are here, Chantel."

"Me, too."

★

"Let's all welcome Chantel to the group," Ms. G announced, as she handed me another piece of paper that she said would be helpful later on.

We were in another beige room. The chairs were set up in a circle so we all faced each other, and there was a white board behind Ms. G's chair that told us in green marker, *be a student of yourself.* I took a deep breath.

Here we go.

The circle was small. I alternated between looking down at the ugly carpet and looking around the circle at the frail young women I was with. *What am I doing here? Maybe this was a mistake.*

Ms. G began the discussion with the ground rules:

Whatever is shared in the group is confidential and never leaves this room. In order for group therapy to be effective, trust is the foundation.

Do not interrupt someone while they are sharing. Even to give a Kleenex. Everyone should feel safe to share, and even compassionate interruptions can hinder the process.

Allow the person sharing to finish before you offer support. All feedback should be positive. Be mindful of how you offer support. Everyone's journey is different.

The word "fine" is not allowed for describing how we feel.

Ms. G pointed to a poster on the wall: *F I N E = Feelings Inside Not Expressed.* Then she then pointed to another poster that provided a list of positive and negative feeling words that we could use to express emotion. "We want you to work on being able to express how you are feeling in order to understand yourself better," she said.

As someone who had always expressed my feelings simply as good or bad or *fine*, I couldn't help but snicker a little thinking how Mike might react if I told him that I was feeling *jubilant* or *afflicted* this afternoon. When it was my turn to share how I was feeling, so many things welled up inside me that I could have torn down the poster and circled them all. After a few moments, sitting in the uncomfortable silence, I finally spoke.

"I am feeling unsure right now," and then I corrected myself. "No, actually, I am embarrassed." I was shaking. I felt like a geyser ready to burst. I needed to say it. "I am too old to be here. I should have been able to get over this shit back when I was in high school. I am a wife and a mother. I am ashamed of myself." The room was quiet. I could only look down. I wiped my tears and my running nose with my hand because everyone followed the rules. "Anyone have a Kleenex?" I asked.

The girl next to me quickly reached behind us to grab a few.

"I guess I should give up wearing makeup for the next few weeks, huh?" I joked. I was relieved when the group smiled at that.

"Does anyone have anything to say that might help Chantel look at this process a little differently?" Ms. G wasn't playing. She looked around and waited. The silence was painful.

I wanted someone to say *something*, but I was convinced none of these girls could possibly know how I was feeling or what it was like to be me.

Then I heard a soft voice.

"I can't relate to what it must feel like to be your age, Chantel. I'm only 16. But what I can say is that I am a daughter of a mother who will never admit that her unhealthy relationship with food and exercise is why I'm here. Being able to admit that you have a problem and get help might save your kids from having to be me."

I didn't know what to say, so I nodded a thank you. The sadness in her eyes reminded me of my own. I may have been a lot older than these girls, but when it came to how we felt on the inside, we were the same.

★

After process group, we dispersed to different rooms. My next assigned destination was my therapist's office, which was another beige room, but it was cozy at least. Dr. C had short blonde hair and round, wire-rimmed glasses. She greeted me warmly and asked me to get comfortable as she got my file together. I noticed as she started to fill out my assessment form the top of her pen cap was chewed up. I chew my pens, too.

"Have you ever had individual therapy before?" she asked, after I sat down.

"Yes, a few times."

"Would you mind sharing with me what for and when?"

"Does a high school social worker count?"

"All of it counts. Let's hear it."

I liked her directness. "Okay, four times since I was 17," I told her. I adjusted myself, trying to get comfortable, and watched as she wrote in her notes.

"Let's start with the first time and why."

"In my senior year of high school, I received a pass to skip my favorite gym class that day and head to the school's social worker office instead."

"Did you request to meet with the social worker?"

"No."

"Okay, then, how did it start?"

"Someone made an anonymous phone call to the school about some bruises they saw on me." I tried to downplay it.

Ms. C paused and looked at me with concern. "What were those from?"

I felt like a child. I was uncomfortable talking about this.

"I would hit myself when I felt like I ate too much or said something stupid. But it wasn't as bad as the few times I had put cigarettes out into my wrists."

"Did you tell your school social worker that your burns and bruises were self-inflicted?"

"Yes."

"Were your parents ever notified?"

"Yes. Apparently, my mom told the social worker that I would be fine, and that she'd keep an eye on me."

"What did your parents say to you about it?"

"Nothing." I watched her write more. "Listen, I know how this sounds. But my parents just didn't ask about it. They had their own issues to deal with."

"How long did you go to your school social worker?"

"A few months before I graduated, but I stopped before we had time to figure some things out."

"Would you like to share what that was?"

I sat there for a moment and thought about how I was going to say this out loud.

"I had some stuff happen to me when I was a kid," I said. I searched for the next words. "And at the end of my freshman year of high school, I let this guy into my house, an ex-boyfriend—I really don't feel like talking about this right now. I don't know how this has anything to do with me being bulimic."

"Chantel, do you like to write?" she asked.

"Yes. I used to like to write a lot. I haven't in a long time. But I still have some of the things I wrote."

"How would you feel about writing out some of the stories that you are not comfortable

sharing with me here? Then, if you choose to, you can bring them with you to your sessions for us to process together. Writing can be a powerful healing tool."

"I have a lot of stories," I warned. "How many would you want me to write?"

"Whatever you want! Maybe start with the reasons that brought you here?"

"Well, I have everything going for me, and yet I still feel like I have to throw up my food to feel something." My reply was almost automatic. "Is this required? I have three children at home that I will now hardly see because I'm here."

"Well, you are responsible for your own recovery, so you can choose to do the work or not. But think about it this way, your children will be grateful one day that you took this time away from them to heal."

I nodded and grabbed a handful of tissues. "The day isn't over and all I've done is cry. I'm such a baby." I mopped up my face and tucked the others in my purse.

"You're not a baby; you're choosing to heal. So many people will never do the work, and if it doesn't kill them, it kills everything around them."

"I just don't want to feel the way I do anymore." I gathered my things to leave, but she stopped me at the door.

"I look forward to our journey together, Chantel. Try to write if you can. You'd be amazed at how healing it can be."

"I'll try," I said, and stepped out into the hallway. The glowing exit sign to my left called to me, but art therapy was next on my schedule, and I always loved art.

EPILOGUE: BATTLE WOUNDS

I never imagined that the day I walked out of treatment in May of 2007, it would take me nineteen more years to articulate all of the reasons I ended up there to begin with. I thought the clarity and the healing and all the answers I needed would arrive once I had the right tools. But the truth is, the clarity I had been searching for was never something that could be uncovered in 30 days. Honestly, if someone would have warned me back then about how long the journey was really going to be, I might not have done it in the first place.

The program gave me a foundation. It opened my eyes to the beginning of healing. It taught me how to nourish my body properly and how to sit in a room with people I did not know and vulnerably share things I had never said out loud before. It taught me a new language to speak about my struggles. It helped me become more aware of my triggers and the tools needed to overcome them. By the end of those four weeks, I knew that in order for me to truly heal and recover, I would have to face the stories of my past that I was most afraid of.

On the last day of process group, I remember hugging my fellow patients, who were now friends, and feeling unsettled. As I read the card they had given to me on the car ride home, I knew that the real work didn't happen inside of those hospital walls. It would begin the moment I stepped back into my life at home. Whenever I was alone with my thoughts, I was going to have to put into practice everything I had learned, but there wouldn't be a therapist sitting across from me to help me process them.

In the beginning, I focused on what was manageable for me, and who I needed to be most. Walking into my home for the first time knowing that I was no longer going to be provided with the structure that treatment gave, it didn't take long for me to become overwhelmed with the fear of how I was going to now create a similar structure for myself on my own. I never had a problem creating structure for everyone around me. Making sure the kids were fed, bathed, loved, and nurtured came easy to me. But to create a healthy environment for myself as well? That was going to take some work. Even if I hated living in survival mode, it's what I knew. I had to accept that what helped me to survive as a child, wasn't going to work now that I was a grown adult with a family. If my providing everything to everyone would eventually lead me to burnout and meltdowns, then what good was I really? I was going to have to learn to ask for help.

Those first few weeks back at home were difficult. I felt a lot of shame for being gone even though I knew how well my kids were cared for. If it weren't for my baby sister (just 22 at the time) rearranging her entire life and work schedule to be home with my children when Mike was at work, I couldn't have done this at all. I will be forever grateful for that spunky little redhead that used to make me hide my face behind a cereal box every morning. Back then, I would have never known that she would be one of my biggest supporters during the most difficult time of my life. But when she went back to work, and life did what life does, I wanted to rush right back into it full speed hoping to make up for the feeling that I was trying to mask. A feeling that screamed that I had failed as a mom and wife for needing this treatment at all. Having spent so many years numbing my pain by seeking perfection and engaging in my eating disorder behaviors, I was completely unprepared for what it would feel like to face my thoughts without doing what I had always done to soften the impact. The weekly outpatient groups and individual therapy appointments helped, but it was definitely a lonely struggle.

One of the most beautiful things that came out of my going into treatment was realizing how much Mike was willing to learn about how to help me. He went to family group sessions. He listened to the therapists with me. He showed me I wasn't too much, and it gave me hope that I would one day be able to heal. He knew a long road was ahead. Instead of walking away from the mess that I was, he chose to walk with me through it all, when I had nothing to offer but my existence. Maybe it's a trauma bond, maybe it's because we truly are soulmates, maybe he is a glutton for punishment. Maybe it's all of that and the sheer insanity of not finding a good enough reason to give up. But what I can say is that our relationship never looked the same after treatment. He is the only man I have ever been able to count on, through thick and thin. I wish I could say I acknowledged this immediately, but navigating this new journey took time for the both of us. I had to learn to surrender and he had to learn to take the reins in ways he never had before. We had always been crazy about each other, but for me to love him like I should, I needed to learn to learn to at least like myself. Even though I wanted to receive the love I knew he had for me, I couldn't help but look for anything that might reflect the marriage I saw growing up. Waiting for the shoe to drop kept my walls up for a long time.

Even though there were only a few people that knew I had gone to treatment, I couldn't stop the awkward and naked feeling I had. I didn't know how to be around regular people for a long time afterward. Being someone who rarely spoke about the things I had struggled with, to then talk about my deepest darkest struggle every day in process groups, to then have to reenter the real world realizing that most of the people I knew my entire life didn't really know me at all, was really strange. I didn't know what to say to them if they should ask me about what I had been doing, and I was afraid of what their response would be if I told them the truth.

My weekly outpatient group and individual therapy sessions were spent talking a lot about boundaries in the beginning so that I would not be unnecessarily pouring salt on my open wounds by oversharing my story with people who didn't get it and could possibly hurt me even more. But setting boundaries was so uncomfortable for me in the beginning, so I chose avoidance instead. Mike and I made the decision to pull back from people and any gatherings that felt like it could expose how fragile I really was until I felt more normal again. Spoiler alert! Normal never happened, but I did eventually reenter the world, and there were a lot of hard lessons I needed to learn along the way.

I used to hate the cliché "time heals" because patience has never been a virtue of mine, but it turns out there's some truth to it. Learning to find grace for myself in this process took a long time. My therapist back then would constantly remind me, Chantel, it took you thirty-two years to get here, change isn't immediate. I hated hearing that.

Peeling back the layers of my story hurt like hell. I had hoped that once I fully understood how my childhood had shaped me, that everything would become easy to fix. If only it were that simple. Every time I shared more about my past, the more broken I felt. It felt strange being pressed for details about things no one had ever cared to ask me before. I never realized how much I minimized the pain I really felt inside in order to be more acceptable to the people around me and how much I was trying to hold it all together for them. It made me angry. It made me sad. I felt robbed and selfish for having to do this now. Therapy had my wounds open, raw, and left me short tempered at times. Even though I never subjected my children to the same physical abuse that I had growing up, there were still days when arguments got heated and I lost my cool and failed big time. I know that affected them because it affected me when I was a child. Failing days felt like hell. That was when my biggest demon, shame, tested me the most. I eventually learned to bite my tongue until it bled, but it wasn't easy. The unhealed version of me that my children sometimes witnessed is where my deepest regrets still live. Even if I knew better and did better than what I came from, I was far from the mother I wanted to be. I fucked up alot. The fuck ups might've been different than my parents', but they still did damage. Damage I promised myself I would never do. Not being able to meet my own standard of healing perfectly, prolonged my healing, and ate me alive inside. It didn't matter how much grace anyone had given to me. I couldn't receive what I didn't think I deserved, and it took a long time to figure out why.

My mom came to a family night once while I was still in treatment. I was surprised and genuinely grateful that she was trying to understand me. It felt like a step in the right direction and that things could be different between us. But the understanding she had come to when she learned about my eating disorder didn't easily carry over into real life. Old patterns like talking about weight and dieting were quick to resurface. When I told her I no longer wanted to engage in those conversations (especially when we are sitting down to eat) she seemed perplexed: what else was left for us to talk about? When I began asking her direct questions about my childhood and needed her to take some ownership and responsibility, things between us became very messy. Although I was proud of myself for being clear about what I needed from her, it was still difficult for me to not allow her to make me feel like a villain. It took me a long time to accept that being vulnerable and straightforward with her wasn't being mean, it was teaching her how I wanted to be treated. I was now choosing self-respect over approval. I wanted to change. I wanted to heal. I wanted my mother to understand that my boundaries were about me loving her so much that I wanted a healthy relationship with her. But getting her to understand this, someone who did not have the tools herself, made the process, at times, excruciating for the both of us.

I had always understood that my mother carried her own history of trauma. Knowing that had been why I could never fully stop myself from trying to take care of her. But her using that as a way to excuse her and my father's role in my trauma was where I had to draw a firm line. I needed to step out of the role I played in her life for 32 years and reclaim my own identity. In order to disentangle myself and see my experiences clearly without the weight of guilt or the need to justify why it all happened the way it did, we did spend some time apart without contact. There seemed to be no other way. We were both emotionally immature, and because I was raising littles myself, being consistent and stable for my children had to be prioritized. The seasons of no contact sometimes went a few months, the longest was over a year, but deep down I knew I could never allow it to go on forever.

The terms enmeshment and parentification though common today, had never been a part of my vocabulary. I didn't realize how deeply my identity was tangled up in my parents' trauma and high-conflict marriage until I tried to separate myself from it. I needed time to tend to my own wounds before I could even begin to understand or feel compassion for theirs. What I wanted most was acknowledgement, an apology, something that named what I had experienced growing up. But when that did finally happen, there was nothing that my parents said that made me feel any better. The resentment I carried for them grew deeper as I faced each traumatic experience head on while still being a wife and mother learning to handle things differently than they did. As I walked through each painful experience, I grew closer to understanding that the only way to move forward was going to be by finding a way to accept what was. I just had to figure out how to get there.

Time heals, right?

This healing journey has been extremely layered and grueling at times. Even though I now understand all the reasons why I have struggled so much with pleasing people, emotional regulation, and the biggest one, boundaries; I have finally accepted that I will be forever working on them. When I realized I could no longer look to anyone else to help me and that I had to do the work myself is when things finally shifted in a better direction. I'm learning that love doesn't ask me to abandon myself, and that healthy relationships can survive honesty even when it's hard. It's this truth that has guided my decision not to pursue a relationship with my father. I had tried a couple times after treatment to repair what had been broken. He even agreed to attend a few therapy sessions with me, but in order for healing to happen, you have to believe that healing is needed. My father's outlook on healing, our relationship, and the world has convinced me that there isn't much more that can be done. All I have is control of myself. I cannot make him see the things he refuses to acknowledge. His love for me (if I can even call it love) has always felt conditional and I have come to accept that. As a little girl I loved him deeply, and I admired him. But as an adult, that love doesn't erase the reality of who he has been to me and my family. I have chosen to protect the family that Mike and I have built by setting a firm boundary with him.

I know we live in a world that says we should have no regrets. I feel differently about it. My regrets have taught me so much. No, I don't live in them, but it is my regrets that keep me from ever wanting to go back to the person I was. The messy moments are what taught me where I still had work to do. I am grateful for those who have forgiven me and given me grace when I didn't deserve it, and I am grateful to those who haven't. They all have taught me valuable lessons on who I want to be.

When I look back at my childhood wounds that affected me growing up, specifically my relationship with Rose, I realize clearly that she had her own painful story, too. All the hurt I had carried came from the little girl that didn't understand what friendship or trust really looked like. I think she could say the same. We were both just trying to survive with what we knew. Now that I understand myself, I understand her. I never felt like I truly ever had a best friend, but looking back she was the closest thing to it for me. I will always love her and be grateful for her in my life. I am still working on releasing the shame of how I have handled situations and relationships throughout my life. I did not understand myself like I do now, and I only have today and every day after to be better.

Learning what grace looks like and accepting that healing isn't about erasing my past or fixing all of my flaws has helped me figure out more of who I am and choose a different way to live regardless.

So where am I today? Well, I am 50 years old, and Mike and I have become first time grandparents of a beautiful baby girl who we can't get enough of. We are empty nesters trying to figure out this new chapter of our lives, and while at times it feels uncomfortable, it's also exciting to do all the things we couldn't do when we were kids just trying to figure it out. We are best friends and will always be. It would take another book for me to explain how we made it through everything. There really is no reason why we should have made it, but we have, and I am damn proud of us.

As for my adult children, we are close. Our relationships are changing as they grow and become the people they want to be, but the one thing that will never change is that I will always be there for them. I will always be their biggest fan. They taught me more about the person I want to be than anyone I have mentioned in this book. I am so proud of each one of them and the lives they are creating. Being their mother is the most important role I have ever had in my life and the reason I have fought so hard to heal.

As for the relationship with my mom, this scorpio daughter loves her with all of my heart and all of her Libra-ness. I have reconciled with the fact that there will be things I will never understand about her. She loves differently than I do but I no longer dismiss it because it's different. I have grown to accept what was and have forgiven her. I have also asked her for forgiveness for the years of disrespect and anger I had not controlled. We are good. We talk and see each other when we can.

I want to leave you with this. Life really goes on. Shit happens, yes. It really is cliché to say but, in the end, it doesn't matter what happened in the past, what matters is how we rise. I wish I figured this out sooner, I wouldn't have put myself through this hell of writing this book. But late is better than never, right? So, here's to always keeping it real, falling in love with life every day, forgiving myself when I fail, and never EVER giving up. #myheartseeshope

Jer 29:13

Acknowledgements

To Mike, the love of my life and best friend-Without you by my side, I would never have been able to walk through these memories all over again. Thank you for believing in me when I couldn't. I'm so grateful for your annoying positivity and continuous reminders of the light at the end of the tunnel on the days when my frustration blinded all hope that this book was even a possibility. I chose to stay the course on the days I wanted to quit because you somehow were able to convince me that I could even though I didn't feel it. I love you forever, Babe. #chantelnmike4life

Ashley Cardona – My editor, my coach, the one who became my therapist on some of the hardest days of this process, I know full well that God knew precisely who I would need to help me bring this book into the world. Your talent and brilliance along with your unwavering encouragement as we worked through each story healed me in ways that I could never anticipate. Thank you for being one of the few women in my life that stuck with me until the end. I will forever be grateful for you and your heart. I truly love ya girl. We did it!

Dani – My sister, girl, thank you for being the one chick who not only gets me but gets "it". Because of your love, encouragement, and forgiveness, it gave me the permission I needed to be brave and vulnerable to share my part in our crazy family story. You will always be my baby sister, but being able to call you my best friend today means so much more. Thank you for walking through life with me all these years. Now it's your turn to write (hint, hint).

Mom – Thank you for giving me your blessing when I told you I would be writing this book. I am very proud of how far we have come and grateful for the lessons we learned along the way. We are proof that if you do the work and don't give up, healing is possible. I love you and always will.

Becky – Thank you for being the one family member who suggested that I write this book to begin with. Your support and encouragement showed me that I had a story that mattered before I realized it did. Thank you for being the cheerleader and friend I needed all of these years. You will always be one of the best memories of my childhood and my favorite cousin. I love ya girl.

Amanda Botfeld and the entire team at FGYBD – Your professionalism from start to finish has far exceeded my expectations. I am incredibly grateful for you and your team for all the work you have put into helping me finally get my book done!